STONED

A FATHER AND SON'S QUEST TO UNLOCK
THE SECRETS OF CRAZY HORSE

DANIEL D. LEE

STONED

A FATHER AND SON'S QUEST TO UNLOCK
THE SECRETS OF CRAZY HORSE

DANIEL D. LEE

WYⵔDAKTANA
PUBLISHING

Nashville, Tennessee

Photos have been reproduced with the permission of the respective copyright holders, they meet the requirements of fair use as outlined by the Library of Congress, or are from the personal collections of the author. Photo of Julia McGillycuddy and baby Courtesy of the California History Room, California State Library, Sacramento, California. Crazy Horse Memorial Image by RJA1988 from Pixabay.

For contact information, visit www.WyodaktanaPublishing.com.

Hardcover: 978-1-7378415-1-7
Paperback: 978-1-7378415-2-4
Kindle: 978-1-7378415-3-1

Cataloging-in-Publication Data on file with the publisher.
Library of Congress Control Number: 2021917943

WYODAKTANA
PUBLISHING

Printed and bound in the United States of America
10 9 8 7 6 5 4 3 2 1

This book is dedicated to the first, my Mother, a mom in all senses of the word. Without her sharing of knowledge, encouragement, unconditional love and support throughout my life, it would not have come to fruition; and secondly, my son, Brody. I hope I have been the father to him as she is a mother to me. Mom, the backbone. Me, the middleman. Brody, the hero.

PART I

"If you find yourself in a hole, the first thing you do is stop digging."

—Will Rogers

I INTENTIONALLY STOPPED using all e-mail and voicemail months ago, and now I dread opening any kind of mail. Even snail mail. It's become a phobia. Too often it's been a legal notice of some kind—delinquency, eviction, insufficient funds, notice to appear, failure to appear, etc. I look at the flat box on the table that came yesterday by personal courier from a law firm in California. I had to sign for it, and it's causing anxiety. Get over it, man. Open it.

I take a paring knife from a kitchen drawer, hold it to the tape and take a reflective pause. Two years digging a hole. I must be getting close to the bottom because, financially, my shovel is hitting bedrock. To go any deeper will require dynamite, meaning everything gets blown up. Check No. 1040, along with signed divorce papers, went in the mail a few days ago. Once she cashes that check, my finances will look something like this: no savings or retirement plan, a house in foreclosure, bad credit, $5,000 in credit card debt, and not much more than that in checking.

It wasn't always like this. People who knew me in a previous life probably wonder what led to my demise. I understand how it must look from the outside. I welcomed a life change but didn't anticipate the possibility of bankruptcy, or losing my son, when I decided to resign from a lucrative corporate attorney position. My marriage was already dead. Years of mutual frustration, anger, and argument morphed into a period of modest attempts at reconciliation and ultimately to complete apathy with me sleeping on the daybed. I told my now ex-wife of my intended exodus from the corporate world the day before pulling the trigger. I started digging. The conversation:

"I hate my job… I hate being a lawyer… I'm tired of the travel… I'm stressed… I've been busting my ass for twenty-five years… I'll find something else."

"I'll divorce you if you quit."

"I'm quitting not to spite you, but in spite of you."

"Move out."

I complied without protest. After packing a few things, I held our dog, my old dog, who had slept between my legs most every night for 17 years and said goodbye. "I love you, Jake. You're the best. Such a good dog." Kiss on the nose. Tears. Thus, began my search, my then-selfish search, to "find something else."

A little background. As a new Second Lieutenant, my Commander recommended I let the Air Force deduct $100 from my first twelve paychecks in exchange for future VA educational benefits. I reluctantly agreed. Twenty-five years later, I discovered that that $1,200 investment now entitled me to 36 months of free education with a housing allowance. Open to anything new and exciting and wanting to escape, I explored my options and found a Golf College in California. There really is such a thing. I was going golfing for a year. With excitement, I pulled out of the parking lot of the cheap motel that had been "home" for the past six months with clubs stowed and headed west. I left with quite a bit in the bank. By the time I crossed the Wyoming/Utah border, not so much.

Golf College was top soil. Easy digging. A nurturing layer of warmth and richness. Classes until noon. Playing golf every afternoon. I was around quality instructors and interesting people from all over the world, enjoying competition again and improving my golf game. Money now tight, I supplemented my monthly housing allowance from the VA by coaching golf at two elementary schools. I also perfected the art of crockpot cooking; ham, beans and rice becoming my specialty.

It takes longer to reach the bottom digging through rocks. While I was playing in the sun, my son, Brody, in his senior year of high school, was drinking and using drugs heavily. He stopped going to school. His mother kicked him out of the house. Homelessness, substance abuse and lack of food and sleep took their toll. Six months earlier, I had left a strapping six-foot one-inch man child with a mane of dishwater blond cherub-curls falling below his shoulders. I returned for the holiday break to find a sunken-eyed, black-dyed, hair thinning, 115-pound skeleton. I took him into my arms and held him tightly. "What happened?" His answer hit hard. "Dad, I know you had to leave, but there's been times I could've used a fuckin' dad."

Damn. I didn't go back to California. I thought that my presence alone would be enough to turn things around. How naïve and narcissistic of me as this running list of events over the next six months demonstrates: I got him an apartment, he got a job, he got drunk, late for work, pills, weed, drunk, late for work, fired, totaled my truck, emergency room, week-long bender, anxiety attack, emergency room, new job, pills, weed, drunk at work, fired, trashed apartment, eviction, homeless again, moved into some girls' apartment, drunk at work falls and hits head, blood, fired, dragged him out of a car and carried him up three flights of stairs to a bed, pills, cocaine, alcohol, nonresponsive, ambulance, beg him to go to rehab, he tries to fight me, cutting, cocaine bender, girls evicted from their apartment, homeless again, living on the floor of new apartment, more cutting and blood, cocaine, pills, weed and hard alcohol his staples. My prognosis for him in September was this: Soon, my son will take too many Xanax while drinking a bottle of Jack Daniels, resulting in respiratory system failure and death.

That is no longer my prognosis. Today is Christmas Eve, and I need no gifts other than that which I already thankfully have. I have my son, whom I love more than anybody or anything in this world, and there is nothing he could ever do or say to change that. Brody doesn't remember much about that hellish period, but he knew he had a loving dad by his side every painful step of the way, and he knew enough to pull himself from the brink. Since then, we've moved to a new city, and he's living in an apartment with me. He's holding down a job, got his GED, put on twenty-five pounds, his scars are healing, and he's experienced extended stints of sobriety. I couldn't be prouder of him. It's not over yet, I know. As with all young men, and all addicts, there will be setbacks and disappointments for sure, but he's with me now, doing well, and a special bond has been formed—there will never be a cross word between us.

Two years digging a hole. I'm tired. I'm broke. I'm divorced. Two years digging a hole, but I'm not burying my son in it. We reached the bottom. We're not going any deeper. It's time to climb out.

Exhale. Open the damn box.

━━━━

I stab the tip of the knife through the packing tape, apply pressure, and proceed with intentions to separate the two top flaps. After cutting an inch of tape the dull blade hits the shipping label and slips from under the corrugated edge of the box. Frustrated, I drop the reading glasses from my forehead, put my index finger firmly on top of the blade and slide it, deeper this time, into my initial incision. Working now with conviction in a sawing motion, I cut through the label and remaining length of the packing tape. A faint smell is released, not quite of dankness, but surely of age. I bend the flaps back, exposing the contents consisting of a one-page letter, short in wording, lying on top of what appears to be an old leather satchel. I remove the letter noticing its texture and weight—high-quality paper—embossed with a raised gold logo and maroon letterhead proudly identifying a law firm in Berkeley, California. Great.

I lay the letter on the table without reading it and turn my attention to the satchel. It measures about 12 inches high by 18 inches wide. A large flap covers the top half. Two straps with tarnished brass buckles connect it to the bottom. There's a separate, smaller exterior pouch between the two straps with its own cover and brass buckle. All buckles are fastened. The satchel is generally brown, but a spiderweb of cracks spreading top to bottom breaks up the consistency of its color—darker along the cracks with lighter sinew exposed below. It has obviously protected its contents from the elements for many years—almost white in places where raindrops hit long ago. The previously indistinguishable scent now makes sense. This thing is old.

The letter:

Wiederstein, Staub, & Smith, P.L.L.C.

601 6th Street

Berkeley, CA 94710

Dear Mr. Lee,

Enclosed, please find the possessions of Dr. Valentine T. McGillycuddy, your ancestor, that have been held in trust in accordance with his Last Will and Testament, bequeathed to you, as his rightful heir.

Interesting. A pleasant surprise. Brody will get a kick out of this.

———

The key hitting the lock and the door opening is a soothing sound to me now, no matter the time. He's home. I look at the clock—11:02 p.m. Not bad. "Hey, Dad."

"Merry Christmas, Bro. How was your day?"

"Good. Merry Christmas. I'm hungry as fuck."

"I made chili. It's in the fridge. I'll make you a bowl."

"Right on."

"We'll open presents and feast tomorrow."

"Hell yeah."

I instinctively observe his walk and talk—both look and sound good. His ripped jeans, as was the fashion, are thankfully getting a little tight, and I remember that his Grandma has sent a gift card to his favorite store so we can get him a new pair soon. He's wearing the jean jacket I wore in high school—now stained, frayed and tattered beyond repair—that he's embellished with a red, spray-painted Anarchy symbol on the back. His mother had given it to me as a Christmas gift.

I open the refrigerator and carefully remove the to-the-rim-filled crock pot saying over my shoulder, "We got a box today. Look at that letter." Knowing his routine, I'd moved the box to the coffee table in front of the couch that also serves as his bed, both located in our small living area just off the kitchen. Brody leans forward, looks inside, and takes the letter. The two strands of white bulbs on the small artificial Christmas tree to his right give off just enough reading light. Awaiting his reaction and response, I go about preparing his food. He asks, "What is it?"

"It's an old satchel. I don't know what's in it yet. I think I inherited it. I was waiting for you." I hit the start button on the microwave and lean back against the counter.

Half-smiling, Brody says in a sarcastic tone, "Dude's name is Valentine. Did you know him?"

"No. Never heard of him. Look it up."

Brody references the letter again, "Dr. Valentine... T... McGillycuddy," saying each word as he types it into his phone. A short pause, and then he starts reading.

Valentine Trant McGillycuddy (1849-1939) was a surgeon who served with expeditions and United States military forces in the West. He was considered controversial for his efforts to build a sustainable relationship between the United States and Native American peoples.

Early Life: Valentine Trant O'Connell McGillycuddy was born on February 14, 1849, in Racine, Wisconsin. When he was 13, his family moved to Detroit. He graduated from the Detroit Medical School at 20 years of age. He began working as a doctor at the Wayne County Insane Asylum and practiced medicine for one year. Next, he began teaching at the medical college. McGillycuddy's longstanding love for the outdoors led him to leave the city.

Career: From 1871 to 1874, McGillycuddy worked for the United States Boundary Survey Commission. He became a topographer and surgeon for the International Expedition. This group headed an expedition to define the border between the United States and Canada along the 49th parallel. They began their expedition in North Dakota, where the ground had frozen due to a wet season. In order to keep their feet warm, the men wore several pairs of socks, wrapped their feet in square blankets, and wore oversized moccasins. After the expedition ended, McGillycuddy returned to Washington, D.C. He was soon sent to Wyoming to continue his career as a topographer.

The following year, in 1875, he was invited on the Newton-Jenney Party. As the surveyor for the expedition, McGillycuddy was the first person to record his climb of Harney Peak (now Black Elk Peak) in the Black Hills of South Dakota. He was responsible for mapping the topography and geology of the region, while the expedition assessed the area for major gold deposits."

The "beeping" of the microwave interrupts Brody's reading and frustrates my intrigue. Opening its door and seeing the dark splatters throughout, I realize I forgot to cover the chili. I make a mental note to clean the mess later while also trying to attach some schema to what I've just heard. I move the hot bowl to the counter, give a quick stir, and grab the corn chips and shredded cheese to perfect his late-night meal. I glance right and see Brody leaning forward, looking at the old satchel. He's curious. He pulls his phone to his face and starts reading again.

Upon returning from the expedition, McGillycuddy married Fanny Hoyt. He was recruited as the Contract Surgeon with General Crook during the Battle of the Rosebud (June 17, 1876). McGillycuddy was appointed Assistant Post Surgeon at Fort Robinson in Nebraska. He was known to the Lakota at the Agency as a "Friend of Crazy Horse," a notable Lakota leader. McGillycuddy treated Crazy Horse after he was fatally stabbed by guards who said he was trying to escape. After Crazy Horse's death, McGillycuddy went to Washington D.C. to lobby for more humane treatment of Indians at Fort Robinson.

McGillycuddy was appointed as Indian Agent in 1879, when he was 30. He served at the Pine Ridge Agency (now Pine Ridge Indian Reservation in South Dakota). He did not manage to achieve such friendly relations here as he had with Crazy Horse and other Lakota. Red Cloud, a major chief, accused McGillycuddy of mismanagement, leading to several investigations of the Agent's administration. Despite this, McGillycuddy established an Indian police force and set up a boarding school to educate Indian children of the region. However, persistent claims followed of his tyranny, fraud and the graft typical *of the "Indian Ring," including one in the Boston Advisor claiming that he had been in receipt of annuities for 2,600 more people than actually lived at Pine Ridge, a loss to the Government of $284,700. McGillycuddy was suspended from his position in October 1882.*

Listening intently, I approach presenting in my mind the perfect bowl of chili adorned with melted cheddar cheese and corn chips. Brody stops reading. "Thanks, Dad."

"It's still pretty hot." I set the bowl on the coffee table. "What do you think?"

"Looks great."

"No. About this guy."

"It's nuts. Wild West shit."

"It is." I smile and sit next to him. As I hit the couch, he immediately jumps up and moves toward the refrigerator. I look again at the old satchel, and still trying to make sense of it all, say in a questioning tone, "He was friends with Crazy Horse?" Brody retrieves the hot sauce, comes back, and gives the chili a generous four-shake dousing. I wait to ask until he's done stirring it in. "Is there more about him?"

"Yeah." Brody repositions himself on the couch, bowl in lap and feet on the coffee table. He takes his first spoonful, swallows, and continues.

After leaving Pine Ridge, McGillycuddy settled in Rapid City, South Dakota. He would later serve as president of Lakota Bank and as Dean of the South Dakota School of Mines and Technology. He was also appointed as South Dakota's first State Surgeon General. While living in Rapid City, he built a mansion in 1888, which is still standing. In 1890 McGillycuddy was elected as a delegate to the South Dakota State Constitutional Convention. Continuing his activism in politics, he was elected mayor of Rapid City in 1897. McGillycuddy died in Berkeley, California, in 1939. He was cremated, and his ashes were entombed at the top of Black Elk Peak. A plaque was installed that reads: "Valentine T. McGillycuddy, 'Wasicu Wakan,' 1849-1939." (In Lakota, Wasicu Wakan means 'Holy White Man'.)

Brody stops, tosses his phone aside, and takes another spoonful. He swallows. "That's it.... we're rich as fuck."

═════

It's Christmas morning. I've been up for a while, turning on the Christmas tree lights, taking out the ham to thaw, having two cups of coffee, and cleaning the microwave. Third cup of coffee in hand, wearing gray sweats and my favorite sweatshirt, I sit in the lounge chair a few feet across the room from Brody's "bed," resigned to wait patiently for him to wake to open presents and the satchel, probably around 11. This kid can sleep, and I'm glad. It wasn't long ago that he would go for days without it, first from excessive stimulation and then out of fear of the withdrawal-induced dreams and night terrors. He hasn't had them in a couple of months. I look at my boy, covered, lying on his back, bare left leg protruding from the blanket and hanging off the couch, his foot grounded firmly on the floor. His hair pulled back into a man-bun exposes the scripted tattoo over his left brow, reading "*Unlucky.*" His head is jammed against the armrest and cocked sharply to his right toward the back cushion. Light snoring. Pillow on the floor. I've told him several times the couch is a hide-a-bed, but he's never pulled it out. He's assured me more than once that he "loves" his couch, but c'mon… that can't be comfortable.

I set my coffee on the table, turn the TV on, and hurriedly lower the volume to almost mute so as not to wake him up. The box containing the satchel is arm's-length away, it's still where we'd left it the night before. I've been thinking about it all night. Fifteen minutes turns into thirty (done with third cup) and then forty-five. While the package had sparked Brody's interest, the messages, pictures, and videos received from girls and friends last evening took precedence and demanded his immediate attention. I was itching to find out what was in the satchel but reminded myself that I was 19 once. Duty called. Opening the satchel could wait.

Forty-five minutes turns into an hour. "Bro… Bro." Brody moves for the first time since I've been up, pulling his leg back onto the couch and rolling his head into a more natural position on his left shoulder. He mumbles something with a slight teeth-grind. Just let him sleep. He never was one of those kids to wake up at the crack of dawn to see what Santa brought. His mother was always far more excited to get the day started, and being unable to wait any longer, she would wake him, remind him of the special day, and coax him into going downstairs.

She went to great lengths to make sure everything was perfectly in place as to make the most impactful first impression. I know it always blew me away. Heaps of neatly bowed presents were stacked under the tree. Three stockings always rested against the couch's backrest, the seams of each stretched to their limits. Hundreds of smaller gifts of candy, food, toys, and other interesting things, each selected for Brody with careful thought and each positioned with the utmost care, surrounded them. Brody loved the spectacle of it all, but if the Christmas bonanzas of his childhood weren't enough to make him want to get out of bed, this year's modest bounty, in comparison, certainly won't do the trick.

I replay in my mind what I'd learned about Valentine McGillycuddy. He certainly had an interesting life, and it did sound like he was a man of means, so who knows, maybe I did fall into some money. But he died in 1939, so why am I getting something now, 80-some years later? It doesn't make sense. Only one way to find out. I push my hand along the box's edge, press my fingertips under the satchel, grip, and lift. Tightly fit, the box comes off the table, necessitating the use of my other hand to free it. I rest the satchel on my lap, undo the buckles to release the top flap from the body, and open the interior pouch. I see a book that I remove carefully for inspection. It's fairly old, about two inches thick, with a tan cloth cover, slightly stained, with red lettering reading: "McGillycuddy Agent." Below the title, also in red, depicts a plow—an early horse-drawn plow—and crossing below diagonally, a feather-adorned Native American peace pipe with smoke billowing from its bowl. I look at the spine that reiterates the title but also provides: "Stanford University Press." I lay it gently on the table.

The second item I remove is a leather-bound folder measuring about 10" x 12" with tarnished, triangular brass tabs protecting the corners furthest from the spine. Compared to the satchel, the leather is darker, softer, and in much better condition. It might be buffalo hide. McGillycuddy's name is stamped in gold lettering into the lower right corner, some of which has flaked away over the years. I open the folder's cover to reveal this old photograph:

This must be him. McGillycuddy. I gaze at the face of this unknown relative… serious… resolute… and then I focus on the eyes… intense… and maybe it's just the downward turn of the heavy lids matching the downward turn of his mouth… a bit of sadness, perhaps. Bald, like me. The raised left hand is a little Stalinesque. I wonder when men started pulling the shirt collar down over the tie? Collar-up isn't a bad look.

There's more in the folder, and it's probably not money, but this is all definitely interesting. Too interesting to go forward without Brody.

"Bro." More forcefully, "Brody... wake up. Merry Christmas."

Brody opens his right eye to look at me, and with left eye still closed, says tiredly, "Merry Christmas, Dad."

"I opened the satchel." I hold up the photograph for him to see. "Look at this." Feeling a little guilty about opening it without him and also for waking him, I try to joke, "Say hi to Valentine."

Something about Brody—sober Brody—that has always amazed me is how quickly he can go from a state of complete comatose to complete lucidity. He tosses the blanket off, sits up, places both feet on the floor, pulls out the man-bun, and combs all ten fingers through his hair. With squinted eyes, he looks at the photograph for no more than two viewing seconds. "Looks like a dick." I quizzically raise my eyebrow. Brody nonchalantly affirms his initial assessment nodding his head, "He do." I bust out laughing. It's going to be a good day.

———

Not surprisingly, the fact that it's Christmas morning doesn't change Brody's normal routine in the least. He throws on a black hooded sweatshirt taken from the floor, and in his boxers, grabs his cigarettes and sidesteps through the sliding glass door and onto our small balcony to smoke. I push my glasses up from the tip of my nose, look down at the open folder in my lap, and read the opening line of an enclosed letter, while also mentally deliberating how to kick off our Christmas Day:

To be opened and read by my heir, as designated in my Last Will and Testament, 80 years after my death, to the day.

After Brody finishes that first cigarette, he'll be in the bathroom a while, and then I'll ask if he wants to open presents. I keep reading.

Dear Trusted Messenger,

My second wife, Julia B. McGillycuddy, who as a child asked my first wife, Fanny, if she thought I would marry her when Fanny died, has listened to my stories since her earliest childhood. After our marriage, I jestingly requested that my reminiscences be recorded for posterity. Now I'm the only one of the old crowd left. At the age of 87, as I ever near my journey "over the divide," there is less jocularity and more urgency to my requests. I have related the stories of my life on the Frontier—my altercations with the government, the press, and with men, both white and red, to Mrs. McGillycuddy, and she has sworn that any future publication will not deviate from the facts as dictated to her. I have instructed that you receive said published memoirs so you may gain a better understanding of my life.

In conjunction with my project with Mrs. McGillycuddy, unbeknownst to her or anyone else, I wrote a less extensive but more focused memoir (now also in your possession) containing facts of historical significance pertaining to Crazy Horse, a famous Sioux Indian, that heretofore have been known to only a few other men, all now deceased. You will soon understand that prudence dictated the need for an extended hiatus before its release to society.

I deliberated how best to bring the full extent of my experiences to light. In most instances, one would entrust the memoir to a university,

16

historical society or museum. I elect not to do so, as first, the subject matter is highly sensitive, and secondly, doing so would not be very interesting. An initial revelation to an unknown descendant intrigues me far more. I hope that you feel you are being bestowed a gift and not a burden. From my experience, life on the move and in the open is vastly preferable to stagnation and closed quarters. In the event you have an adventurous spirit, like me, I encourage you to visit the places where these events occurred. No doubt much has changed since my days as topographer, contract surgeon, and Indian Agent, but any sights, sounds, and smells of Dakota Country still present will only embellish the experience.

Words of warning. Exposure of these writings will surely cause much consternation and debate between white and red men alike. My character, and likely yours, will be called into question, but know that all that I have written is true and accurate. My life was history and must be exact. I was deemed "the most investigated man of his age" by the papers, so I suspect my memoirs may also rekindle questions regarding my efforts to establish the Indians as citizens of this country. I, like all men, have regrets but given a chance, there are few things I would change. I was young and full of courage. I was a clear thinker. I made decisions quickly, and I was always unswerving in my purpose. Let history judge me accordingly. Finally, if anyone expresses resentment in my actions or inactions to you, assure him that I was sincere in my judgments and that the responsibility rests solely with me and not with you, my Trusted Messenger.

V.T. M'Gillycuddy
Ta-sunko-witko-kola, The Friend of Crazy Horse

━━

Strange letter. I start reading again from the beginning. The sliding glass door opens, and I catch the familiar whiff of his last lingering puffs as Brody announces today's weather conditions as "cold as hell." I nod, letting the faulty metaphor slide without comment. "We rich?" he asks.

My head goes from nodding up and down to shaking side to side. I look up. "Don't think so. We got that book. This folder doesn't have anything in it other than a letter and a bunch of old pictures that are pretty cool. The only other thing is a… a journal or something" (that must be McGillycuddy's private memoir). True to routine, Brody heads to the bathroom, and I reread the letter in its entirety, noticing an increasing feeling of reluctance. I'm intrigued, but this doesn't feel like a gift, McGillycuddy. I look at his photograph again. I don't know if I want to know your secrets. A simple fat inheritance would have been preferable.

Brody finishes his business, grabs an orange energy drink from the refrigerator and asks if I want to open presents.

"Yeah. Let's do it."

He removes two gift bags from under the tree, one for me and one for him. Open, appreciate, comment. Next. Open, appreciate, comment, repeat. The entire present-opening process takes 15 minutes. I appreciate the sentiment of the gifts, and these are all very nice things. But in all honesty, the mess we've made and the disorder of things randomly lying about now bothers me a bit. Brody loves it all: cologne, clothes, money, food and candy, a plethora of gift cards to stores and restaurants, but especially the new headphones from his aunt. His mother sent him a nice box. The card and $50 from her boyfriend, who Brody has met once for about five minutes, was odd. I replaced Brody's old wallet that he'd lost a couple weeks earlier with a new one. It contains a crisp $100 bill. I'm glad I didn't skimp and go with $50. "Guard this one with your life, Son. May it always be full."

He smiles, "I will, Dad. Thanks." He's happy, and that makes me happy. It's definitely a good day.

═══

It's early afternoon on New Year's Eve. I'm sitting in "my spot," the lounge chair, and half-watching a college football bowl game through watery eyes. Brody and I are recovering from colds. He came down with his first, and as soon as he started blowing his nose, I knew from experience that I was in trouble. I'd taken extra precautions this time to avoid his bug, like trying to keep my distance (which is hard in a one-bedroom apartment), taking a cold tablet before symptoms hit, drinking orange juice, and wiping the door knobs with disinfectant wipes. But my efforts proved futile. The die had been cast. He's pretty much recovered now, but for a slight cough. I need two more days.

"Bye, Dad."

"Got everything? Cigs… lighter… wallet?" I scan his area to see if he's forgotten anything.

"Yep."

"Want some medicine?"

"Na. I'm good."

"Wash your hands a lot. You don't want to get everyone sick."

"I will. Always do. Bye."

"Proud of you. Love you, Buddy."

I can tell he's excited to go back to his job as a prep cook, and more recently, the added responsibility of line cook. He's tired of being cooped up. Even though the Italian restaurant is only three blocks away, I normally give him a ride, to be nice, but mainly for the opportunity to pass on some advice and a few encouraging words before starting his work. When he first got the job, I pained over the message I wanted to convey—know the importance of hard work; take pride in your work; be excellent in everything you do; don't get frustrated when things get tough; roll with the punches, think about that paycheck, etc. Regardless of what I'd come up with for that day, it always ended with me telling him how proud of him I was and that I loved him. To his credit, the pep talk has gotten shorter and perhaps somewhat repetitive over the last three months, but today's "proud of you… love you" that I threw out as he was going out the door was highly condensed.

The football game uninteresting; I look for something else to do. I see McGillycuddy's photograph still staring from the coffee table… next to the cough medicine. I take a swig. Alright, Valentine, what do you want to tell me? I again inspect the leather-bound journal for the second time since its arrival. It's about 6" x 8" in size, bound twice by a thickly fibered goldish-colored ribbon. I untie and unwrap it, open the cover, and notice that, unlike the previous communications, this one is neatly handwritten in cursive black ink. Resigned to a slow day, I read:

Dear Trusted Messenger,

I trust you have first read my published memoir, but…

Nope. I haven't. It's still on the table.

… as an introduction to my private memoir that you now hold, reserved solely for you, and to refresh your memory and expound in further detail, I first rehash the events from my first encounter with Crazy Horse to his death at Camp Robinson in Nebraska, as purveyed by the historical record to date. If you wish to fully embellish the experience by visiting the places where these events occurred, as I have suggested you do, I have clearly identified the pertinent locales for your convenience.

Rosebud Battlefield, Montana

On June 17, 1876, I, as a contracted Field Surgeon with the U.S. Army, accompanied the Big Horn and Yellowstone Expedition—a 1,051-man column consisting of fifteen companies from the 2d and 3d Cavalries, five companies from the 4th and 9th Infantry, 261 Shoshone and Crow allies, 250 mules, and 106 wagons, all led by General Crook, with the charged purpose of finding and eliminating Sitting Bull, Crazy Horse, and the hostile Sioux threat (see photograph #1 enclosed).

I'd previously thumbed through the old photographs but hadn't noticed that each was numbered on its back. #1 is on top. #2 is next. #3. Good. Looks like they're in order.

That day's march had commenced at daylight. We had marched through an elevated, undulating tableland, mantled with emerald green

grass eagerly nibbled by our horses and mules. Without possessing any decided beauty, its picturesqueness was very marked and pleasing. A little brook coursed down every few rods to pay its tribute to the Deje-Agis, as the Crows call the Tongue River. Having marched thirty-five miles the day before, this morning at eight o'clock a.m., after four miles, General Crook permitted the troops to rest near Rosebud Creek in present-day Montana. No timber, except an occasional small cottonwood or willow, could be seen along the banks, but wild roses by the thousand laid their delicate beauties at our feet.

A greater state of unpreparedness would be hard to fathom. Soldiers were sipping coffee from their tin field cups, and some were napping. The horses were grazing on the soft grasses—not a one saddled or bridled for battle—when two shots rang out to our west, followed seconds later by six of our Crow scouts racing from the hilltop to the lounging army below. Lakota! Lakota! The bugle sounded, and this being the first face-to-face Sioux encounter of the Expedition, all scrambled to prepare for the impending attack. Eyes wide with excitement, heads swiveled rapidly looking for boots, weapons, and the hostiles.

A mounted silhouette appeared on the bluff's horizon, its arm raised to the sky with the rifle in hand and loudly declaring, "It is a good day to fight; a good day to die! Strong hearts and brave hearts to the front; weak hearts and cowards fall back!" These were the first words I ever heard from Crazy Horse. Yelled in Lakota, I did not understand his prayer for bravery at the time. Little did I know at that moment that the Sioux warrior would later become my friend, nor that he would have such a significant impact on my life.

Crazy Horse gave a whoop; his horse turned full circle and funneled into a hillside ravine leading directly to my position in the center of our bivouacked encampment. Running downhill, the warrior covered the ground quickly generating a cloud of dust in his wake. Reaching the flats and inside thirty yards of our pickets, I had a clear view of his appearance before turning the grunting brown and white stallion southward and racing it parallel to our lines. Crazy Horse's complexion was unusually lighter than most Indians, so the zigzag streak of red earth from the top of his forehead, along the side of his nose and to the point of his chin, was visible. Crazy Horse's waist-long hair and single eagle feather, worn upside down, flew freely and parallel to the ground behind him. He rode shirtless and without leggings, a breechclout his only clothing. Bullets filled the air, but despite Crazy Horse's proximity, he was not hit.

I learned in later years from interviews with the old Indians like Eagle Elk that such acts of bravery were not unusual for Crazy Horse. Eagle Elk reported that on one occasion, Crazy Horse said: "Just keep away for a little while. These soldiers like to shoot. I am going to give them a chance to do all the shooting they want to do. You draw back, and I will make them shoot. If I fall off, then you can do something if you feel like it; but don't do anything until I have run by them." The first time he ran by them, they shot at him many times, and he passed by safely. He rested a little while and then came again, this time closer to the soldiers. He was not hurt."

It would be incorrect to assume that Crazy Horse was suicidal. Quite the contrary. He would later tell me that he believed he was bulletproof so long as he performed a certain ritual before going into battle. A medicine man named Woptura had granted him this power, his wotawe, after Crazy Horse was shot in the arm by a Ute warrior. The ritual consisted of Crazy Horse rubbing dirt into his hair and moistening more dirt to paint his face with the powerful symbols of the Thunder Beings—a red zigzag line to represent lightning and random white dots representing hail. The medicine man also gave Crazy Horse a small white stone that he was to wear behind his left ear in battle. The medicine was supposed to protect Crazy Horse from knives as well, as long as his arms weren't being held. Crazy Horse would convey his special power to his horse by rubbing streaks on its hide and throwing dirt into the air, letting the cloud of dust pass over it.

Captain Mills of the Third Cavalry would later declare that the Sioux "were the best cavalry soldiers on earth" because they would hang on with one arm around the horse's neck with only one leg over the horse's back. This made for a very small target, but the Sioux could still shoot from this position by firing from underneath the horse's neck. Crazy Horse demonstrated this skill of horsemanship masterfully on his second pass, which was unfortunate for Sergeant Maher (Co. "I," 2d Cav.) who was standing and firing close to my position. The slug from Crazy Horse's rifle shattered his right arm just above the elbow. Seeing his lower arm hanging limply, attached only by a strand of tendon and skin, almost spinning as it hung, Maher dropped into a sitting position. I scurried to the soldier, and using my belt as a tourniquet, stopped the bleeding, and proceeded to conduct the simplest of amputations. One swipe of my field knife severed the limb from his body.

I had joined General Crook's Expedition only eight days before, and this was the second time I found myself belly-down since my arrival. Two months earlier, I had been in Washington D.C. when I received a telegram from Crook asking if "McGillycuddy's service can be secured for the field. Stop. If so, send him at once." Despite having to leave my new bride, Fanny, I longed to return to the Great Plains, and I jumped at the opportunity. The previous summer, I accompanied the Geological Expedition of the Black Hills, the purpose of which was to confirm the presence of gold in the Hills as reported by Custer in 1874. Being the topographer for the Expedition, I knew the country, and I had created many of the maps Crook would use to track down Sitting Bull and the hostile Northern Indians. Being a doctor was an added bonus.

After reporting in and receiving a warm welcome from the General, I went to the hospital supply wagon to take inventory of the medical equipment. I eyed a folded cot in the wagon, and thinking it would make a decent bed, I moved it to my tent. I had lived in the field before and knew I could endure hardship as well as the next, but I saw no reason to avoid comfort if it was at hand. I did not suspect my bed would cause such a stir among the ranks. That afternoon nearly every officer in camp stopped by my tent to comment on my luxurious quarters. The Sioux would soon let me in on the joke.

Bones weary from having ridden over forty miles that day, I looked forward to the ensuing slumber in my new bed. I rested my head on my field pack as a gunshot rang through the night, followed shortly by a slug ripping through my tent's canvas and hitting a metal wash basin a mere few feet from my head, releasing a loud clang. Instinctively I rolled off the cot and lay belly to the ground as the firing continued for several minutes. Two soldiers were hit that night, but the "wounds" were of little consequence, not more than bruising and welts, as the bullets were fired from the bluffs on the other side of the Tongue River and were largely spent by the time they reached the camp. After treating the soldiers, I returned to my tent. I kicked the cot to the side and laid my blanket on the ground—-the ground being much safer in Indian country. Smiles all around, General Crook greeted me at breakfast the next morning with a devilish grin: "Sleep well, McGillycuddy?" (See photographs of our camp near Whitewood, Dakota Territory, 1876 (#2), and General Crook (#3).)

I look at the photograph of the camp and pause to reflect and appreciate that McGillycuddy has included these pictures to add color to his story. When he described his "tent," this is not at all what I had pictured in my mind's eye. I pictured something much larger, more in the shape of a modern hunter's tent, square at its base, canvas sides wrapped around four corner posts, and tops stretched up to a taller center post. Certainly, something large enough to stand up in, with a cast-iron stove inside perhaps. I look now at my humble apartmental abode. Not bad, compared to those "tents." I pull out the next photograph, photograph #3 of General Crook, give a quick look, and set it on top. Tired and sick, I let my eyes close and fall asleep.

The key hitting the lock and the door opening wakes me. It's a soothing sound to me now, no matter the time. He's home. I look at the clock—9:17 p.m. "Hey, Dad. Brought ya food. Good shit."

"Thanks, Bro. Glad you're home."

He struts to the refrigerator with a covered plastic container and says proudly, "A little prime rib and salmon, beans, and rice." I instinctively observe his walk and talk—both look and sound good. "Rafael was going to throw it away. Thought it was overcooked, but you like it done, so I took it."

"I do. Thanks." Brody plops on the couch and gives an exaggerated sigh of relaxation. I've never met Rafael or any of Brody's co-workers, for that matter, but he works closest with Rafael and talks about him the most. Just waking from a deep sleep—and lacking Brody's ability to click the lucidity switch—it takes me a second to pull what I know about Rafael from my memory banks. Rafael is the head assistant chef, Columbian, about forty years old, who has worked at the restaurant for over ten years. Brody admires his cooking skills. Everything I've eaten that he's made has been excellent. Given Brody's numerous descriptions of Rafael as being "such an asshole," said usually with a wry smile, I assume he's tough and runs a tight ship. When Brody started, after about a week, the manager somewhat apologetically told Brody that he would have to work in Rafael's kitchen (the restaurant has two kitchens). Brody told her that he didn't have a problem with Rafael and that he'd rather work there. The manager was surprised, saying, "Nobody wants to work with him." Brody didn't tell the manager the reason for his preference, but it was because several female cooks who he described as "gossipy bitches" worked in the other kitchen. I don't know, but I suspect Brody got off on the wrong foot with one or more of them, said something, and complaints dictated Brody's working solely for the unlikeable Columbian hard-ass. I have no complaints. Whatever Rafael is doing is working. Brody likes his job.

"How was work?"

"Good. Busy as fuck. Rafael was glad to see me. When I walked in, he stopped cooking and put his hands on my shoulders and said, (Brody speaking now in a heavy Mexican accent), "Where you been, fucker? I only had these lazy fuckers. Feel OK, brother? You need to eat something. I'll cook for you. I don't cook for these other fuckers, only you." Brody starts laughing, and I join him. "How you feelin'?" he asks me.

"I'm fine. I'll be better tomorrow. I started reading the journal. It's interesting. He's talking about the first time he saw Crazy Horse." I give Brody the thumbnail version of what I'd read so far and show him the photographs of the Expedition and the camp. He sums up his close examination of both photos with "that's cool." I pick up the next photograph and hand it to Brody, knowing it will get a reaction. "That's General Crook. He was in charge of the Expedition."

Brody chuckles. "Why do all these dudes look so pissed?" Brody strikes a pose with his arms extended, hands fisted, with a grimace on his face and says in the scratchy voice of an old man, "I gotta get back and feed them hogs." Immediately recognizing his obscure reference, I bust up laughing. Brody goes back to flipping through the photos. I'm not prone to laughing much, less so as I get older. Not many things strike me as truly being funny anymore, but the way this kid's mind works amazes me, many times in a humorous way. If he's interested in the subject matter, he has an almost photographic memory, and he certainly knows how to use it to find my funny bone. I've never participated in any kind of social media, and until Brody started living with me, I'd never watched an online video. He recently introduced me to Norm MacDonald, probably most famous for his stint on Saturday Night Live doing the Weekend Update. "Dad, I think you would like this guy." Since that introduction, I've watched many of his videos, and Brody was right; I do like his cerebral storytelling form of comedy.

Finished looking at the photographs, Brody jumps up. "I have to get ready."

Shit. "I didn't think you were going?"

"That waitress wants me to go with her. She's pretty hot."

"You should eat something first. There's a little chili left." I remind myself that I need to move the last of the chili to the freezer tomorrow.

"Na. I'm good. She's gonna be here in a minute. Don't want my breath to stink."

A couple of days ago, Brody briefly mentioned the waitress he was interested in and that his restaurant was having a New Year's Eve party downtown. I started gathering as much information as I could. Where's the party? I get the name of the venue. Check. How would he get there? Uber. Check. What kind of party is it? Fancy. No blue jeans. Black jeans are acceptable if they don't have holes or rips. We discussed what he could wear. Is alcohol served? Dumb question. I expressed my concerns about the dangers of being on the roads on New Year's and so forth, but didn't go overboard as not to come across as controlling or untrusting. I was relieved earlier in the day when he said he wasn't going to the party because he was tired and thought it would be boring. Still, I knew from experience that a teenager's plans can change quickly, especially if a girl is involved. I remained hopeful, but my gut told me there was a good chance he'd come back from work with a different mindset. When he didn't mention it right away, I thought I was in the clear. My gut was right.

Brody jumps into the shower, and I find the restaurant's address and location in the city. I note that I need to try to get the girl's name and phone number. After a quick shower, I hear him shuffling through the closet, getting dressed, and spraying his new cologne. He looks handsome. His hair is back. He's wearing his best clothes—new black jeans, untucked white dress shirt patterned with small black designs, black buttons and black stripes at the collar and cuffs, and new red shoes.

"You look nice, Brody. That's a sharp outfit."

"Thanks." He grabs his phone.

"Phone charged?"

"Yeah."

"Take your charger."

"The waitress's name is Ally, right? Give me her phone number."

"I don't have it. Just met her." He puts on his coat.

I get up to say goodbye. "You still taking an Uber?"

"Yeah. We're meeting some other people at the restaurant."

I don't want him to go, but I have to let him. He's done everything I've asked of him for three months. Show a little faith. Just throw together a quick pep talk—a few words laying out your expectations but keep it positive. Don't damper his excitement. "Alright. Have fun. Be safe, Son. Keep it straight. No issues." I hug him. His new cologne smells good. "Love you, man."

"Love you too, Dad."

"Text me later and let me know what's going on."

The apartment goes quiet again, but my thoughts are loud in my head. This is going to be a test. Please make good decisions. Be thankful that he's with you, I tell myself. If he were at college, you wouldn't have any clue what he was doing. Think about something else.

I search "Norm MacDonald's last Letterman appearance" and find the video with the joke Brody referenced earlier. Norm says: "What about in the old days when they took pictures of you—way back—you know when they pulled that thing, and it exploded and stuff. I got a picture of my great grandfather, the thing took six hours, uh, to take your picture… and, uh, uh… and the picture of my great grandfather… one… every guy only had one picture back then… and it's just him sitting like (Norm strikes the grimacing pose that Brody replicated minutes before). I gotta get back and feed them hogs…. Who's gonna feed the hogs? Somebody gotta feed them hogs. Now…," I stop the video, impressed as much with Brody's using this reference to convey his impression of the old photographs, as with Norm's comedy.

I still don't have much of an appetite, but realizing I haven't eaten much today, I heat a portion of the food Brody brought. Nice job, Rafael. Well-done prime rib and salmon. Perfect for my liking. I settle back into my spot, resigned to stay up until Brody gets home.

I remember where I last left McGillycuddy—sudden attack and pinned down by the Sioux. I start reading again.

Unlike those of eight days before, these bullets had plenty of steam. Sioux warriors owned the summit of the steep bluff to our west. From the protected cover of small piles of rock, they rained bullets down for several minutes while Crazy Horse made his passes at us. Uninjured, he returned to the top of the bluff; the Sioux stopped shooting and appeared to take flight. Lieutenant Bourke, aide-de-camp to General Crook, to his credit, rallied a detachment and the soldiers, still mostly on foot, stormed the bluff.

The battle would rage on for the next six hours. It had separated Crook's army into three separate factions; as such, his first order of business was to consolidate his command. His second was to recover his casualties and bury the dead. All able bodies were ordered to the battleground. I worked my way to where I had been summoned when I came upon a soldier kneeling beside a log, aiming his rifle into the distance. "Put your gun down, soldier. The battle's over." No response. I touched his shoulder and could feel his body was rigid. Leaning forward, I saw the soldier's face—a bullet had pierced his left eye and passed through his brain, causing instant paralysis and death.

I proceeded to where several officers had gathered around a wounded Captain Guy Henry of the Third Cavalry. The Captain sat on the ground with mouth wide open as one of his colleagues surveyed the damage in amazement, "If you ain't the luckiest son-of-a-bitch I ever met." Lucky indeed. A bullet had pierced the fleshy portion of both cheeks. It was a bloody mess, but other than losing several teeth and a good chunk of his tongue, it appeared the Captain would recover.

Unfortunately, the bullet had caused more damage than was at first readily apparent. It damaged his optic nerve that would later render him blind in his left eye. While examining and treating the Captain, I was made privy to certain details of the recent battle. From behind, I heard the young officer who had inspected Captain Henry's wounds, "I thought ya'll were done for sure."

Lieutenant Bourke responded, "The cowardly whelps wouldn't give us a fight in close quarters. Every time we got near 'em, they would turn and run for the next ridge. We had 'em on the run, but then it all went south." Witnessing the Sioux withdraw from the bluff, I too assumed our men had taken control of the fight. Another young officer, not cautious in his comments in the least, made me think differently. "They weren't on the run. He fooled you. Fooled Royall for sure (referring to Lt. Col Royall, who commanded the Third Cavalry). That Crazy Horse is a sneaky bastard. He kept falling back until you were too far out, then he sent a hundred around your left flank and a hundred around your right. You were surrounded before Royall knew what was happening." Bourke was quick to defend. "You think those primitives planned that? Impossible."

I would later learn from Crazy Horse that the unrestrained officer was correct in his assessment of the day's battle. Crazy Horse had followed a proven tactic of scattering, dividing the troops into small units, drawing them away from support, and then turning on them in force. Casualties that day, while significant, could have been much worse. The number of casualties of all kinds was fifty-seven, including ten killed outright and four mortally wounded. While military experts would likely deem the battle a stalemate, the Sioux had succeeded in *forcing Crook's prong of the Expedition to come to a halt to resupply. This was not insignificant, for Crook was planned to join forces with Custer and the Seventh Cavalry in a few days. The delay at the Rosebud resulted in Custer and the Seventh Cavalry having to go it alone at the Battle of the Little Bighorn seven days later, thirty miles away, where Sitting Bull and Crazy Horse would wipe the Seventh out.*

"Bing." Text from Brody. 11:10 p.m. "This is so formal."

Good, I think. Response: "They usually are."

Fort Robinson, Nebraska

On October 24, 1876, the Big Horn and Yellowstone Expedition was disbanded after Crook's army surrounded Indian bands led by Red Cloud on the newly-designated Red Cloud Agency, seizing all horses and firearms belonging to the Indians. Crook then ordered me to report to the commanding officer at Camp Robinson, where I was assigned to serve as assistant post surgeon. Camp Robinson at that time was a rough frontier outpost. Located on the north side of the parade ground, I lived in one of a row of small adobe duplexed houses that were quite comfortable compared to the living accommodations of the field. The commanding officer's house, two stories high and more resplendent than the other officer housing, was at the west end of the row. The camp benefited from the open winter and devoted many hours daily to drill and other instruction, which commenced every morning and consisted of instruction of the Manual of Arms, skirmish drills, and occasional sabre exercises and target practice. Across the parade ground to the south were the barracks, adjutant's office and guardhouse. (See photograph #4.)

Longing to have Fanny join me, I applied for a leave of absence without pay to get her in Detroit and accompany her back to the post. General Crook, to his credit, arranged instead that I be commissioned for the purpose of taking an insane soldier to the National Asylum in Washington, thereby furnishing me with traveling expenses and salary. I wired Fanny to meet me in Chicago, and she thereafter joined my insane patient and me on the remainder of the trip to Washington D.C. Completing my mission, we enjoyed a short visit in the Capitol before proceeding by train and stage to the remote Camp in northwest Nebraska, arriving in December 1876. I had concerns about how she would respond to seeing the remoteness of the location and her modest living accommodations, but as always, she did not disappoint. "Our little home looks very cozy, and seeing you cheerful and happy; my happiness is complete."

At Camp Robinson, I labored under the direction of Dr. Charles E. Munn. The lead doctor spent his days in the post hospital treating soldiers, stationed both at Camp Robinson and Camp Sheridan, about forty miles to the northeast. I, as a young subordinate, would assist him at the hospital, but I also had the duty of treating those who were ill or injured away from the posts, including the Sioux living on the Red Cloud and Spotted Tail Agencies. A routine day began with a sick call at seven o'clock in the morning, after which I spent the remainder of the day treating Indians in the outlying camps.

I took no issue with my duty to treat Indians, as I viewed it not only as a legal obligation because the government had promised the Sioux medical care as a condition of surrender, but also a moral obligation under my Hippocratic Oath to administer care to all men, white and red alike. Not all—indeed rather few—believed the same as me, most adopting the view of General Sheridan, who famously stated, "The only good Indian is a dead Indian." I had personally witnessed this type of ignorant detestation for the Indian at the battle at Slim Buttes in present-day South Dakota, earlier in September of that year at the tail end of my assignment to Crook's Expedition.

The day before, Captain Mills' detachment had come across a Sioux village. Waiting in a sunken depression in the earth less than two miles from the Indian camp, the soldiers hunkered down through the rainiest of nights before attacking before daylight. Seventeen warriors evaded the soldiers taking refuge in a creek ravine where they were soon surrounded. Interestingly, the troops entered the tipis in the hastily abandoned camp and recovered a guidon that had been carried by the Seventh Cavalry at Little Bighorn, a gauntlet that had once belonged to Captain Myles Keogh, along with three horses from the Seventh. Attempting to remove the remaining warriors from the ravine, soldiers threw burning poles into the gorge to no avail.

The soldiers remained relentless in their efforts and rained bullets down on the trapped Indians throughout the day. Eventually, the Sioux informed the soldiers they were bringing out an injured man. Carried by two men, a weak American Horse soon emerged with the butt of his rifle pointed at us. A blood-soaked blanket covered his midsection. I laid the warrior on a patch of wet grass and removed the blanket to discover his intestines spilling out. It was a mortal wound. I prepared to give American Horse a shot of morphine to ease the pain when one of the soldiers demanded, "Put a knife through the son-of-a-bitch. I ain't got no use for a doctor that'll do anything for a goddam Injun." I kept steady as I administered the morphine injection. Once done, I turned on the soldier and within inches of his face let him know what I thought of anybody who could see a man or animal suffer without giving aid (See photograph #5 of members of the Third Cavalry in front of a tipi that I used to treat the wounded at Slim Buttes. The recaptured guidon from Custer's Seventh Cavalry is clearly visible resting against the front of the tipi.)

Threeee... Twoooo... Oneeee!!! Happy New Yearrrr!!! I've had the TV muted but turned up the volume just before midnight for the ball drop. The camera pans from couple to couple kissing, celebrating revelers, and then returns to the celebrity hosts. I never understood the draw of standing for hours in freezing weather in the middle of Times Square with nowhere to use a bathroom. They look like they're enjoying it, though. I send Brody a "Happy New Year" text and hope he's having as much fun as the people in New York. Back to mute. I continue reading McGillycuddy's journal.

Starting in early April 1877, all the talk around the Camp was whether Crazy Horse would surrender. The winter had been especially brutal on the hostile Sioux bands that had remained in the North. Soldiers occupied the hunting grounds depleting food supplies, and the Indians never knew when the soldiers might burst into their village. Most had succumbed to the pressure, surrendered, and relocated to either the Spotted Tail or Red Cloud Agencies near Camp Robinson. General Crook was busy sending out peace-talkers for the few remaining resistants, in conjunction with the army's relentless pursuit. His first offers were simply for unconditional surrender, but this got little response from the likes of Crazy Horse and Sitting Bull. Crook changed his strategy and induced Spotted Tail, the powerful Brule chief who had been granted his own Agency, to convey more favorable terms to Crazy Horse, including a general promise to do his best to secure an Agency for Crazy Horse in the Powder River Country in the North along with the possibility of future buffalo hunts. Of course, the surrender of all weapons and horses was still required. Spotted Tail returned to Camp Sheridan, the post nearest his Agency, on April 5th and reported success. The various camps, excluding only Sitting

Bull's band, were slowly creeping toward the Agencies, their progress hindered by poor grazing and lack of supplies. Sitting Bull had moved North into Canada.

Over the next month, Sioux scouts continually reported Crazy Horse was moving toward the Agency. These reports were later confirmed by army delegations sent to encourage his continued advance with gifts and supplies. On May 6, 1877, Crazy Horse and his followers marched into the Red Cloud Agency and camped about five miles from Camp Robinson. Fanny and I joined the crowd that had gathered to witness the arrival of the infamous Sioux. Among the onlookers were many of the Agency Indians as well as Indians from the bands of Touch-the-Clouds, Roman Nose, and Young Man Afraid of His Horses, who had fought with Crazy Horse during the Indian Wars and had surrendered only one month before.

Indians travel loosely and are not closed up like military columns. As such, the one-mile-long procession with its great herd of ponies, packs of dogs and crowds of women and children had an irregular breadth of one hundred and fifty yards to half a mile. A military contingent, with which Chief Red Cloud rode, led Crazy Horse's band in. Crazy Horse, mounted on a different horse than when I first saw him on the Rosebud, followed directly behind. Two hundred highly-adorned warriors riding in eight loose lines, approximately twenty-five abreast, rode behind Crazy Horse. Taking up the rear were about seven hundred women, children and the elderly, all on foot. When Crazy Horse was within viewing distance as to clearly see his dress and features, Fanny leaned toward me and asked quizzically, and perhaps with disappointment, "Is that him?"

Indeed, based solely on appearances, one would not believe that this stoic Indian in his mid-thirties, slender in build, unpainted, his hair braided in fur wraps, with only one feather hanging from his head, and wearing a plain buckskin shirt with blue flannel leggings, was the ferocious warrior I had told her about and who had wiped out Custer's Seventh Cavalry. As the procession neared the Agency, the men of Crazy Horse's band burst into song with the women joining shortly thereafter, the women singing one octave higher than the men, their voices filling the flats and echoing off the sandstone bluffs. One of the army officers near me complained, "By God, this is a triumphal march, not a surrender."

———

Brody hasn't responded to my midnight text. It's now 2:00 a.m. I text him again. "On your way home soon?" I assure myself that he's fine and rationalize that the party probably didn't get going until midnight, and like the televised broadcasts from Times Square, things are probably now just starting to wind down. I look at the lit Christmas tree, still standing in our living area. Earlier that day, I told Brody that I would take it down and was pleasantly surprised when he protested. "Na. Keep it up. It ties the room together. We can hang stuff on it."

Ten minutes roll by without a response from Brody, and I'm becoming more anxious. C'mon, man… text me back. Steadily, worrisome thoughts start to take hold. When things were so bad with Brody, I was always able to deal with the situation, emotionally and in actuality, once I knew what the situation was—whether it required me to talk to his landlord or boss, pick him up at some shady location, carry him, clean him, take him to the hospital, or just hold him. The "not knowing" was always worse than the reality because, after enough bad experiences, it became easier and easier to imagine the worst-case scenario. What if he doesn't ask for your help this time? What if he can't? What if it's too late?

I try calling him again, and his phone goes straight to voicemail, triggering a flashback to the most frightening night of my life. After receiving his drivers license, I bought Brody a 1979 Dodge van. It had a decent stereo, swiveling captain's chairs and a fold-out couch in the back, an upholstered ceiling, and rust-colored carpet throughout. He loved it while it lasted. In hindsight, it probably wasn't the best vehicle choice for a teenage boy. As expected, the van started needing more and more repairs, of which I was unaware since I was in California. When I returned, the van needed a new radiator (due to some sort of minor accident), the heater didn't work, and the driver's side window wouldn't close. Kicked out of the house, it was also Brody's sleeping quarters. The interior was trashed. Given the cost of repairs, my financial situation, and Brody's living habits at the time, I elected to wait to get him another vehicle. We scrapped the van for $600. After that, I got him an apartment downtown so he could walk most places, but I would also let him use my truck on occasion. One day he asked if he could use it to take a girl on a date. I obliged. We planned that he would be home around midnight, he would stay with me that night, and I'd take him to his apartment in the morning.

Midnight came and went. I started texting him, but all went unread until about 1:00 a.m., when he responded, stating he was on his way. Knowing you can get anywhere in the city in no more than thirty minutes, my annoyance with his tardiness turned to worry when he wasn't back at 1:40. I tried calling him. Straight to voicemail. I called again. Voicemail. An overwhelming feeling that something bad had happened swept over me. Three more attempted calls. Nothing. I couldn't reach him, and I had no vehicle to look for him. Feeling desperate and completely helpless, I started calling the hospitals. The conversation with the receptionist at the third hospital went something like this:

"I'm looking for my son. He told me he was on his way home an hour ago. His name is Broderick Lee."

Ten-second pause. My heart pounded.

"White male, nineteen years old?"

I gagged. My breathing stopped, and tears welled up in my eyes. I didn't want to hear the next words from this woman because I was certain I knew what they would be… "He's dead." I forced myself to answer. "Yes."

"He's here. He's being treated in the ER."

I released my breath. My worst nightmare had not been realized. He was alive, but the momentary sense of relief was short-lived. Panic again ensued, and I urgently interrogated the receptionist, demanding to know his condition.

"Is he OK? Was he in an accident?"

"He's being treated for a face laceration."

"He's OK, though?"

"He's talking. He's getting stitches."

It's been a worry-filled start to the new year, and I'm concerned that he hasn't responded, but I don't have that overwhelming instinct that something bad has happened like I did the night of his accident. I decide a good next step is to call the restaurant hosting the party. I reach for my phone when the key hits the lock, and the door starts to open. It's a soothing sound to me now, no matter the time. He's home. "Brody." No response. I get up from my chair and move toward him. "Brody." He mumbles something and slumps against the wall in the entry. Dammit. He's shitfaced.

———

It's the morning of New Year's Day, and I'm lying in bed after six hours of restless sleep. The steady sound of morning traffic usually present is absent today. The apartment is quiet but for the hum of the fan spinning above me. Conditions conducive to thought, I replay in my mind the events of the early morning hours and plan how to address matters. Although unsteady, he could make it to the couch and take off his shoes without my assistance. I started to grill him, but I let things rest after hearing his badly slurred confirmation that he "Didn't take no fuckin' drugs." I rolled him onto his side, which he resented, and set the garbage can next to him. I'm concerned. It's certainly a setback. I'm disappointed. This was his first real test, and he failed miserably. But despite these negatives, I'm also pragmatic—he's not the first person to get drunk on New Year's Eve, and I try to find a silver lining. I'll have to dig further, but if it's true that he didn't take any drugs, that's a positive. I have time to come up with my bullet points. He probably won't get up until 3, at the earliest.

I haven't heard any movement from him this morning, so I get up to check on him. He's lying on his back, and his sinuses are still stuffed. He's snoring through his open mouth. I take the trashcan back to its designated location in the kitchen and contemplate whether I want to make coffee. My laziness trumps my need for caffeine, and I elect to wait. My cold symptoms have lessened, but I still feel weak. With the college bowl games not starting for several hours, the thought of a long morning in bed is appealing. I grab McGillycuddy's journal and photographs, get back into bed, prop my shoulders against the headrest, make pillow adjustments, drop my glasses, and read on.

———

When the whole of Crazy Horse's party reached the place where their camp was to be pitched, it looked for all the world like a swarm of black ants. The tipis were soon erected, about one hundred and fifty in number, nearly all of them small and badly worn. The village was arranged in the form of a loose circular pattern with a parade ground of about two hundred yards in the center.

That evening, the officers gathered for dinner awaiting the return of Lieutenant Clark, who had led the military detachment escorting Crazy Horse's village onto the Agency and who had been charged with disarming the hostile band. The mood among the ranks was high for with Crazy Horse's surrender, it was believed that the Sioux threat had been, for all intents and purposes, extinguished. Lieutenant Clark soon arrived at the Officer's Mess and proudly reported on that day's events. Clark made the first contact with Crazy Horse's band about eight miles from the Agency where Crazy Horse met him in silence but not ungraciously. The pipe of peace was smoked. Crazy Horse smoked with his hand covering his heart as a symbol that the peace now made would last forever.

One of the warriors, who I learned in later years to be He Dog, gave Clark a war bonnet (a war-shirt trimmed with scalps) buffalo robe, and a pony. Crazy Horse offered no gifts stating that he had given all he had to Red Cloud. Lieutenant Clark brought the war shirt with him to the dinner gathering. It was passed around the room for examination to great acclaim. Once the village had been erected, the warriors laid down their weapons without incident other than to note that the Indians, at first, only surrendered a portion of the cache, seventy-six arms, under the supposedly mistaken belief that Colonel Miles had in previous negotiations told Crazy Horse that if he went to the Agency, he could keep his new weapons and need only give up his old ones. Lieutenant Clark told Crazy Horse firmly that such was not the case and that he must lay down all his weapons. Clark began a search of the tipis with no resulting disorder or bad feeling. He ultimately recovered one hundred and seventeen arms in total, the greatest in number being the government carbine and Winchester rifle most likely reclaimed by the Sioux from the battlefield at Little Big Horn. All was now quiet at Crazy Horse's camp.

With Fanny by my side, Lieutenant Clark approached after dinner to inform me that Crazy Horse's wife had been ill for some time, and he was open to experimenting with the "white man's medicine" to cure her. I assured the Lieutenant I would make the visit to Crazy Horse's camp a priority. On the short walk home to our humble quarters after dinner, Fanny requested, to my surprise, that I allow her to accompany me to the Crazy Horse camp. I protested in adamance, but Fanny was equally determined to change my mind saying, "Oh, Valentine. So *dreary and lonesome is camp life. It is no wonder men do go so mad,"* undoubtedly referring to the insane patient who had accompanied us from Chicago to Washington D.C. in the winter. All reports indicating that Crazy Horse desired peace, knowing all had been disarmed and that the village was now calm, I reluctantly relented to her request.

The next morning, I, accompanied by Fanny wearing her green riding habit, and John Provost, my interpreter, the mixed-blood son-in-law of Crazy Horse's uncle Black Elk, embarked on the five-mile ride to Crazy Horse's camp. A clear day absent of the nearly constant winds that plague the plains, we were able to travel swiftly, and we soon arrived at the village. A swarm of curious children and dogs escorted us the last one hundred yards. Provost, assigned to my cause since my arrival at Camp Robinson, had proven to be a sound interpreter and trustworthy servant. Knowing the ways of the Sioux, he was able to identify which of the multitude of tipis belonged to Crazy Horse. He led us toward the village center.

I was accustomed to being somewhat of an oddity in the Indian villages, but Fanny was now drawing far more interest than I ever had. A woman riding sidesaddle, much less in a green habit, I am certain is something these Sioux had never seen before. More and more of the women and children gathered to follow our advance. The attention did not seem to bother Fanny in the least. Indeed, she seemed quite at ease, acknowledging her gazing onlookers with an occasional soft smile and gentle nod of her head.

It was quite apparent, riding slowly through the camp, that these people had felt the effects of the army's relentless pursuit of them. The beautiful massive tipis I had seen so many times dotting the horizon in the past were nearly all now gone, most having been captured and *confiscated. Their blankets and clothing were tattered and worn, and sparingly a buffalo hide could be seen, all sure indications that the close pursuit of last summer and the fall had prevented Crazy Horse's band from securing its wonted comforts.*

As testament to this condition that was common to all the Northern bands surrendering to the Agencies, I offer a photograph of Old Man Afraid of His Horses with his wives and children, taken at his village on the Red Cloud Agency one month before. Old Man Afraid of His Horses was a respected chief and Sioux warrior fighting alongside Crazy Horse, Sitting Bull, and Red Cloud throughout the Indian Wars. The Chief proudly displays articles of war no doubt acquired from past battles. He and his son, Young Man Afraid of His Horses, would later become staunch allies in my efforts to civilize the Sioux while I served as Indian Agent of the Pine Ridge Reservation. (See photograph #6.)

I hear Brody move. His hangover makes him break his normal routine. No nicotine cravings this morning. He gets up and walks to the bathroom. I note the sound of his uneven gait. He's still half-drunk. He urinates for such an unusually long time that it becomes almost comical—like a scene from a bad movie. No doubt feeling dehydrated, he takes an energy drink from the refrigerator, cracks it open, and takes several gulps.

"There's aspirin on the counter," I tell him in a voice loud enough for him to hear from my bed.

"I'm good."

"How you feeling?"

"Horrible."

"Sleep it off. We need to talk later."

I hear Brody climb back onto the couch. Content being in bed and knowing he'll sleep for several more hours, I keep reading.

———

Provost led us around a tipi where a couple of squaws busied themselves making coffee and preparing a meal. I then saw Crazy Horse seated on the ground. His face was quiet, rather morose, and his expression was melancholic. Seeing Provost, he stood and gave him a hearty grasp of the hand. He stood about five feet eight inches in height, his frame slight and sinewy. He wore the same clothing as when he arrived at the Agency the day before, a plain buckskin shirt and blue broad-cloth leggings. I could now also observe that he wore finely-beaded moccasins. Two braids of fur-wrapped light brown hair hung to his waist. Provost, speaking in Lakota, gestured toward me, and Crazy Horse turned to allow me to see his face. He was a handsome Indian with hazel eyes and a complexion lighter than that of his people. His face was disfigured by a distinctive scar starting just under his left nostril and extending down his cheek to just outside the corner of his mouth, giving it a drawn and ever-present fierce or brutal expression.

I removed my black medical satchel from the saddle bag. Fanny, still sitting sidesaddle, was surrounded by interested squaws, several of whom tentatively reaching out to touch the fabric of her green riding habit. Fanny confirming her comfort, I moved toward Crazy Horse to receive a handshake and the general Lakota greeting of "hau." I returned the salutation and turned to Provost to gain what information he had secured. Crazy Horse's wife was named Black Shawl Woman, and from the description of her symptoms, she likely suffered from what we then called consumption, and now call tuberculosis. Provost motioned to the tipis opening, and Crazy Horse returned to his sitting position with his face going back to its previous dogged and resolute disposition.

I entered the open front flap to the smell of burning sage. Provost followed. A small fire pit had been constructed in the center of the tipi, next to which stood a small altar consisting of a flat stone resting on two smaller stones, upon which smoldered a twisted wad of sage. A thin ribbon of blue smoke rose to the vented tipi opening above. Blankets and a buffalo hide lined the outside of the circular base upon which Black Shawl lay to my right.

The interior of the tipi was surprisingly well-lit as the sunlight pierced through the almost translucent skins stretched tightly around the fifteen or so structural pine poles. A hand-painted mural of horses of all hues of black, brown, and red lined and decorated the backside of the tipi. Pieces of clothing and leathered bags of various sizes, some plain and some beaded, hung from a line tied between two tipi poles.

Provost leaned over Black Shawl Woman and told her that I was a white medicine man. She acknowledged my presence with a nod and wheezy cough. Her black hair was braided and parted down the middle, exposing her forehead beaded with sweat. Unnecessary to confirm her feverish condition, I laid my hand on her. I sat her up and then used the stethoscope against her back to listen to her breathing. As expected, it was shallow and congested. I recommended horizontal rest and to keep the fire going inside the tipi to dehumidify the air as much as possible, but my prognosis for her recovery was not favorable. I stood by as Provost relayed the unfortunate news to Crazy Horse. If he was disappointed with his introduction to the white man's medicine, he did not show it, his gloomy state remained unchanged. I told Provost to tell him that I would come back the next day to check on her condition, to which Crazy Horse nodded his affirmation and consent.

Crazy Horse then requested I attend to one of the younger women in the camp who was suffering problems in childbirth. From experience, I knew Indian women did not want any man present when in confinement, much less a white man. Provost again led us through the camp. The Sioux women, having satisfied their initial curiosity with Fanny, did not follow. We rode to the edge of the village where the tipis were further separated. A burning heap of sagebrush around which a group of medicine men crouched, all droning incantations to the steady beat of a drum, identified where we were to go. Provost dismounted to inform an older squaw that Crazy Horse had sent the white medicine man to assist. I entered the tipi.

The smell inside was stifling, and I told Provost to fasten back the tent flap. The girl lay on a pile of buffalo robes with half a dozen older squaws around her, her mother among them. Their bodies stank. Sweat rolled down the girl's face. Her pulse was one hundred thirty beats per minute. I asked for the girl's age. The mother said she was eighteen. Provost, on my behalf, communicated that an examination was necessary to which the squaws muttered their disapproval. Provost argued with them for some time until their mutterings stopped, which I took as an indication that I could proceed with my examination.

The child was dead, and I would have to make a delivery with instruments. I told them the girl would die if I did not take the child. The squaws grumbled and shook their heads, believing "it would bring down the anger of the Great Spirit." I was not inclined to start a commotion on my first visit to Crazy Horse's camp. I told the women to think about it but firmly reminded them that the girl would not live long unless the stillborn child was delivered.

Fanny and I rode outside the camp about a quarter of a mile to lunch among the herd of grazing Indian horses scattered across the landscape. Provost stayed behind to visit. Fanny prepared our meal of buttered bread, dried beef and canned pears. It was a pleasant respite, but my lack of conversation evidenced that my thoughts were still on the girl.

Fanny tried to lighten my mood by conveying her happiness with her new life, that she was thoroughly enjoying herself that day, and that she would like to accompany me on future visits. After about an hour, Provost rode to our location to inform me the girl's condition had worsened, and the women were now willing to let me perform the necessary procedure. I jumped onto my horse, leaving Provost behind to escort Fanny back to camp.

The medicine men outside the lodge were now quiet. The girl lay unconscious on the buffalo robes making it quite easy to position her properly. Piece by piece, I removed the bones of the skull of the child. The squaws, uncomfortable with what they were seeing, started muttering their "hump-hump-humps" again. When I had finished, the girl slept quietly. I was always curious to learn more about the Lakota, and I asked the mother via Provost what they did when the babies didn't come.

"They always come," the mother answered.

"This time, it didn't," I replied.

"That's because she was raped by a white man," the mother explained. "Their heads are too big."

———

"Touchdown!" but not for the team I'm rooting for. I have one of the college football bowl games playing on the TV, and I'm eating the last of our chili. I decided to finish it off rather than take the time to freeze a single serving. It's over a week old, and there's not much hamburger left in it, but it still tastes fine. I think it tastes fine. I really can't tell, given my cold-stunted sense of taste and that the only thing I can smell is the vapor of menthol coming from my chest and neck.

Brody continues to sleep, but he's moving more and starting to awake from his drunken slumber. I now have the aspirin readily accessible on the coffee table next to his already opened drink. I suspect he'll need it. I mull over the points I want to make when we have our talk—how proud I am of the progress he's made over the past three months. He slipped, and I'm disappointed, but it's not the end of the world. I'll confirm he didn't take any drugs. How he responds is what's important. "Touchdown!" This game is over.

Eyes still closed, Brody raises his left hand to his face and presses his thumb and middle finger into the corners of his eyes. He lets out an exaggerated groan.

"There's aspirin on the table if you need it."

Brody sits up, plants both feet on the floor, and leans forward to drop his head in his hands for a few seconds before reaching for his cigs. He sidesteps onto the balcony, and I contemplate how horrible a cigarette would taste with a hangover. Brody finishes his smoke, and probably anticipating that I'm there to talk, he initiates the conversation about last night. "Felt like Hugh Hefner," he says. I don't respond, keeping my stern demeanor intact. "Ally had a nice little black dress, and I had two cute waitresses on the other side. Girl's so hot."

"Sit down. We need to talk." Brody complies. Other than his hair being a matted mess, he looks surprisingly refreshed after 12 twelve hours of sleep. The recuperative ability of a nineteen year old's body is an amazing thing.

"Where's your coat?" I'd previously taken inventory of his things. His phone and wallet are on the coffee table.

"Huh?" His memory is foggy, and I can tell he's struggling to remember. He looks to the chair in the kitchen, where he normally throws his coat over the backrest. "Ah, shit. I couldn't find my ticket so the girl wouldn't give it to me. Told her what it looked like. I started to get pissed, so I told her to donate it to Goodwill."

"What? That's a nice coat."

Brody replies disingenuously. "I know. Sorry I'm such a fuck up, Dad."

"Knock it off." I make a mental note to call the restaurant about his coat. "I didn't want you to go. Things have been going so well."

"Why you comin' down so hard? It's not like you've never been drunk."

"Brody, I can't remember the last time I was drunk like that." Not true. I can. I cringe inside. It was about ten years ago during the attempted-reconciliation period of my marriage. My then-wife had gotten us tickets to see a live performance of a rather famous chef who had a television show. As she explained it, the chef told funny stories and took questions from the audience. Prior to the show, we stopped at a restaurant with a bar down the block from the Performing Arts Center. We sat at the bar and ordered drinks. A beautiful woman—certainly always to me—she looked especially attractive that evening in her low-cut blouse. The young bartender apparently thought so, too. She was flirtatious and obviously enjoyed the attention. I didn't say how I truly felt, and I laughed along with them, pretending not to care. But I did. Bottomline, I hid my insecurities by knocking back seven or eight doubles. The full effect of the alcohol not yet hitting my empty stomach, I made it to my middle seat, theater center. It wasn't long until I started to feel especially warm. Minutes later, the show in progress, I knew I was trouble. I made it, rather the contents of my stomach made it, about halfway to the aisle. Undoubtedly it was the most humiliating moment of my life. Reliving the shame in my mind, I change my tone. Leaning toward Brody, I say, "Son, I love you, and I only want the best for you. We can't go back… I can't do it again. I need you to make better decisions."

Brody looks me squarely in the eye and then drops his head. "I'm sorry."

I appreciate the sincerity of his apology, and I let a few silent moments pass to ponder how to proceed. In the recent past, such an apology would have ended the conversation. Many apologies before were equally sincere, and when said, I have no doubt he intended to do his best to amend his ways. Unfortunately, addiction is a bitch. Determined to be a "fucking dad," I press on. "What happened? First, did you take any drugs?"

"No.

"Promise?"

"Yes. Told you I'm not doin' that anymore."

I believe him. "You can't. What happened then?"

"It was an open bar. Y'know I was gonna drink."

"You're always going to be around alcohol, Bro. An open bar doesn't mean you drink as much as you can. They were serving you?"

"No. Some girl's boyfriend was giving 'em to me. Ally's pretty, but she don't talk. Girl's so shy. She didn't wanna dance. I was bored, so I drank."

"Was she drinking?"

"Na. She don't drink. She's a good girl."

I hope that's true. There have been a few "good girls" in his past, and I've always far preferred them to the wild, partying, stripper-types he's normally attracted to. It doesn't matter how pretty Ally is, though. From experience, I know she won't last long if she's too shy to talk. At the same time, her apparent shyness and unwillingness to dance could just as easily be explained by her date acting the drunken fool. I hope it wasn't the latter.

"Was she mad that you got drunk?"

"I wasn't that bad until the drive home. We'll hang out again. She wants to go to a movie tonight."

We'll have to see how Ally plays out. She may be one of the "good girls" who tries to fix the broken "bad boy," or she may be the kind who just likes the novelty of being with one. I've seen both. The first type encourages and rewards good behavior. The second type wants the bad boy to live up to his name. I hope Ally's a "fixer," and maybe this time, Brody is a willing participant. "Alright. You slipped. It can't happen again. Get back on track and keep doing what you've been doing."

"Being bored as fuck."

"What?" I wasn't expecting this. "What do you mean?"

"I hate it here. I don't have any friends."

This isn't good. My immediate concern is that Brody will tell me that he wants to move back to our old city. I have no doubt that all the gains he's made will all be for naught if that were to happen. "It's only been three months. You'll start meeting more people."

"I don't think so. I don't fit in here."

"C'mon. You like your job. You're going to the movie tonight." I'm suddenly rooting for a girl named Ally whom I've never met. I need her to step up her game ASAP to keep his interest. We sit in silence. I question where this is coming from. He's been happy, at least I thought so. I stand up and turn on the Christmas tree lights, hoping they may somehow brighten his suddenly sullen mood, perhaps attributable in part to the depressive effects of large amounts of alcohol, perhaps in part to feelings of guilt. "What do you want to do? You can't move back."

"I know. I don't wanna… but I sometimes miss it… the rush of everyone crazy… bitches everywhere… hella fun."

"I'm sure it was fun sometimes… but it almost killed you too." Neither Brody's facial expression nor body language indicates that he in any way disputes what I just said. "Listen. I'm so proud of you… and thank you for coming to live with me. I don't care about this place. If you don't like it, we can go somewhere else. Nothing is tying us down. We can go anywhere you want. Pick a spot anywhere, and we'll go." I pause to let what I just said sink in. I can see the wheels are turning in Brody's mind. "Let's order a pizza."

"Right on."

═══

Apparently, a lot of people crave pizza on New Year's Day. It's certainly not the best day to order delivery if you want it in thirty minutes or less. I tasked Brody with making the order. His initial call went unanswered for several minutes. Frustrated, he tries a different franchised location. This time Brody's call is answered, but based on the conversation, I assume he's told that our apartment is outside the delivery range. Annoyed, Brody holds the phone away from his ear. I hear, "You'll have to call the one on Hatcher Road." Holding the phone in front of his face, Brody yells, "I tried, but the phone rang off the fuckin' hook!" He hangs up.

"Why's this so hard?" Brody makes a third call and places his order for a large pizza, half Hawaiian and half hamburger and onion. No doubt the worker is busy, but whatever he's saying, Brody doesn't appreciate it, and his voice and temper again rise quickly.

"Don't be a dick," I say. "I don't want them spitting on our food."

He pulls the phone away from his face and shoots a look telling me that he's annoyed with me questioning his handling of the situation. "I won't," he says. Brody goes back to his call. "An hour? Alright. Thanks." Brody disconnects and asks, "Remember that time we called in a pizza, and they said it would be four hours."

I smile. "I remember." We were about 15 minutes away from the pizza shop and thought we would swing by and pick up a pizza en route to his apartment. Brody called in the order and was told it would take four hours. Brody said, "That's bullshit," and suggested we keep going and order from the counter. Intrigued by what he was thinking, I complied. I parked, and he told me to let him handle it. Brody approached the counter and placed his order.

"It'll be ready in about 15 minutes."

"Didn't I just talk to you on the phone?"

"I don't know. Did you?"

"Yeah, I did. I recognize your voice. You told me it was gonna take four hours."

"It's busy."

"Not that busy. I gotta pizza coming in 15 minutes. Get the manager." Not too far back in the recent past, I was negotiating multi-million dollar deals, but for some reason I felt far more nervous watching him handle this awkward situation over an eight-dollar pizza.

Brody takes out his phone and holds it up as if recording the twenty-something manager coming to the counter. "Can I help you?"

"Yeah, I just called in to order a pizza, and your boy here told me it would take four hours. I came in and ordered, and he said it'll be ready in 15 minutes. Give me a corporate complaint form. This shit going viral."

The manager looked at his worker. "Did you say that?"

"We were busy."

"I apologize. This one's on us."

"Thanks." Brody put his phone back into his pocket and turned, flashing a devilish grin. "These guys don't give a shit."

===

Brody's on his phone catching up with the messages, pictures, and videos from friends he's neglected for over 12 hours. I quietly reminisce about our shared pizza experience and note that there are a couple more things still hanging out there that I need to address. It can wait. On reflection, he probably is bored. That's not entirely a bad thing. He's experienced more excitement in his short life than most ever will, and I'm confident he would acknowledge that a respite from his days of "hella fun" has been beneficial. Still, working 40 hours a week and just hanging out with dad the rest of the time is far too docile a life for a 19-year-old male. A week of us hunkering down in the apartment with cold symptoms has probably also contributed to any growing feelings of boredom, but what Brody expressed earlier was deeper than just needing more friends or more fun. He's searching for something. I realize that Phase 1 of "Operation Save Brody" has come to an end, and I mentally rebuke myself for not having the least bit of a Phase 2 ready for implementation. I have work to do.

Something on Brody's phone strikes him as amusing, and he laughs. Whether it be the message or video he just saw, the prospect of pizza, spending time with Ally, his hangover going away, the Christmas lights, relief that I've stopped talking about last night, or a culmination of it all, his mood is improving. I realize I could stand to get out of the apartment and have a little fun too. "Want to go bowling this week?"

"Hell, yeah."

"I always liked to bowl. Haven't done it in years. We went a few times when you were little. Do you like it?"

"Yeah. We bowled in PE."

"I'm really good. Bet you ten bucks I can average twice your score over three games."

Brody smiles. "Aright. Bet." He jumps off the couch and strikes his rapper pose. "Pizza comin' in an hour... time ta shit and shower. Ohhhhh!" He pretends to "drop the mic," throws his arms out to his sides and struts to the bathroom.

I call the downtown restaurant hoping they didn't act on Brody's recommendation to give his coat to Goodwill. A recorded message informs me that they are closed for the holiday. Brody occupied, the football game a blowout, and having time before dinner's arrival, I read on in McGillycuddy's journal.

Despite having an enjoyable first visit to Crazy Horse's camp, the returning winds of the plains and resulting dust clouds influenced Fanny's decision to bake instead of accompany me the next day. After completing my sick call duties, Provost and I embarked on the five-mile trek to the village, intending to first check on the status of the young girl, and then Black Shawl Woman, before attending to any other ill and infirm.

Fanny absent, and despite a strong headwind, we were able to ride at a fast pace and soon arrived at the girl's tipi. We were met by a large group comprised primarily of women, but including some men, wrapped in blankets of every color and design worn high on the shoulders behind the base of the neck and wrapped in front to cover their arms. Circling the main body were children playing with the dogs that ran wild throughout the whole camp.

We slowed our gait, and as we approached I must admit my first thoughts were those of uncertainty and concern. We dismounted a fair distance from the crowd when from the center broke Crazy Horse striding toward me, previous dress unchanged, a sordid expression on his face. It was then that I learned not to assess Crazy Horse's mood by his facial expression, as it rarely changed, and his furrowed brow in conjunction with the nasty scar on his left cheek always presented a menacing appearance.

Not knowing his intent as he approached, I was relieved when he stopped squarely before me and extended his arm and hand in welcome. I reciprocated by offering my hand that he shook more vigorously than he had Provost's the day before. "Pilamaya, Pilamaya. Hau Wasicu Wakan." I looked to Provost, who explained it was an expression of gratitude, a thank you of sorts, and that the Indians believed I was a miracle man. I then suspected the girl must be recovering well. Hands still embraced, I nodded at Crazy Horse to express my understanding and appreciation of his kind words. I proceeded through the gathering that separated as I walked toward the girl's tipi to facilitate my entry. I was pleased to find her sitting upright and in good spirits. Knowing the squaws' likely protest, and my candid assessment of the girl's condition, I elected to forego any examination. I smiled and nodded at the women before exiting the tipi. I then told Provost to convey to Crazy Horse that I wished to see Black Shawl Woman.

Crazy Horse, on horseback, led us through the village to his tipi. We rode slowly. With Crazy Horse directly to my front, I was able to make a close observation. He sat rigidly upright, one feather dangling behind his head, a small white stone dangling from behind his left ear. His head remained straight ahead, not turning left nor right unless called upon. Sometimes he stopped to engage in a short conversation, sometimes only nodding in acknowledgment. At all times, you could feel the respect from his people as he passed. Provost had informed me on the ride that while the Sioux found him strange, a mystic of sorts, often going for days without eating, all gave him a high reputation for courage, for which I can personally attest from my experience on the Rosebud, and that he is always generous, never keeping anything for himself. He is always taciturn and rarely jokes or smiles. So too, I can attest.

To my surprise, as we approached Crazy Horse's lodge, I saw Black Shawl Woman standing alone outside preparing food, the exact nature of the meal I did not know, but I suspected it likely a dog stew that was common fare with the Sioux. The party dismounted. Crazy Horse was immediately approached, tentatively but loudly, by several Sioux women. I asked Provost what the discussion entailed. Multiple voices speaking simultaneously, Provost struggled to make sense of it all. "They want food. Their children are hungry. They want the white man's gifts they were promised." Crazy Horse remained void of emotion as the women squawked. He listened intently for thirty seconds or more until he interrupted and said firmly, "Wiconi." Two silent seconds passed. An older squaw attempted to reengage, to which Crazy Horse raised his hand as if telling her to stop. She complied, and Crazy Horse turned and walked toward his lodge.

At first appearance, one would believe that Crazy Horse had ended the discussion. Such was my belief, and I took a step to follow him intending to assess his wife's condition, but Provost took me by the elbow to stop me. The squaws, not speaking, waited patiently. Moments later, Crazy Horse returned with the steaming sheet-iron kettle of stew that he presented to one of the older squaws. She thanked him and accepted the pot in her blanket-covered arms. Crazy Horse then said, "Yahi cha philamayaye." Later that day, I asked Provost for the translations of Crazy Horse's words. Provost translated the meaning of "Wiconi" as "Life." His final words were those of thanks, "Thank you for coming."

My prognosis the day before was that Black Shawl Woman, consumed by consumption, would most likely die in the next two weeks. My medical attention the day before had nothing to do with her seemingly improved condition. Her fever had broken during the night, and the relief therefrom was completely fortuitous. I listened to her chest. Nothing changed my initial prognosis, and I reiterated my initial instructions of horizontal rest and dry air. Crazy Horse and Provost then sat and talked briefly, with Provost carrying the conversation. I feigned the appearance of being occupied with the contents of my medical satchel. Provost then demanded my attention and informed me that the first rations were to be issued the next day; Crazy Horse was hosting a feast and he wanted me to attend as his guest. I told Provost to relay my gracious acceptance.

No other Indians needing attention, Provost and I proceeded back to Camp Robinson. The winds dying considerably since the morning's ride allowed us to converse easily. Given the prominence of the scar on Crazy Horse's face, I asked Provost if he knew the source of the wound, anticipating it was likely the result of a battle. He did, the story being well-known amongst all the Sioux. Apparently, Crazy Horse had fallen in love with a young Sioux maiden from another band, named Black Buffalo Woman, when he was a teenage boy. He never forgot about her, and years later when ready to take a wife, it was she that he chose despite that she already belonged to another man with whom she had borne three children. Crazy Horse, joined by a small party of warriors, rode into the camp of Black Buffalo Woman in the middle of the day, and made his desires and intentions known to her. Black Buffalo Woman consented and left with him. To do so was undoubtedly her right as a Lakota woman.

They could go with any man—at any time—of their choosing. There were some social ramifications, of course. She could never again join the dance of the Only Ones performed by those who had only had one man, but many honored women of the Lakota were barred from that dance. Two nights later, Crazy Horse's party stopped to lodge and feast with a friend. There was a commotion in the camp, and moments later, Black Buffalo Woman's man, No Water, threw open the tipi's front flap, pronounced, "My friend, I have come!" and shot a bullet from his revolver into Crazy Horse's upper jaw that ricocheted downward off the bone tearing through the facial tissue of his left cheek. No Water immediately fled, as did Black Buffalo Woman, who climbed out the back of the tipi to run to nearby relatives for protection. For several days it seemed unlikely that Crazy Horse would live, and his fellow warriors prepared to avenge his death in accord with Sioux tradition. Crazy Horse eventually recovered under his mother's care. To keep peace between the Sioux bands, the leaders decided that No Water should give Crazy Horse two of his best horses and Black Buffalo Woman should return to her husband. Many of the Sioux credited his not being able to take Black Buffalo Woman as his wife as the reason for Crazy Horse's strange behavior, melancholy demeanor, and unwillingness to speak much.

A picture worth one thousand words, if I possessed a photograph of Crazy Horse alive, I would so provide. In recent years I have communicated with historians of the Sioux and the noted photographer of Indian life, D.F. Barry, and I am convinced that Crazy Horse never knowingly allowed himself to be photographed. Barry told me he had repeatedly tried to bribe Crazy Horse to sit for one, but he could not be bribed, Crazy Horse saying, "Friend, why do you wish to steal my shadow?" In 1927, the Photographic Division of the War Department in Washington issued a photograph alleged to be of Crazy Horse. I have this photograph in my possession and can attest that it is not him. Crazy Horse was a strange-looking Indian whom I could identify anywhere.

===

Ally is expected to arrive soon for tonight's movie. Brody's fresh, dressed, pressed, and ready to go. Hoping to curtail the onset of heartburn from the pizza, I look for the antacid in the shoebox that holds our medicine. I see a dark spot in the shower from the corner of my eye. I turn to look. It's a hairball that Brody pulled from a comb he uses to detangle his curls and that he's slapped against the shower wall. A closer examination of the tub's base reveals his hair loss is accelerating. It's not alarming in the least. It has nothing to do with environmental factors. I'm bald. My maternal grandfather was bald. His maternal grandfather was bald at 19. He knows that his baldness is inevitable.

"Brody, come clean the shower."

Brody has, from before he can remember, enjoyed the attention his hair afforded him. I reminisce about him sitting in a highchair in a restaurant, maybe two years old, his long, then-golden cherub curls hanging from his head. I was in law school at the time. He pointed to our young, blond waitress and said, "Like her." His very cute infantile attention didn't go unnoticed. The smiling waitress commented on and touched his curly locks. Because his hair has always been such a source of his identity, one may think he would take losing it hard. Surprisingly, we've discussed the looming reality of his baldness and it doesn't seem to bother him. His plan: "I'll just shave it and get head tats."

Brody never had a haircut in his first thirteen years. It was a thick mane of the tightest corkscrew curls hanging to the middle of his back. His dislike of school really became apparent in the eighth grade. Despite testing in the 90th percentile in all categories on national aptitude tests, his grades were not good. I took him for his first haircut two weeks before starting his freshman year of high school. My rationale for shorter hair wasn't punitive in the least. Rather, the basis of my decision was twofold. First, I believed that Brody's long hair was propelling a self-fulfilling prophecy of sorts— if he looked like a rebel, he was going to act like a rebel. Secondly, I didn't want his high school teachers to make snap judgments of his aptitude or intelligence based solely on his appearance.

Interestingly, Brody was on board with cutting his hair. Whether or not it was just to please me, I don't know, but he wanted to donate it to a charity that made wigs for children with cancer. Upon our arrival, all the beauticians surrounded him to feel his hair, many commented how jealous they were, and all looked at me as if I was crazy when I said we wanted to cut it.

Concerned that this may be against Brody's wishes, the gal tasked with the unenviable job asked him, "You sure you want to do this?" Brody answered in the affirmative. The beautician showed Brody some pictures of different styles, and they agreed on a shoulder-length cut. She then wet his hair, thoroughly combed it out, and twisted it into a thick ponytail. She removed large shears from her drawer at which the beautician at the next station pronounced in very dramatic fashion her need to leave the room. The decisive cut was made. Whop! At first, it appeared the cut was to the desired shoulder length. As his hair dried, his curls twisted tighter and tighter. The length got shorter and shorter until it was painfully apparent that she hadn't accounted for the shrinkage. Even on top, she'd cut it too short. I felt horrible. He didn't look like Brody anymore. I asked him what he thought. Brody's words were on point. "I look like an old lesbian."

We tried to salvage the situation by shaving the sides and leaving a curly mohawk on top. I readily agreed when he asked if he could dye it blue. It was at that moment I knew I would never again try to dictate Brody's appearance. So tonight, as I look at him prepared to go on a movie date, he looks perfect to me—painted black nails, tattoos on his hands, neck and face, padlocked chain around his neck, earring dangling, and thankfully, hair grows back, his long curly hair. If head tattoos are in his future, so be it.

"She's here."

"Got everything? Have money?" I scan his area.

"Yeah."

I stand to see him off. "No issues tonight, Bro. No drinking."

"I'm not gonna drink."

I put my hands on his shoulders and look him squarely in the eyes. "And if I call or text, I expect a response. Seriously… got it?"

"I will."

I pull him in for a hug. "Love you, Man."

"Love you too, Dad."

"Come home after the movie. We need a good night's sleep. You work tomorrow."

"Not gonna be a late night."

I certainly hope that's the case. I make a cup of coffee, settle into my spot, and read.

My duties at the post hospital completed in the evening, I was anxiously excited to tell Fanny of the day's events at Crazy Horse's camp—that the young Indian girl was in good health and that Crazy Horse had invited us to a feast. She listened intently and summarized my report by saying, "Imagine that. Valentine McGillycuddy, miracle man of the Sioux." Of course, she was thrilled at the prospect of attending a feast at Crazy Horse's invitation. She planned to wear her beaver jacket over her best riding habit and fox fur pillbox hat. Given that rations would be issued in the morning, we planned to go to the Agency headquarters before proceeding to Crazy Horse's village. I would attend to my duties of care before partaking in the festivities later in the morning.

In addition to the standard rations of flour, hard bread, coffee, sugar, and interestingly for that day, strawberries and cream, the Sioux were also to receive the usual proportion of cattle. The glory of warfare departed, the ridiculous habits of savagery continued to manifest themselves when possible. Crazy Horse requested a favor that the herd of wild Texan cattle be turned over to them alive so his people could enjoy a sensation like that of a buffalo hunt. The request was granted, and about twenty steers were turned loose on the plain, and the Indians, armed with bows and arrows and mounted upon ponies, gave chase. All the thrilling whoops of battle were shouted, and the terrific feats of horsemanship and hunting skills with the rudest of weapons were exhibited.

Having secured their rations, the Indians started the short journey back to the village. Provost, Fanny, and I followed a good distance behind. Upon arrival at the village around mid-day, my first stop was the young girl's tipi who I had treated in childbirth but two days before. I was pleased to find her working busily outside, likely in preparation for the day's events. Fanny, knowing the girl's story, was dumbfounded that she was standing, much less working. I informed her this was not unusual for Sioux women, who under normal circumstances of childbirth do not lie in bed at all, but resume without delay their ordinary avocations. Not having personally witnessed this, I have been told by scouts and traders familiar with the ways of the Sioux that when moving with the village, the Indian woman will simply remove herself to the bushes for two or three hours and reunite with the village later with a papoose on her back. Staying mounted, I performed a candid assessment of the girl's condition, noting her good color and that she appeared to move absent any pain.

Outside her tipi, a wretched cur stretched at full length upon which a small boy comfortably reclined. The young boy and the big dog are two principal features of every Indian village. From my observations, the Indian boy is far ahead of his white contemporary in health and vigor. Looking at the matter as a boy would, I do not know of an existence with more happiness than that of the Indian boy from eight to twelve years old. With no one to reproach him because his face or hands are dirty, to scowl at him because his small allowance of clothing has run to tatters, and no long-winded academic lessons, his life is one long, uninterrupted gleam of sunshine. The Indian boy, a brat no doubt to our standards, knows every bird's nest for miles around, every good place for bathing, every pile of sand or earth to roll in. With a pony to ride and a bow for shooting, I am confident he would see little in the schools of our civilization to excite him.

It has often seemed to me that we are going ahead too fast with our boys. While we are teaching them matters of great import found in our books, nature's great secrets and beauties have been withheld. Our cities are filling with tallow-faced children; tallow-faced children grow up to be tallow-faced leaders; tallow-faced leaders make tallow-faced laws, and these laws lead to a tallow-faced country. Still, it would be immoral to not accomplish the elevation of the savage and illiterate. Such elevation could most assuredly be brought about by first teaching the children our language in which our ideas can be much better conveyed than through the medium of the Sioux tongue, which from the paucity of its vocabulary and infeasibility of its grammatical construction, is not suited for the advanced ideas of modern civilization.

As was our standard procedure, Provost had gathered information from the squaws to ascertain who was in need of medical attention. Provost mounted, and Fanny and I followed him through the village to our next stops, all inflictions uninteresting and minor in nature. Upon Provost's recommendation, we then proceeded to the ceremonial parade grounds. In the center of the parade ground, a company of warriors milled about—around thirty in number—accoutered in every mode of fantastic invention. Some were naked except for a breech-clout. Others wore red or blue leggings. Their faces and bodies were painted in all colors and in all patterns of green, blue, yellow, striped black and red, speckled and spotted in every conceivable design. Every costume was trimmed with small sleigh-bells. All wore feathered headdresses. On the far side of the diameter sat five older men, all holding switches, around a drum supported on a tripod. Five men mounted on ponies—masters of ceremonies of sorts—painted as oddly themselves, but wearing magnificent war bonnets that hung to the ground, faced Crazy Horse and his guests. Lieutenant Clark, or White Hat as named by the Sioux, the officer who had led Crazy Horse onto the Agency two days before, sat immediately to Crazy Horse's right.

Provost instructed that I should present myself to Crazy Horse, and he would direct where I was to sit. Seeing me, Crazy Horse extended his hand in greeting, saying "Hau Kola" or "Welcome, friend" and then "Kitala Putihi," the meaning of which I did not understand. I took his hand and repeated his greeting of friendship. He then pointed that I should sit to his right. Lieutenant Clark slapped me on the leg as I walked past to take my place. Between the Lieutenant and me sat Frank Grourard, Lieutenant Clark's interpreter. We sat on a couch made of a bed of twigs and small willow branches covered with buffalo robes and blankets. A cotton sheeting painted with crude drawings of horses, mounted men, and buffalo covered the modest backrest. It was quite comfortable. Fanny and Provost took positions on a blanket behind the couch directly to my rear. I turned to ask Provost what Crazy Horse had said after his initial greeting. Provost responded, "He called you Little Beard."

Moments later, the center-positioned horseman uttered some words, which was perhaps a short prayer. Touches the Clouds, sitting immediately to Crazy Horse's left, then stood, drawing the attention of all. His name fit; Touches the Clouds was the largest Indian I had ever seen, standing over seven feet tall and weighing well over three hundred pounds. Two long braids hung over the highly decorated blanket that covered his shirtless torso. Like Crazy Horse, he wore only one feather, but he wore it in an upright position on the back of his head, unlike his cousin. He was reputed for his bravery, strength, skill in battle, and *diplomacy in council. A modern-day Goliath. He had only recently assumed chieftainship of his band after the death of his father and surrendered at the Spotted Tail Agency just one month before. Touches the Clouds commenced speaking in his low, powerful voice. While he never looked at Lieutenant Clark, the message of his speech was directed at him, which according to Provost's later translation, centered around reforms he wished inaugurated at the Agencies. (See photograph #7.)*

Crazy Horse spoke next. He did not stand but turned to face Lieutenant Clark. Provost interpreted his words as follows: "You sent tobacco to my camp to invite me to come in. When the tobacco reached me, I started and kept moving until I reached here; my face always turned toward the fort. My heart has been happy. In coming here, I picked out a place where I wish to live, and I put a stake in the ground

to mark the spot. There is plenty of game in the country. All these relations of mine that are here approve the choice of the place, and I would like them all to go back with me and stay there together. This is all I have to say."

Frank Grourard interpreted Crazy Horse's words for Lieutenant Clark. I was acquainted with Grourard; he having served as a scout and interpreter on Crook's Expedition. By all accounts, he had done more perhaps than any other one man to subdue the Northern Indians, except for General Crook himself. Of note, he was the scout to locate the Sioux village at Slim Buttes previously discussed. Given his eventual influence on Crazy Horse's life and mine, I find this an appropriate place at which to elaborate on this man.

Grourard was consummated from the marriage of a Mormon missionary and Polynesian woman. He moved with his parents to the Utah Territory in 1852 before moving to the Montana Territory to become a pony-express rider and stage driver. At the age of nineteen, while riding the express, he was captured by the Crow. The Indians did not kill him but abandoned him without mount where Sitting Bull found him, took him as a prisoner, and later adopted him. Grourard lived in the camps of Sitting Bull and Crazy Horse for the next seven to eight years. He married a Sioux woman, and for all intents and purposes, became Sioux in speech, custom, and behavior.

For reasons of which I do not know, Grourard escaped the Sioux to volunteer as a scout and interpret for General Crook. This did not sit well with Sitting Bull, who had made it known that he would kill Grourard if given the opportunity in battle. There had been some discussion, raised by Grourard, whether he should join Lieutenant

Clark for Crazy Horse's arrival to the Red Cloud Agency. The Lieutenant demanded his presence, and according to Clark, from all appearances, Crazy Horse harbored no animosity against him.

Despite the warnings from other Indian scouts, primarily Crow—that Grourard was not trustworthy—General Crook trusted him implicitly, stating one evening around the fire at which the Expeditionary officers gathered each evening, "I would sooner lose a third of my command than Frank Grourard." Not all of the officers shared in General Crook's admiration. Captain Mills, in a moment of solidarity with other lower-ranking officers, stated, "Grourard has a splendid knowledge of the country and knows the ways of the Indians, but I regard him as a coward and a big liar." (See photograph #8 of Frank Grourard with mounted Sioux Indians, 1878.)

Lieutenant Clark was the last to speak. He stood and spoke in animated fashion, a bit of a showman by nature, loud enough for all around the parade grounds to hear. After every sentence, he paused to allow Grourard to translate. "My friends, I want to say a few words. The buffalo are getting scarce and cannot last but a short time. A few years ago, the country was filled with them, but now the whites are crowding in, and settlements are springing up everywhere. For that, I am glad you have come in for your own good. I am glad you have listened to reason and come in. By doing so, you have saved your lives. I am glad you have come in now while you can get such good terms. If you waited, the Great Father would not give such good terms, and he would have sent more and more soldiers until you were all killed. But now that you have come in, the Great Father wants the best for you, and he wants to meet all of your great chiefs at his house in Washington D.C. If you have friends still up north (no doubt referring to Sitting Bull's band), you had better send out now and tell them they must come in at once. I am very glad to see you and glad you have come in with the good feeling you seem to have. Hau! Hau! Although you have been up north fighting against us, now that you have come in to live at peace, you will be treated well like the other Indians here. Hau! Hau! Hau!"

═══

I'm driving slowly back from the city-center in a light rain, anticipating that it could turn to ice at any moment. We had no issues last night. He was home early after the movie, allowing us both to get a good night's sleep. He opened the door to proudly inform me that he'd received a goodnight kiss. "She's got braces. Don't think I told you that. Didn't feel 'em, though." His good spirits carried over into the morning as he readied for work.

"Want to go bowling tonight?"

"Yeah. Sounds good."

After dropping Brody off at work, I called the restaurant where he had left his coat, and was relieved to learn that they had it and that they would hold it for me. I think about our conversation from the day before and try to start formulating Phase 2. Brody clearly expressed growing feelings of restlessness; and while Ally may serve as a temporary band-aid to alleviate his boredom, unless I can get Brody excited about something, help him find something to want to get out of bed in the morning, I'm concerned he'll decide to just return to his life of "hella fun."

My immediate thoughts center around the possibility of him going to college, but I quickly dismiss the idea. He didn't like high school, so why would I think that college would be any different? Besides, unless he knows what he wants to do, I don't think it makes sense for him to take out thousands of dollars in student loans for a general liberal arts education. I've heard many stories of kids graduating from college, in massive debt, and living at home because they can't find a high-paying job. Maybe he'd like something more hands-on—a trade, perhaps. I've heard that there's a national shortage of skilled plumbers, electricians, welders, etc. They make good money, and the unions offer apprenticeship programs that pay you while learning the trade. He likes cooking. Maybe culinary school?

My favorite job was building houses. I ponder the possibility of Brody doing that. After changing colleges three times in four years and having hundreds of credits from dabbling in every possible course of study, my academic advisor scanned my transcripts and responded to my question of "what's the fastest way for me to graduate" with "psychology major." Psychology it was. Nearing graduation two years later, I realized that an advanced degree was necessary to make any decent money in psychology; and while I found aspects of the field interesting, I certainly wasn't interested enough to study it for two more years. On a whim, I walked into the Air Force recruiter's office. After looking at my transcripts, the recruiter convinced me to apply for Officer Training School. Upon graduation, I waited to hear whether I'd been accepted to the Air Force, and needing a job, I approached a carpenter at a construction site and asked if he was hiring.

"Have any experience?"

"No."

"Can you start now?"

"Sure."

"Start picking up all the scrap and nails."

I went on to work for the carpenter for the next eight months, six days a week. I bought basic tools, proved my reliability and smashed my thumb more times than I can count. Steadily I became more competent, and over time I was given more responsibility. Sometimes being first on-site at 6:30 a.m. on a frigid winter morning to set up the compressors, lay out frozen hoses, and prepare the nailing guns and tools, I questioned what I was doing. Overall, I thoroughly enjoyed cutting wood and pounding nails. I found the end of the workday especially satisfying. I could look at what I'd built that day, and over a couple of beers, the carpenter would lay out the next day's plan of attack. We were nearing the completion of our second house when I broke the news that I'd been accepted to Officer Training School. He made me a generous offer. If I stayed on for two years, the carpenter would make me a full partner. I wonder how my life would now be different had I accepted. Back at the apartment, I hang Brody's coat in its designated place over the backrest of the kitchen chair. We have time to come up with a plan. We'll figure it out. I note that he won't be done with work for several hours, and I have nothing else to do until we go bowling. I make a cup of coffee and read on in McGillycuddy's journal.

———

Lieutenant Clark finished speaking and sat. Crazy Horse pulled from his side an elaborately carved wooden pipe, about three feet long, and from the stem hung several feathers. Crazy Horse handed a tightly-twisted bundle of brush to a squaw who proceeded to the large fire burning at our diagonal over which a large pot hung from a tripod of pine poles. The squaw returned in haste, bundle burning, and handed it to Crazy Horse. Crazy Horse lit the pipe, and it was thereafter handed mouth to mouth. I took a modest pull and handed the pipe to Grourard. The pipe returned to Crazy Horse, and he turned to give it to Black Shawl Woman standing behind him. My immediate thought, which I quickly suppressed, was to object to her smoking. I noted that she looked surprisingly well, and it was not the time or place to render medical advice. Crazy Horse was the last to smoke; he took a small whiff. When the pipe was emptied, he turned to shake Lieutenant Clark's hand.

The mounted headmaster of ceremonies recited another short prayer, and then a striking evidence of generosity was exhibited before the feast. An old Indian, ragged, wrinkled, and fairly tottering in his weakness, entered the circle, introduced by a fiery young warrior. The warrior said that his aged companion should be fed and otherwise cared for and that it was a shame that such feasting should be indulged in by the young and strong while the old were suffering. Touches the Clouds stood and presented his fine blanket to the old man. A group of old squaws then congregated closely together and covered the ground with pieces of calico, blankets, and other textures, which were immediately taken up by younger squaws and distributed among the most destitute of the Sioux.

The distribution of cloth and clothing still in progress, the master of ceremonies heralded in the feast with the loudest of prayers. After his utterance, a group of young men strangled about half a dozen large dogs, singed off the hair, and artistically carved the carcasses. Gruesome sights and sounds indeed. I heard Fanny gasp behind me. Shoulders, ribs, heads, feet and tails were thrown into the large pot. The old men started drumming, accompanied by others shaking gourds filled either with shot or small stones. The mounted masters of ceremonies turned in unison to remove themselves from the grounds, with the dancers flooding in behind them to take center position. Provost leaned forward to inform me that the dancers were about to perform an Omaha dance. I observed that many of the dancers were scarred in the shoulders and arms, evidencing Sun Dances past. The skin had been pierced through with thongs of rawhide fastened to buffalo heads strewn over a tall tree. They had danced and strained until the ropes pulled through the tortured flesh. The dancers started to circle in a slow two-stepped movement, with one of the dancers occasionally stepping outside the circle in animated fashion, giving in pantomime, as Provost later explained to me, a very graphic depiction of his achievements in battle, while the chorus of voices from the other dancing warriors chanted a verbal account of the same.

Enthralled by the dancing before me, a strangely grand sight and as gorgeous and gaudy a combination of movement and color as I ever saw, I did not at first notice the squaw approaching with a steaming plate of meat—beef and dog in combination—the evening's meal. The Sioux men to my left were the first offered their choice of the selection. Touches the Clouds, I observed, had a particularly bad habit of removing a piece of meat, and finding it not to his satisfaction, putting it back onto the plate. I found the food quite acceptable, sampling a piece of beef and a slab of dog's ribs, that I can pronounce to be of equal quality as mule meat. I, with the Expeditionary forces, had eaten mule for several weeks out of necessity at the tail end of the Campaign, whose mission it was to subdue these very people with whom I now was breaking bread.

I turned to Fanny to see her looking at me incredulously, her eyes filled with worry. A squaw with basket in hand stood over her and was offering her the tail of one of the curs only minutes before carved and boiled. I felt for her, but had it not been my beloved, I would have found the predicament most humorous. I gave her a slight nod to encourage her to accept that offered, as not to do so would have been an unpardonable insult. Fanny, to her wonderful credit, complied, pulling the steaming piece of gray cartilage from the squaw's knife.

In the end, it was a delightful evening, with Fanny thankful for the strawberries and cream that followed the main course, and Crazy Horse presenting me a very elegant tobacco bag and nicely worked pair of moccasins. Crazy Horse and all of his people received us in urbanity, as a virtue common to all Indians I have ever seen. Their treatment of visitors is fully equal in essentials to that of white men, even if they do not know as much of the minor points of etiquette.

When did bowling become so popular? I haven't been to a bowling alley in years, and I'd imagined we'd probably have the place to ourselves. Far from it. The parking lot is packed. I consider the possible explanation that families are looking for a final activity to extend the holiday season. Brody was talkative on the drive, filling me in on the highlights of his shift—the most interesting thing being that he and Rafael bet $50 whether Rafael could "land" the new African-American waitress in the next two months.

Brody's always been more verbal in the truck, or as he calls it, the "Kiva." He first used the term to reference our truck years ago when we were driving, and I was talking about my childhood. I don't remember the specifics of the story, but it involved me explaining how after family meals, four families in all, the women talked upstairs, and all the men would congregate in the basement. Brody said, "The kiva." I had no idea what he was talking about. He'd learned the term in school and explained that a kiva is a room used by Native American men, primarily the Pueblo, for religious and political discussion. Brody then made the connection saying, "This truck is our kiva." We're now on our third Kiva, all previously used, basic two-wheel-drive pickup work trucks. The first was a 1997 model we ran into the ground with over 260,000 miles. The second totaled. The third is going strong.

Having waited about 15 minutes for a lane to clear, we choose our weapons, my selection tedious and deliberate, Brody's not so much. He accepts as satisfactory the first ball he finds. "All right. Ten bucks on the line." I secretly like Brody's odds of winning our bet. I can score 75 as easily as 150. It's highly unlikely I can double his score over three games unless he gutters everything, which I hope doesn't happen. Brody opens the first frame knocking down seven pins and picks up one more on the second ball. I match him. His play is solid, but we're both struggling to find the headpin consistently.

End of game 1: Brody 114. Dad 118. May as well give him the tenner now.

Brody starts to find his groove in the second game. His stride is smooth, and he can effortlessly generate a lot of ball speed with his long arms. I observe that his shoulders are getting wide, and his upper body is bulking up. What I wouldn't have given to have his body when I played baseball. I exposed him to all the sports during his childhood, but he never showed any great interest. His disinterest wasn't based on a lack of athletic ability, quite the contrary. The kid's hand-eye coordination was excellent. He was hitting golf balls over 100 yards on the driving range when he was seven years old. At six, after watching an older neighbor boy in a conjoining backyard miss a teed baseball after three attempts, he asked if he could try. The boy's father, obviously frustrated, was hesitant, but I backed up Brody's request. Positioning his feet and his hands on the bat that was far too long and heavy for him, he squared it up on his first swing lining the ball over the father's head.

Brody rolls a strike. "She cute," he says, tilting his head to his right.

Girls have always intrigued him far more than sports. I remember watching one of his soccer games when he was about ten. The coach, trying to get him into the game, yelled, "Brody, you're in." I was excited to see what he could do. Coach: "Brody, get out there!" I looked to see what was causing Brody's delayed response. He sat with his back to the pitch, smiling and perfectly content talking to three girls in front of him. Finally taking notice of his coach's third demand to enter the game, Brody jumped up with his curls bobbing as he ran onto the field to immediately find the ball coming toward him. Brody planted his feet, took two steps and kicked with all his might. The ball went ten yards; his untied shoe flew twenty.

I pick up a spare. Brody follows with another strike. I'm scoring better in the second game, but so is he. Brody takes aim for the seventh frame and rolls it perfectly. "Turkey! Hell yeah!" Fist pump.

Game 2: Brody 148. Dad 136. Brody, proud of his win and beaming ear to ear, says, "Can't believe I beat you."

"I'm not surprised at all." I shake his hand in congratulations and hand him a ten-dollar bill. "You're going down next game."

I squeaked out a win in the third game, pulling my left glute in the process. On the ride back to our apartment, I share my recollections of the athletic prowess of his youth, including the soccer story. He questions the story's authenticity, and we share a laugh after I remove his doubt with, "Yes. That really happened." We ride in silence for about a minute, both of us, I think, reflecting on days gone by.

"Thanks for taking me, Dad. That was fun. We have to do it again."

"It was fun. Thanks for going." I extend my arm across the Kiva, give a pat, and rest my hand on his shoulder.

══════

Two days later, having just completed my sick call duties, Provost informed me that Crazy Horse was outside the hospital asking to see me. I exited to find him, six of his warriors, and a group of fifteen or more boys gathered around an electric machine I had set up for the Camp's amusement. Crazy Horse and I exchanged our normal greeting; he again called me Little Beard and asked if I would show him the machine's "magic."

I placed one of the poles into the metal basin and poured in a bucketful of water. I then threw in a handful of cent pieces telling the youngsters that if they would take hold of the other pole, they should have every penny they could snatch from the bucket. From experience with many previous contenders, I knew that this was about as good a contract as any Indian boy could wish. The boys looked at the shiny coins, and their bright eyes grew brighter. Smiles of expectancy played upon their dusky countenances. The old stagers could not be prevailed to touch the electric battery, but they would sit closely by for hours waiting for some "greeny" to come along. Crazy Horse's first visit to the Camp, in and of itself, drew attention, but his interest in my machine collected a larger than usual gallery. A courageous boy stepped forward, ready to collect his treasure. He gripped one pole in his hand and plunged the other into the water. His immediate howl of pain was drowned by the yells, cries, and laughter of the spectators. The boy, while receiving a significant shock, was fine. Crazy Horse was at first taken aback, but realizing the boy still possessed his full faculties, smiled faintly in amusement. This was the only time I saw Crazy Horse smile.

After several more failed attempts to grab the coins, Crazy Horse engaged me with the purpose of his visit. The transition from a diet of buffalo and other game, fish, and wild berries, bulbs, and grasses to Agency rations—the white man's food, of which he had heartily consumed since his surrender, had locked his bowels. I took a tumbler and filled it half full of water at the temperature of the room, poured in a few drops of tincture of camphor, just enough to give the water a slight sapidity, then filled the remainder with water. He drank it trustingly. I instructed Provost to inform Crazy Horse that it would not be unusual—and he should not be concerned—if he found an uncontrollable need to relieve himself on his ride back to his village.

━━━

"What's happening now?" Brody mentioned on the ride home from bowling that he'd noticed I'd been reading McGillycuddy's journal a lot. I brought him up to speed with a condensed synopsis of the battle on the Rosebud, Crazy Horse's surrender, McGillycuddy treating the Indians, and the feast, to include eating boiled dog. My recounting must have sparked his interest because, after only a few minutes of continuing my readings since our return to the apartment, he asked for an update. I tell him about McGillycuddy's electric machine and that Crazy Horse is constipated because he can't eat buffalo anymore.

"What was that joke Francie used to tell?"

"What joke?"

"About the constipated Indian and the doctor."

Somewhat surprised he would remember such a thing, I slowly start to recall his grandfather's joke. "Give me a second; I'll get it… Alright. An Indian was constipated, so he went to the doctor. He told the doctor his problem. The doctor gave him two pills and told the Indian to take them and come back the next day. The Indian did as told, and the doctor asked, 'Did you move yet?' The Indian said no, so the doctor gave him two more pills and told him to come back the next day. The Indian came back, and the doctor asked, 'Did you move yet?' The Indian said no, so the doctor gave him two more pills and told him to come back the next day. The next day the doctor asked the Indian, 'Did you move YET?" The Indian said, "Me have to move, tipi full of poop."

———

Over the summer months of 1877, I made a point of visiting Crazy Horse's camp weekly, often two or three times a week. Out of respect for him as leader and a personal desire to develop his friendship, I always made my presence in his camp known to him. Fanny accompanied me often, she becoming quite friendly with Black Shawl Woman. Many an hour I would spend in Crazy Horse's tipi, and as his trust in Little Beard grew, more and more he graciously exposed his thoughts, beliefs, and plans for his people. By the end of summer, I can say with all sincerity that I had spent more time with him and knew him better than any other white man had ever, thus earning me a second title among the Sioux of Ta-sunko-witko-kola, The Friend of Crazy Horse.

The months of May and June were quiet on the Agencies, and Crazy Horse and his people were gaining a reputation among the whites as being quite sociable. Crazy Horse continued his pursuit of securing his own Agency in the north, and he waited patiently for the promised buffalo hunt later in the summer. In early June, it was suggested to a collection of chiefs gathered at council that they should move to Fort Randall on the Missouri River. Of course, such a move was desirable to the government as one dollar at Fort Randall would go further than three or four dollars at the present Agencies. The chiefs resoundingly rejected the suggestion, and it was after this council that I first noticed that Crazy Horse was becoming more and more disenchanted with his decision to surrender.

Despite the initial shock that there be any discussion that his band relocate to any place other than the north, as had been promised by General Crook to entice his surrender, Crazy Horse remained committed to join a delegation of chiefs to Washington to meet with the newly-appointed President Hayes to discuss the matter. On my previous visit to his village, Crazy Horse stated that he believed he should learn the way of eating with a fork before he went to Washington. On my next visit, two days later, I brought with me two sets of utensils for training purposes. I first assessed Black Shawl Woman's condition. While she was still far better than when I first laid eyes on her, the deterioration in recent weeks was readily apparent. She was not fevered, but her breathing was again more belabored. Completing my examination, I requested via Provost that she set out two plates, each with a small serving of meat, one before her husband and one before me. I unwrapped the eating utensils, forks, spoons, and knives from two cloth napkins and handed half of the set to Crazy Horse. Focused now on Crazy Horse, who was distracted with the unusual pieces of silver in hand, I observed that Crazy Horse was without a shirt and wearing only a tanned breechclout, it being a hot day. Like many of the dancers

I had observed at the feast, Crazy Horse's arms were severely scarred, but in difference, he was also scarred across his upper pectorals. Each about three inches in length, the two scars protruded from his chest in puffy white skin.

I commenced the lesson. The best description I can provide is like that of trying to teach a toddler how to hold and utilize a pencil correctly for the first time. I first demonstrated the proper technique of cutting a small bite with knife and fork, resting the knife on the plate, and then using the fork to raise the severed morsel to the mouth. Crazy Horse looked at me sternly with his ever-present scowl. I repeated the process and motioned for him to give it a go, which he attempted and fumbled. I leaned forward and positioned his fingers on the fork, and nodded for him to try again. Failure again ensued. Although somewhat humorous, Provost nor I displayed any emotion. Black Shawl Woman chuckled from the corner. Crazy Horse calmly set the fork on the plate. He removed his hunting knife and stabbed the piece of meat, raised it to his mouth, and took a generous bite. He then said he did not understand all this foolishness when the point of a hunting knife was as good as a fork to catch the meat, and it didn't have to be specially wrapped for travel; a knife was always handy at a man's belt. I nodded thoughtfully in agreement.

Crazy Horse continued to speak seriously about wanting to know how Indians would travel to Washington, how a man could relieve himself, and how he could sleep. I answered his questions in the most reassuring manner possible. My duties fulfilled and our lesson completed, I left behind a set of utensils for Crazy Horse's continued practice. He then asked Provost to join him on his trip to Washington as he knew both the Sioux and white man's ways and spoke with straight tongue.

The month of January passed in silence. Gray, wet, and uneventful, Brody working, me holding down the fort, preparing the best meals I can muster, keeping his clothes, the toilet, and the apartment, in general, clean. Ally has kept Brody's interest, and the more time he spends with her, the more I start to appreciate her. I haven't met her yet. I want to, and Brody has invited her to come up to the apartment, but he reaffirms that she's extremely shy. All I know is that she's 18, a waitress at the restaurant, a "ginger" as Brody refers to her red hair, has braces, lives with her parents, and she must be home by midnight. I have no complaints. It's been quiet. Oh… and "she's hot."

I paid rent this morning and took a good account of my finances. I'm paying the minimum on the credit card. I have enough to cover our basic expenses for another two months, maybe slightly more if we keep it tight. I've applied for dozens of jobs and had a couple of interviews that I thought went well, all without success; but I've been in enough hiring positions to understand that in addition to me having no connections here, a comparison of my resume and the lower-level jobs I'm applying for are likely raising eyebrows and questions like "What's wrong with this guy?" I pull up my resume and read through my lifetime of work. I think back to when the General Counsel of a billion-dollar company commented before hiring me that my resume was "quite impressive." Well, the resume isn't working now. Time to change tactics. Tomorrow I'm dumbing it down. I convince myself that it's not lying if you take information out, right? The words "lie of omission" run through my head.

Phase 2 of Operation Save Brody has always been in the back of my mind, but I still don't have a plan. Brody engages me in a conversation that moves the topic to the forefront of my thinking.

"I hate this tattoo. Stupid as fuck." It's an accurate description of what he's staring at on his right forearm, given it's a rough homemade tattoo in large, uneven, black capital letters reading "**FUCK!**"

"I agree. It's bad."

"Next paycheck, I'm gettin' it covered. I'm tired of hidin' it. Scarred up arms too. I'm gettin' a sleeve." The fact that Brody acknowledged that he's been hiding the tattoo, and the scars, strikes me. He's wearing a short sleeve tee shirt now in the apartment, but he always wears long sleeves in public. "I remember when I showed it to you and asked if you liked it. You didn't say shit."

"Should I have?"

"Na. What'ya mean. Wasn't nothin' you could've done about it. I was stoked. I liked it at the time."

"How much does a sleeve cost?"

"I don't know. Not cheap."

"Let me see it." I move to sit by Brody on the couch and roll his forearm over to get a better look. "I'm sure they could cover it. What are you thinking?"

"I don't know. Maybe a snake. Rattles goin' into my palm or something."

I push the sleeve up his arm to look at his scars and see that they have largely healed. Most are smaller white scratches crisscrossing his arm that are not very visible anymore. He still has one running up his bicep that must have been deep because the skin running the length of the four-inch scar is still white at its center, surrounded by still-healing pinkish skin. I don't know if the color will become more natural over time or not. "Want to go to the tattoo shop tomorrow and ask about a cover-up? Your birthday's coming up; I'll split it with you."

"OK. Thanks."

"I think it's a good decision. You don't want that on your arm."

Brody laughs and says sarcastically, "Yeah, will impact my job opportunities."

"It would."

"And face tats, won't?"

He makes a good point, but the tattoos on his face have become such a part of his appearance that I really don't notice them anymore. Most people probably do, I'm sure, and so would most employers. "I don't know. You see more people with them all the time. When I was in the Air Force, you couldn't have any visible tattoos. Now every soldier I see has them. The stigma of face tats will probably go away too."

"Maybe. Don't matter if you're a cook, though."

"Or a chef. I'd think only the food matters. Ever thought about becoming a chef? There's a good culinary school here."

"Na. Cook's a great job. Chef is horrible."

"Why's that?"

"A chef has to order all the food, hire and train cooks. They're always stressed out. To cook, you just hav'ta make good food… and you can always find a job anywhere."

"Well, if you decide to be a cook, that's fine, but you're smart enough to do whatever you want." I'm not just trying to stroke his ego. I'm stating a fact. He is smart. I don't know many people who could skip half of high school and pass the GED on their first try. "Ever thought about what you might want to do?"

Brody looks at his inked forearm again. "Not really. What's it matter?"

"It matters a lot."

Brody looks me in the eye. "I mean, look at you." Something in my face must reveal that his words have bite. "Just sayin'… I'm not bein' disrespectful… I mean, what's it matter. You did everything you were supposed to do… and you've done more than I ever will… I just don't see the point."

I let a few moments of silence pass as I take in what he just said. "I don't think you're being disrespectful. Well, you don't have to decide today. Just think about it… I'm glad you want to cover that," referencing the tattoo on his forearm with a downward nod of my head.

"Yeah. It's stupid."

I put my hand on his leg, and with a wry smile, say, "You might feel the same way about head tats someday. Just sayin'."

Brody smiles. "I hear you."

Brody's at work, and I'm occupied making a batch of my specialty—ham, beans, and rice in the crockpot. I cube the ham and add it to the pan to brown with the slightly cooked onion, green pepper, and celery. It's not one of Brody's favorites, but he likes it more now that I give it a generous dose of cayenne pepper and hot sauce. I like the dish, but more important than taste, I appreciate that I can get five or six hearty meals out of it for about ten bucks.

Stirring the ham and vegetables, in a moment of self-reflection, I think about what Brody said earlier. His words made me pause, not because I was offended—I know he had no intent to disrespect me, but because I don't think I'd ever been asked, or asked myself, what was the point of all my hard work? I still ended up poor. What **did** it all matter?

I spoon the ham and vegetables into a bowl. I think what makes my beans and rice dish unique is that I cook it in a roux base. I didn't have cable television in California, and Brody had not yet turned me on to the wonders of online viewing. I had my choice among one local station, public television, three Spanish-speaking channels, and one channel each in Japanese, Vietnamese, and Chinese. Of my limited selection, public television was my favorite and where I learned how to make a New Orleans roux. Six teaspoons of butter melted in a pan. Slowly add six teaspoons of flour and stir, stir, stir over low-medium heat. I remember the host of the public cooking channel sharing a story from his childhood that all the kids would wait until "Mama" made the roux before engaging in any mischievous activity they had planned, knowing that once she started, she couldn't leave the stove.

I run through my resume in my head. Distinguished Graduate Officer Training School. Company Grade Officer of the Year Air Forces in Europe. Master's Degree with honors. One of six in the Air Force selected to attend law school for free while on active duty, law school Honors Graduate, Order of the Coif. Chief of Military Justice of the largest Command in the Air Force. Never lost a trial. Respected corporate attorney for ten years. Golf College student. Delivery driver. A divorced middle-aged man on the verge of bankruptcy... who makes a damn good roux.

An image appears in my head. I know the Indian name Crazy Horse would have given me. "Rock of Gibraltar."

I see the roux is just starting to brown and keep stirring, knowing I can't stop until it has the color and consistency of peanut butter. The moment of mental levity at my own expense now passed, I let the half of my brain working to unravel my thoughts take control but make a conscious decision to not completely give up the reins as the other half must attend to the roux.

Interestingly, I don't feel like a failure. Not in the least. I'm proud of my accomplishments. I ask myself again the question Brody raised. Why hadn't my 25 years of hard work with achievements throughout translated into wealth, or at least some semblance of financial security? I let the question simmer with the bubbling roux. I know the answer.

Peanut butter. The task-oriented side of my brain stayed alert. I turn the heat to low and keep stirring while I slowly add a cup of chicken stock, the ham and vegetables, and a dash of cumin, garlic powder and black pepper. The ham provides the necessary salt. If it needs more salt, I add it at the end. I keep stirring until the mixture becomes smooth again. I lick the gravy off the spoon... perfect... and pour it over three 15-ounce cans of red kidney beans already in the crockpot. I've soaked dry beans overnight before, but it seems like a waste of time to me. I add water until the beans are completely submerged, taste to Brody's liking with two tablespoons of cayenne pepper, noting that I need to buy more, and three or four shakes of hot sauce. I give a final stir to bring everything together and set the crockpot to high. I'll let it cook for about 2 hours, stir it once after 1, and then serve it over instant white rice.

I start the process of cleaning the kitchen and attend to answering my thoughts. I was never going to be rich, but becoming a millionaire was well within the realm of possibility. It didn't come to fruition, though, for an obvious reason—after ten years of working my way up as a corporate attorney, I quit just when I started making the big money. Dumbass. In a moment of self-reflection, I run through the reasons for quitting. The constant travel was a big one. I would often fly out on a Sunday evening to arrive home at midnight the next Friday, take care of business around the house, and do it again the next week. Grueling. I didn't care for my boss, and I used that as a partial excuse at the time, but he was planning to retire in a year. I no longer enjoyed the job. I didn't feel appreciated at home. The culmination of these factors seemed insurmountable at the time, but running through them now in my mind, they seem kind of petty. I'm sure a lot of people would gladly have traded places with me for what I was getting paid.

Still, even with the divorce and unanticipated expenses of the past two years, after 25 years of hard work and good jobs, you wouldn't think I'd end up technically living in poverty. I could have stayed on the safe path. I realize that had I stayed in the Air Force, right now I'd be pulling in around $75,000 a year in retirement pay. Correction. $37,500 a year. She would get half. I served for thirteen years and held the rank of Major when I separated from active duty. Colonel, at a minimum, was well within my grasp. I had my reasons for wanting to get out, including not wanting to go to Iraq for a year and believing I could make far more money in the private sector. I wasn't necessarily wrong. I just miscalculated how long and how much effort it would take to get to the big money. $37,500 in retirement pay would sure be nice right now. Dumbass. A psychiatrist would probably enjoy delving into the hidden depths of my psyche to understand why I tend to drive myself to my limits to outpace my peers, achieve success, and then bail before reaping the financial fruits of my labors. Who knows, maybe subconsciously, I just want to be the cook and not the chef. I contemplate how I'd look with a face tattoo. Enough self-examination for one day. It's all good. We have cheap food for a week.

———

Throughout the month of June 1877, I continued my social visits with Crazy Horse in conjunction with performing my medical duties in his camp. The circumstances, specifically his growing resentment of life on the Agency, facilitated my access to him. On my last visit, Crazy Horse returned the silverware that I suspected he had not touched since our lesson and said, "It's not good that warriors should have to sit in camp around a fire all day like a squaw." Simply stated, he was bored and no longer able to hunt or fight; he had nothing better to fill a portion of his days than to talk to me.

It being the first anniversary since the Battle of Little Bighorn, at which the Sioux wiped out General Custer and the Seventh Cavalry, I decided I would breach the topic with him. I introduced the conversation by telling Crazy Horse that I first saw him on the Rosebud, where he rode past our pickets under immense fire just one year before. I then asked about the Little Big Horn, or Greasy Grass as the Sioux call it. At first reticent, after some mild coaxing, he agreed to discuss the matter. In the process, he revealed many facts of historical significance. There was much back and forth between us, and the flow of conversation was often disturbed in translation, but this is Crazy Horse's account of events leading into and of the battle itself, told by him in absolute seriousness and without any hint of boastfulness:

> Sitting Bull told all the hunting bands of the Sioux and Cheyenne they should come to the Rosebud for a Sun Dance. In the spring, all came. It was the largest Sun Dance in many years. Sitting Bull gave flesh at the Sun Dance of fifty pieces of skin from each arm. He danced. After many hours he had a vision. He saw soldiers and horses, like grasshoppers, coming toward the Indian

village. They came, and the soldiers and horses were turned upside down, their feet to the sky, their heads to the earth. Their hats fell off. A voice told Sitting Bull that these men have no ears. He meant they did not listen to the Indians' words saying they wanted peace. They will come, and they will all be killed. He told us we were not to steal from their bodies after death. All the Indians were happy because we knew we would win.

Days after the fight on the Rosebud, the soldiers came again. The Indians camped on the Greasy Grass River. Women on the bluffs saw the soldiers riding fast across the flat land. The soldiers started shooting into the village. The men rode out to meet them, and the soldiers stopped and were forced into the timber by the river. Many soldiers tried to cross the river. The river was high and fast, and the Indians shot many soldiers. Some warriors crossed the river and chased the soldiers.

Word spread fast that the soldiers were attacking the village to the west. Many warriors moved back to the village. Many soldiers were on the slope. Warriors attacked from the front and side. Many other warriors approached from behind the soldiers. The soldiers dismounted and fought on foot. Then the Indians acted like they were driving buffalo to a good place to kill them. After we closed the lines, no one but a bird could have escaped. I rode through the middle of the soldiers and split them into two groups. Warriors followed, fighting on the ground. All the soldiers were killed. Long Hair (Custer) was killed. The Indians surrounded a smaller group of soldiers on the bluffs, and we shot at them all day. The Indians let the soldiers who were still alive go the next day after the village moved. The Indians did not follow Sitting Bull's words to not steal from the soldiers' bodies. Sitting Bull told the Indians that because they did not follow his vision, they were cursed. Forever Indians will always want the white man's things.

I observed during Crazy Horse's recitation that he spoke with great reverence when speaking of Sitting Bull. Sitting Bull was a comfortable topic of discussion for Crazy Horse, for when I asked him to tell me about the chief, he spoke freely and at length. According to Crazy Horse, Sitting Bull was a Wichasha Wakan, or holy man, a spiritual leader to whom the Great Mystery spoke in dreams and visions. He was also a warrior. When younger, he was the bravest and greatest warrior of the Lakota, accruing more white and red feathers than any other. Crazy Horse noted that there were many brave men, but what separated Sitting Bull from the rest, in addition to his spiritual qualities, was his "big and good brain," which I took to mean that he was intelligent.

All of the tribes had younger chiefs of high stature and ability: Lone Horn of the Miniconjous, Spotted Tail of the Brules, Red Cloud, and Man Afraid of His Horses of the Oglalas, but all had started to gravitate toward concession with the whites. Only Sitting Bull maintained an inflexible opposition to them. His opposition appealed in particular to the youth. Most of the elders were trying to block the traditional paths to glory by which men rose in honor and status in the tribe. Sitting Bull did not. He understood that peace was not for young warriors.

Given Sitting Bull's unique combination of qualities of holy man, brave warrior, and intelligent strategist, the Big Bellies, the eldest chiefs from each tribe elected Sitting Bull a Supreme Chief.

Such a position had never before existed among the Sioux. Before his appointment, each tribe, each band, and each man fiercely guarded its independence and freedom to do as they pleased, constrained only by social conventions and kinship obligations. But the times had changed. Constant encroachment by the whites and the increased military presence in their land demanded a head war chief with authority over all decisions of war. Four Horns, a big-belly and Sitting Bull's uncle, announced the election saying, "For your bravery on the battlefields and as the greatest warrior of our bands, we have elected you as our war chief, leader of the entire Sioux nation. When you tell us to fight, we shall fight; when you tell us to make peace, we shall make peace."

I asked Crazy Horse why, if all were to follow Sitting Bull's orders, did the Sioux so desecrate the bodies of the soldiers at Little Big Horn. Indeed, the news reports in the aftermath of Custer's defeat sent shockwaves of fear and disgust throughout the nation, reporting that many of the fallen soldiers were found riddled with arrows, nailed to the ground with pickets driven through their testicles, and the ultimate degradation, their male organs severed and stuffed in their mouths. Crazy Horse, in response to my question, showed little emotion. Always stolid, always fierce.

> *Little Beard, you do not understand our ways. Sitting Bull told the Sioux not to steal from the bodies of the dead. Yes, Sitting Bull did not approve of taking the soldiers' things. I told you he cursed them. Our women did the other things you speak of so the soldiers could not fight us again in the next life. Sitting Bull's vision did not tell the women not to do this.*

Crazy Horse continued to educate me of the ways of the Lakota, explaining that even though Sitting Bull said what should be done, it was up to each Indian to decide how to proceed. He continued, "If my warriors follow me into battle, it is because they want to, not because I have ordered them. We defeated Long Hair and killed all his men that day because every warrior made his own decision that he wanted to fight and kill them. We won because we outnumbered the white soldiers. We believed in Sitting Bull's vision that we would win. Every man was mad and determined to save his family." (See photograph #9 of Sitting Bull taken in 1882, the earliest photograph of him that I am aware of.)

That evening back at Camp Robinson, Fanny and I attended dinner with the army officers at Camp Robinson to commemorate the loss of the two hundred sixty-three soldiers of the Seventh Cavalry at the Little Big Horn one year before. Captain Jesse M. Lee, the military Agent in charge of the Brule Sioux at Spotted Tail Agency, of whom we both were very fond, joined us. Upon entry to the Officer's Mess, all patrons were escorted to the head table to view a neat arrangement of artifacts recovered from Indian villages in the aftermath of Custer's Last Stand, to include saddles, canteens, curry combs and brushes, rosters of companies, shovels and axes, two officer's blouses, a buckskin jacket, a gold pencil case, a silver watch, rifles and sidearms—all marked with the letter of the Company, in the Seventh Cavalry, and the name of the soldier it had belonged to. The Seventh's guidon I had last seen at Slim Buttes stood upright center-stage.

After the meal, Lieutenant Clark, ever the flamboyant showman, rose from the head table, tapping his knife against his glass. The room quieted, and the Lieutenant spoke. "My friends. Today we remember and honor those fallen. Those who were willing to make the ultimate sacrifice for the benefit of their country. Many of you knew men who perished on the Little Big Horn. I did." Clark raised his arm, holding a small gold object between his left thumb and forefinger. "This ring belonged to Lieutenant Van W. Reilly, of the Seventh Cavalry, killed in action on July 25, 1876. He was a man of honor, a skilled officer, and my friend. I shall never forget him nor his sacrifice. Many of you in this room remember the trials, hardships, and dangers endured for more than eight months chasing those savages. And you remember how we felt as we tightened the noose, ready to strike the final blow. But, as we feared, Crazy Horse surrendered before we could atone and compensate for our losses. Never forget. Please, all, raise your glasses. Remember the Seventh. Remember the Seventh!" The officers joined Clark's commemorative toast in loud unison, and then a four-piece band played the strains of "The Girl I Left Behind Me," the unofficial marching song of the Seventh Cavalry.

Fanny and I bid Captain Lee farewell and walked back to our quarters. One million stars filled the sky. As was her custom, she took my arm and when comfortable that no ears could hear her words, she spoke. "Husband. I did not care for the Lieutenant's speech. He continues to see them as enemies, but they have been kind to me. I have studied their family relations. They are kind to their elderly and poor. They care for their children. Their ideas are peculiar, but they are strictly adhered to. Listening to the Lieutenant, I fear the great danger of the future is not of the Indian's want of faith so much as our government's indifference to them. If our government will only observe half its promises, I am certain the Indians will comply faithfully." (See photograph #10 of Lieutenant Philo Clark and Little Red Hawk taken at Camp Robinson, 1877.)

It's been a good week. Uneventful. I've applied for a few jobs using the newly modified version of my resume. No bites yet.

Bing. Text from Brody: "Hey, think I can have apartment tonight?"

Response: "Sure. How's it look?"

Brody: "Great."

Ally picked him up a few hours ago to go to the tattoo shop to get his sleeve. Brody had his initial consultation the week before. The artist confirmed he could do a snake-designed sleeve that covered the ugly tattoo on his forearm.

Response: "Is it done?"

Brody: "An hour."

His 20th birthday is in a few days, and I pitched in half of the cost as his present. I'm anxious to see it and potentially Ally, too. Wanting to make a good first impression should the meeting come to fruition, I shave, shower, and change into nicer clothes. I observe that my black boots are starting to look a little worn. I also give the coffee table and toilet a quick wipe down. I had planned to go to the grocery store tomorrow, but Brody's request for me to vacate the apartment has pushed those plans forward. I make my list starting with our staples, visualizing myself working from the back of the store to the front: eggs, milk, big bag of shredded cheddar cheese, chips, cereal, white bread, tortillas, frozen pizzas, lunch meat, bacon, hamburger, bag of frozen fruit, oranges, head of lettuce, and a bag of baby carrots. Coming off a solid week of ham, beans, and rice, these products don't make the cut. I have spaghetti and sauce, macaroni and cheese, and several cans of tuna in the pantry. Pancake mix too. Condiments are in good supply. Brody usually eats at work, so I only plan two "special" meals for the week. I have half a bag of potatoes, so I go with fried pork chops for one of them. Green beans sound good for that meal. The second special meal not readily revealing itself, I decide to wait for an epiphany at the store. I then take stock of any needed cleaning products, detergents, and toiletries. Almost forgot—more cayenne pepper.

Reviewing the list, I note that a nutritionist may question some of our choices. I'm fairly careful about limiting my intake of the cheese, frozen pizzas, chips and the kind, largely leaving them for Brody's lunches and late-night snacks. I don't eat "the roux" very often. All I know is Brody has put on a much-needed 25 pounds, and he's looking stronger and healthier all the time. Eat up, my boy.

Bing. Text from Brody: "Done. Heading home."

Response: "Nice. Can't wait to see it. Door open. I'll text before I come back."

Brody: "Thanks."

I scan the bedside table while feeling the contents of my pockets. I grab my reading glasses, the list, McGillycuddy's journal and head out for my evening at the library and grocery store.

Fanny joined me on my next visit to Crazy Horse's village. On the ride in, I observed the village had grown in size. Many of the younger warriors of Spotted Tail's band had moved camps no doubt drawn to Crazy Horse's reputation as a warrior and continued persistence to secure his own Agency in the north. We arrived at Crazy Horse's lodge, and seeing Black Shawl Woman, Fanny hopped off her sidesaddle, and gayfully approached her friend. Black Shawl Woman smiled heartily, but I could not help but observe that she was unable to maintain her posture; her shoulders slumped, and her body bent slightly at the waist. She took Fanny's hand and led her around the tipi as if excited to show her something. Provost and I lingered as Crazy Horse was not present. I observed that the soft grasses of the plain upon which the Sioux had first set their tipis were now largely absent. Only immediately next to each tipi did they still appear. The grass stripped from the earth by the tread of moccasins, paws and hooves, unable to replenish itself for the lack of sufficient rain in over a month. A layer of dusty soil replaced the soft greenery of three months before.

Crazy Horse soon appeared on horseback, covered only by a breechclout, stoic, as always, but appearing more morbid than usual. He dismounted, and I immediately felt the weight resting on his shoulders. My suspicion as to the source of his foul mood was soon confirmed. He was standoffish and hesitant to talk, but my friendly assurances were slowly accepted, and he started to share his thoughts.

A few days before, General Crook, having returned from Fort Laramie, announced at a special council that approval had come from the Great Father for the buffalo hunt and that the traders could sell guns and ammunition to the Indians for that purpose. The chiefs hounded their approval, and one, Young Man Afraid of His Horses, a chief nearly equal then in stature to Chief Red Cloud, suggested that a celebratory feast be held at the lodge of Crazy Horse. No oral objections by the other chiefs were made, but Chief Red Cloud and two of his followers departed the council in protest.

That evening Red Cloud and two other Indians representing two other bands engaged Dr. Irwin, the Agent at the Red Cloud Agency. Frank Grourard accompanied the Indians to serve as interpreter. Dr. Irwin told the Indians he would attend to no business at such a late hour. He begged them to return in the morning. Still, the Indians were exceedingly anxious to discuss what they deemed the considerable dissatisfaction among many Indians to have Crazy Horse hold the feast. He had only recently joined the Agency, and therefore it was only right and a matter of courtesy that Crazy Horse should come to them, they being more established. Red Cloud told the Agent that Crazy Horse had always been regarded as an unreconstructed Indian; he had constantly evinced feelings of unfriendliness towards the other Chiefs; he was sullen, morose, and discontented at all times, proven by the fact that his common practice was to not attend the councils, just as he had not attended the council announcing approval of the buffalo hunt. Grourard then offered his opinion that Crazy Horse should not be trusted—he seemed to be chafing under restraint and was only waiting for a favorable opportunity to leave the Agency. Once away on the hunt, with his ever-increasing band of warriors, and weapons and ammunition, he would return to the warpath. Dr. Irwin took this information to General Crook the first thing the next morning, upon receipt of which Crook rescinded the order for the hunt and the sale of weapons and ammunition to the Indians.

Crazy Horse spoke. "Little Beard, tell Gray Fox (Crook) and White Hat (Clark) that I am not going to Washington to talk to the Great Father. Gray Fox promised a buffalo hunt before the trip to Washington, and the promise is broken. I will not let them put me in prison there. Touches the Clouds, and I are going north to hunt."

I stressed the importance of Crazy Horse's participation in the Indian delegation, as it was his opportunity to tell the heads of government directly what he desired for his people. I also provided assurance that he would not be imprisoned should he go, but his mind was set, "I am not going." How the details of Red Cloud's and Grourard's conversation with the Agent so quickly reached Crazy Horse, I do not know, but I now suspect that a major source of his information was the mixed-blood son-in-law of Crazy Horse's uncle Black Elk, and my trusted interpreter, John Provost.

I rode largely in silence on our return to the Camp, contemplating Crazy Horse's predicament and how I would communicate Crazy Horse's decision to General Crook and Lieutenant Clark. The news would not be well received nor lightly taken. Indeed, the rescission of the hunt angered Crazy Horse, but I do not believe that is what plagued him most. In the plainest of terms, Crazy Horse was hurt. Chief Red Cloud, the leader of the Oglala, the man to whom, along with Chief Sitting Bull, Crazy Horse had pledged his allegiance, with whom Crazy Horse had fought throughout the Indian Wars, to whom Crazy Horse had given the last of his best possessions upon his surrender, had withheld his approval and participated in a lie about Crazy Horse's intentions. I did not know it at the time, but this was my last visit to the camp of Crazy Horse. As for Fanny's experience that day, it was delightful. Unaware of the tension boiling among the Indian bands, she was simply giddy having spent the day playing with a new litter of puppies.

I've made a conscious effort to deviate from my normal method of grocery shopping, telling myself to bide time and give Brody some space. Tonight, instead of viewing the task as a personal test of speed and efficiency to see how quickly I can get in and out, I walk slowly, starting in the sporting goods section. I look at boots but decide mine will suffice for the rest of the winter. I look at the electronics and finally work my way to the food. Still thinking about how inexpensive televisions are now, I grab a nine-pack of orange energy drink.

I move my way deliberately through the aisles from back to front checking off each item as it's collected in the cart. Realizing I'll have plenty of potatoes left even after our special meal of pork chops and having pancake mix in the pantry, I elect to make a breakfast dinner for our second special meal for the week— pancakes, eggs, bacon, and fried potatoes and onions. It's a Brody-favorite. I'd planned on spending an hour in the store. I dragged it out for 45 minutes. Close enough. It's 8:52 p.m., and by the time I get home, it'll be past 9. For whatever purpose he wanted the apartment, he should be done by now.

I send Brody a text from the parking lot: "Done shopping."

Response: "Give me 20 minutes."

Me: "OK." I back out of my parking space, figuring that it will take me ten minutes to drive back, and then I can wait in the truck to run out the remainder. I pull into the apartment's lot to see Brody and Ally making their escape. They walk into the glare of my headlights. I think, "Oh no, Miss Ally… you're not getting away this time." Brody realizes it's the Kiva lighting him up, and he flashes a big smile. I park, jump out with bag in hand and say, "Hi, Ally. Come grab some groceries." Brody laughs and struts to meet me, with Ally following behind. "Nice to meet you, Ally. I'm Dan." She shakes my hand softly.

"Nice to meet you."

"Here you go." I give her a bag containing a loaf of bread and some hard rolls. Brody and I grab the rest, three or four bags in each hand.

It's apparent why he's been enamored the last month. She's cute as a button. Straight red hair wearing a nice sweatshirt and black leggings. Tiny. Great figure. Shy. Nice. No tattoos or piercings visible. I have a good feeling about her.

We unload the groceries, and Brody scans the contents of the bags to announce, "Hell yeah, good shit. We're set."

I see his arm is bandaged. "Do you like his tattoo, Ally?"

"Yeah. It's nice."

Looking at Brody, I ask if I can see it. "It's just the outline now. I have to go back for more shading and color. Hang on."

Brody heads to the bathroom and I start to unpack. "Can I get you anything, Ally?"

"No. I'm fine."

Brody returns not more than 30 seconds later, smiling and proud to display the new art on his arm. "I love it, Bro. It looks great."

———

"Happy birthday, My Boy." I pat his sleepy head. He's 20 and possibly falling in love. Last night, Ally stayed for about another hour after my return from the grocery store. I took this as an indication that she felt comfortable with me around. Unpacking the groceries, I noticed Brody had turned on the Christmas tree lights in my absence. Wondering if she thought it strange that we still had the tree up two months after the end of the holiday season, I asked for her thoughts. "What do you think of the tree, Ally?"

"It's cool."

"We like it."

I offered to make food, which they both declined, and proceeded to the bedroom with the journal to read and give them privacy. "Goodnight, guys. It was nice to meet you, Ally."

"Nice to meet you too."

I closed the door behind me and climbed onto the bed. I opened the journal, and searching for my readers, I heard Brody start to strum his acoustic guitar. I hadn't heard that sound in quite a while. Being homeless for a period and bouncing from apartment to apartment, Brody lost, or had stolen from him, many of his possessions, but he always protected his guitars from thievery—one electric and one acoustic. The guitars have been resting against the wall since we moved in, but he's played them infrequently and only in short stints. I could tell he was a little rusty, but overall, he played well.

Brody started taking guitar lessons when he was nine or ten. His instructor, a younger man and accomplished guitarist in his own right, intuitively understood that Brody would probably respond best to learning music he liked, at that time, classic rock. Rather than toil over learning to read music and basic cords he started the lessons by teaching Brody to play "Hell's Bells" at Brody's request.

"Brody," I said loud enough for him to hear me through the door and over his guitar. He stopped. "Play 'Hell's Bells'." I heard him chuckle, play a few test cords and bars, pause in silence for a few seconds to retrieve the song from his memory, and proceed to play it flawlessly. He still has it. I took it all in without comment and feeling happy for him, and me… us. I put on my readers and continued with McGillycuddy's journal.

━━━━━

As expected, the news that Crazy Horse was now refusing to join the Sioux delegation to Washington and that he intended to move his village north to hunt along with Touches the Clouds' band was not well received by General Crook. In response, Crook established an arbitrary boundary twenty-two miles north of Camp Robinson. If crossed, it would amount to an act of war and to which the army would respond accordingly. The task of communicating Crook's order to Crazy Horse and his people was delegated to the Oglala Chiefs Red Cloud and Young Man Afraid of His Horses. Whether Red Cloud knew that Crazy Horse was aware of his participation in the cancelation of the hunt and his perpetuation of General Crook's belief that Crazy Horse was plotting to return to the warpath, I do not know, but I imagine Crazy Horse did not receive Red Cloud warmly. Upon hearing from the Chiefs, and no doubt fearing retaliation from the soldiers, half of Crazy Horse's village departed. This left Crazy Horse and his most loyal followers more isolated than they had been since coming to the Agency in the spring.

My duties at Camp completed on September 2, 1877. I proceeded with intentions to visit Crazy Horse's village. En route, I met General Crook's four-mule ambulance coming on the jump towards me from the village. The General halted me and ordered me back to the post for the reason that it would not be safe for me in the camp as there had been trouble in the council. Knowing no danger would befall me at Crazy Horse's village, I requested permission to continue, but the General denied my appeal. That evening I received a visit at my quarters from Louis Bordeaux, a well-respected man of the Territory, to red and white men alike, who in his life had interacted with the Sioux more than any other, first delivering mail between Fort Union and Fort Laramie in 1835 when he was seventeen. His boisterous voice and mannerisms made him known to the Sioux as Louis Mato (Bear). By all accounts, he was an honorable and truthful man. Bordeaux served as an interpreter at the Spotted Tail Agency and had been present at the council with Crazy Horse earlier in the day. Discussing the situation that had developed, Bordeaux shared these details: "Doctor, that damn Grourard raised hell in the council today, for I was there when Crook asked Crazy Horse to take his young men and help the army by going north and helping to round up the Nez Perces."

Indeed, the enlistment of Indians to fight Indians was a great secret of General Crook's success in the taming and management of the wild tribes. He had used this tactic masterfully during the Expedition, having the Crow fight alongside the government against the Sioux and Cheyenne. Now it appeared he was attempting to recruit Crazy Horse and Touches the Clouds for the same purpose against the Nez Perce who remained untamed in the Idaho Territory. Bourdeaux said Crazy Horse seemed confused by Crook's request that he fight the Nez Perce. He then reiterated his desire for a buffalo hunt and for his own land in the north as had been promised before his surrender. General Crook told Crazy Horse all that may be possible, but he needed to join the Indian delegation to Washington so he could tell the Great Father, in person, of the things he wanted and that Crook would do his best to support his efforts. As further enticement, Crook said the Great Father would look fondly on Crazy Horse if he helped him fight the Nez Perce. With this reassurance, Crazy Horse then spoke: "You sent for me. I came in peace. I am tired of war, but now that the Great Father would again put blood on our faces and send us on the war path, we will go north and fight until there is not a Nez Perce left."

Bourdeaux continued stating, "Grourard interpreted what Crazy Horse said as 'we will go north and fight until there is not a white man left.' General Crook bristled upon hearing the mistaken threat, his face turned red, and he stood in anger to depart. Crazy Horse and Touches the Clouds, undoubtedly confused by the General's reaction, looked at each other in wonderment, for they could not understand why the Gray Fox was responding in this manner when they had just pledged to go to war with him to fight the Nez Perce. Bourdeaux immediately realized the mistake and attempted to calm the General and correct the misinterpretation contrasting Crazy Horse's words and Grourard's words in Lakota. Hearing that Grourard had changed "Nez Perce" to "white man," Touches the Clouds, stood abruptly in all his mightiness, loudly reprimanded Grourard calling him a liar, and moved with intent to do the man great harm should he get him in *his grasp. Several soldiers fronted Touches the Clouds with bayonets drawn, allowing Grourard to escape. In the commotion and fearing possible arrest, Crazy Horse slipped out the back of the tipi and fled. Bourdeaux summed up his account of that morning's events by saying, "There's going to be the devil to pay if this thing ain't straightened up."*

━━━

Brody now fully awake, I drop the colorful array of envelopes from family members that have accrued over the past week on the coffee table. Brody opens the envelopes carefully, removes the cards and reads the front of each before opening to reveal the enclosed cash or gift card. He immediately sends a text of thanks to each of his donors. I comment on the generosity of his relatives and then ask how he plans to celebrate. He confirms my suspicions that he and Ally have birthday plans with, "Hangin' with Ginger."

"Going out?"

"Yeah."

"Where?"

"She wants to go to a fancy sushi restaurant."

I wasn't expecting that. Sushi? Never did I think Brody would eat sushi. This is the same kid who worried his parents as an infant because he refused to eat any kind of meat? I remember thinking we had to get some protein into him, so his Mother chopped the tiniest piece of chicken and mixed it into a bowl of mashed peas. He clumsily used his spoon to finish every bite. Just when we thought our trick had been successful, he stuck out his tongue to reveal the morsel of chicken on its tip. "Fancy sushi restaurant. That sounds fun." Not wanting him to have to spend his newly-acquired birthday money, and not sure if he has enough in his wallet to cover a "fancy" meal, I give him $60. "Happy birthday, Son."

"Na, Dad. You already gave me my present," referencing his tattooed sleeve.

"That was part of it. Take it. Happy birthday."

"Thanks, Dad."

I'm the one who's thankful, thankful that we made it to twenty.

Brody left to eat raw fish with his pretty girl about fifteen minutes ago. Ally arrived on time, looking put together, wearing black leggings and a tightly fitted reddish-orange sweater that matched her hair color perfectly. Her makeup was lightly applied and subtle on her fair skin, and tonight, she wore a small gold nose ring. She must feel comfortable here because she opened the front door and walked straight in, no doubt at Brody's texted instruction. Her display of apparent comfort emboldened me to ask for the name of the restaurant and her phone number in case of emergency, which she readily gave up. Brody's rolling eyes notwithstanding, her number is now written on my ever-present notepad, ready for entry into my phone tomorrow. I reiterated my wish for them to have fun, encouraged safety, and have since made a cup of coffee to facilitate my staying awake until their return. I read on.

———

Bourdeaux was adamant that Grourard's incorrect translation of Crazy Horse's words was intentional. He, like others, believed that Grourard feared for his life, thinking that Sitting Bull, or another

Indian on his behalf, most likely Crazy Horse, would kill him in retribution for his desertion and subsequent treason in helping the army against the Sioux. Under such a theory, it was simply in Grourard's best self-interest to put Crazy Horse out of the way. I remained noncommittal, but then Captain Mill's words spoken during the Expedition ran through my head that, "Grourard has a splendid knowledge of the country and knows the ways of the Indians, but I regard him a coward and a big liar."

Upon Bourdeaux's departure, I went to find General Crook to clarify the translation and perhaps avert trouble. General Crook was not present upon my arrival, but several army officers and Indian leaders had gathered in his quarters in his absence to include Lieutenant Clark and Chief Red Cloud. Frank Grourard served as interpreter. They were discussing a plan to kill Crazy Horse. The chiefs agreed they would each select three or four of their top warriors to go to Crazy Horse's camp the next day. The man successful in carrying out the fatal attack would receive three hundred dollars. General Crook soon returned and immediately quashed what had been concocted, saying, "Gentlemen, I fear you have not properly thought through the consequences of such an open killing. The same ends can easily be achieved without bloodshed and setting the stage for a mass uprising. I have telegraphed Washington requesting orders granting permission to arrest Crazy Horse and move him by rail to the Fort Marion in Florida (that being the location of the imprisoned Apache chief, Geronimo)."

I attempted to explain to General Crook how Crazy Horse's words had been skewed in translation, but the General would have none of it, saying there had been no mistake and reaffirming that Crazy Horse planned to go north to join Sitting Bull. Crook's unshaken belief in the veracity of Grourard's translation, despite evidence to the contrary, undoubtedly rested on his trust in the man formed as an Indian scout during the Expedition.

The next morning, General Crook departed Camp Robinson for Fort Laramie, perhaps intending to avoid the trouble about to ensue, for later that day a courier arrived from Fort Laramie with orders from the General stating that Washington had approved his request and that Crazy Horse was to be arrested and put in the guard house (which contained a holding cell). I also received orders to report the next morning before daylight as medical officer to accompany the arrest party. Fanny was visibly distraught by the news that Crazy Horse was to be arrested and sent to a prison in Florida. More so she became upon learning that I was to accompany the arresting party the next morning.

One hour before daylight on September 3, 1877, a force of three troops of cavalry and a field piece left Camp Robinson to make the arrest. According to orders, the cavalry was to surround the camp at first light. A contingent of Sioux leaders to include Agency chiefs Red Cloud and Young Man Afraid of His Horses would appeal to Crazy Horse to surrender peacefully. In the event such appeals fell on deaf ears, the soldiers were to take Crazy Horse by force. The contingent crested the bluffs that overlooked the village just as the first rays of sunlight broke the horizon to reveal an empty plain below. There wasn't a tipi in sight.

The key hits the lock, and the door opens. It's always a soothing sound to me now, no matter the time. He's home. 10:04 p.m. "Hey, Buddy. How was it?"

"Good." I instinctively observe his walk and talk. Both are sound. Brody's holding a brightly colored red gift bag with a large scripted "Happy Birthday" and colorful streamers and balloons adorning its side.

"What's that?" I ask.

"She got me all spiced." Brody sits on the couch, sets the bag on the table and removes its contents to reveal two nice shirts, candy bars, and a card. He displays the shirts proudly for my inspection.

"Very nice. I like 'em. How was the sushi?"

"Good. I had a second plate. That wasabi's good."

Knowing how I prepare his food with extra heat, I'm sure he applied the wasabi generously to flavor the otherwise flavorless raw fish.

"Restaurant was fancy as hell too. She gettin' me all domesticated. Gentrified and shit."

I laugh in agreement. Leaning forward, Brody removes and reads the card that I assume he's already read in Ally's presence. He smiles, still reading. "Ewwww. I like this girl. Not gonna date a crazy girl again."

Speak of the devil. Brody answers his ringing phone and gives his standard salutation of "What's up?"

"What up, fucker." Sitting in the small space, I can hear the conversation and immediately recognize the female voice on the other end. It's his old girlfriend. The stripper. Stripper Jasmine. "My life is so fucked. I'm gonna take a bunch of bars." I've learned that her slang means she's going to take a "bunch of Xanax." I look at the tattooed snake on Brody's arm, red eyes, fangs exposed. It coils tightly around his arm, ready to strike. I imagine her shaking the pharmaceutical bottle in her hand, sounding the tattooed rattles on his wrist. Her voice hisses at me across the room. I say nothing, but I want him to hang up and cut the head off the viper.

There were many "girlfriends," but Jasmine was an almost constant presence during our time in hell, at least physically. Mentally not so much. I remember her answering the door to his apartment, and realizing I must be Brody's father, she introduced herself. I promptly told her I knew who she was as it was our fourth time meeting. That she had answered the door was unusual. Generally, the door went unanswered despite knocking several times, forcing me to use my key to gain entry, always anxious to discover what I may find inside. On my previous three visits, I'd found them sleeping on his mattress in the center of his living room floor, she still in her stripper clothes from the night before, out cold. In all fairness, she did once open an eye, acknowledging my presence with a "what's up" before slipping back into her Xanax-induced slumber. I could generally wake Brody and coax him out of bed. Not that day. That day he was the one out cold.

Brody wanting privacy, grabs his cigarettes from the coffee table and proceeds to the balcony advising Stripper Jasmine in the process, "You don't wanna do that. Stupid." Disappointed that her call has dampened the good birthday mood and that he's willing to talk to her, but also appreciating what he said as he sidestepped to his smoking area, I take a deep breath and read on.

——

On the morning of September 4th, word came that Crazy Horse, accompanied by Chief Spotted Tail, Touches the Clouds, and the Agent at Spotted Tail, Lieutenant Jesse Lee, had reported to the Officer of the Day at Camp Sheridan, forty miles to the east of Camp Robinson. In later years, I learned from my friend Lee of the tense situation at his Agency created by Crazy Horse's unexpected arrival. He described it as follows:

> *This came like a clap of thunder from a clear sky! How could it be that the most wanted of Indians among all others to be secured had made his escape and come to my Agency? The arrival of the Sioux courier from the Red Cloud Indians with word that Crazy Horse had escaped arrest produced great excitement; but when the courier was but a short time later followed by Crazy Horse himself, there was a wild scene that defies description. The bold warrior, the venerated hero of the braves, who had often led them to victory, was in the midst of his devoted friends, and to them now was a hunted victim of rank injustice and cruel prosecution!*

> *There were war bonnets and war shirts in profusion, and I believed we were about to have serious trouble. We took Crazy Horse to the post—or perhaps I would better say that he and three hundred of his friends were taking us there. As we reached the little parade ground*

of Camp Sheridan, Chief Spotted Tail arrived from another direction with not less than three hundred of his trusted Brules, all armed with good breech-loaders, principally Winchesters. The arrival of three hundred 'reliables' gave good solid backing, and with our ninety soldiers at quarters, turned the scales and kept it safely in our favor. The two sides squared off in the grounds, and as if by intuition, the forces split, permitting Crazy Horse and Spotted Tail to advance through their centers, leaving a small space six to eight paces between them.

Spotted Tail, the coolest man of all the assemblage hundreds, in his plain Indian garb without any insignia of chieftainship, spoke a few words, delivered in a clear, ringing voice with dignity and eloquence: "We never have trouble here! The sky is clear. The air is still and free of dust. You have come here, and you must listen to me and my people. I am chief here! We keep the peace! We, the Brules, do this! They obey ME! Every Indian who comes here must obey me! You say you want to come to this Agency to live peaceably. If you stay here, you must listen to me! That is all!"

It is hard to justly render an Indian speech, especially on such an occasion, but had you heard its telling points and pauses, emphasized and punctuated by the clicks of loaded rifles on both sides, you would have thought it one of the most effective speeches ever delivered! Its conclusion was greeted by six hundred vociferous "Haus!"

We then held council with Crazy Horse, who expressed his concern that something bad would happen if he returned to the Red Cloud Agency. He requested I go down without him and fix up the matter. I assured him that we had no thought of harming him and that he owed it to his people to return to Red Cloud to speak with authorities there, peaceably and quietly. All parties ultimately agreed that we would depart the next morning at nine o'clock for Camp Robinson, under escort and the following conditions: First, that neither Crazy Horse nor myself should take arms; and second, that I would tell the soldier chief, Lieutenant Clark, in General Crook's absence, that Chief Spotted Tail and I were willing to receive Crazy Horse's transfer to that Agency if authorized by higher authority.

———

Brody, having completed his call with Stripper Jasmine and smoking several cigarettes in the process, returns to the warm confines of the apartment. I heard him raise his voice a couple of times during the call, and given the time of night, I was close to popping my head out to tell him to keep it down. The call now completed, I'm glad I didn't. I push my glasses to the tip of my nose to bring him into focus and sit silently, waiting to see if he wants to disclose anything of the conversation. He tosses the cigarettes on the coffee table but immediately reaches for them to put the pack in his back pocket. "I'm goin' to work for a minute."

"Why? It's getting late."

"They're closing and want me to come down. Birthday."

"All good?"

"Yeah."

"No issues. Need a ride?"

"Nah."

Crap. Not knowing what's going on in his head after talking to Stripper Jasmine or what they have planned at work, all I can think to say is, "Happy birthday, Son."

"Thanks, Dad. I won't be long." He grabs his coat and walks out the door.

━━━

On September 5, 1877, Camp Robinson was on high alert in preparation for Crazy Horse's arrival and arrest, expected to take place in the afternoon. Lieutenant Lee had been ordered by telegraph to drive Crazy Horse to the Adjutant's Office, located next to the post's guard house. All quartered soldiers, about one hundred in number, were prepared for trouble, and a half dozen line officers with twenty subordinate guards were positioned near the designated arrival location. I was to keep within the limits of the post, as in case of trouble with the Indians, I would be wanted. At least one thousand Lakota from both Agencies milled about the parade grounds, with more arriving and tensions growing, every hour throughout the day. Many were armed with breech-loaders. I do not know how the weapons were acquired as all the Indians had been disarmed at the time of surrender. The smell of trouble was in the air.

The incoming party arrived in the late afternoon, coming in from the north, passing between my quarters and that of my neighbor on Officer's Row to enter the parade grounds. A yellow ambulance in which sat Lieutenant Lee, Bourdeaux, and two of the 'reliable' chiefs from Spotted Tail led the way. Behind on horseback rode Crazy Horse joined by Touches the Clouds and seven northern Indians, friends of Crazy Horse. Lee proceeded across the parade grounds toward the Adjutant's Office as ordered, the swarms of Sioux split like the Red Sea to make way for the wagon and trailing warriors, hump-humping as Crazy Horse passed. The great Lakota warrior acknowledged not a one with even a darting glance, riding firmly upright as always, wearing buckskin leggings and a red blanket, but looking more morbid than ever before. His brow furrowed deeply as if suffering from a terrible headache. The strain of recent events had clearly taken its toll.

Lieutenant Lee had Crazy Horse and his fellow warriors dismount and sit in front of the office. I quickened my pace across the grounds to advance to their position, where I met an agitated and concerned Lee and Bourdeaux. Lee informed me he was going to see if Clark would have a few words with Crazy Horse and said, "I'm not going to be made a goat of in this affair."

Bourdeaux then advised, "If he won't listen and they try putting him in the guard house, we better get out of here. There will be a fight, and we'll get killed for bringing him over here." I expressed my hope for Lee's success, but I feared the die had been cast and there would be no outcome other than Crazy Horse being arrested and imprisoned.

Upon my approach, Crazy Horse recognized me as usual and extended his greeting of 'hau kola' or hello friend. I paced anxiously in front of the Adjutant's Office waiting for Lee's return, which he did a few minutes later to announce Clark's directive to the Officer of the Day, Captain Kennington, that he was to take custody of Crazy Horse and not a hair on his head was to be harmed. Bourdeaux then in his growling voice, as loud as he could muster, informed the gathered Sioux of what was about to happen, stating, "The night is coming on, and the soldier chief said it was too late for a talk; that he had said to go with the Officer of the Day, and Crazy Horse would be taken care of, and not a hair on his head should be harmed." At the conclusion of the message, the Sioux gave a joyous collective "HAU!" Crazy Horse's face lighted up hopefully as he stepped toward the Officer to take his hand in embrace. Bourdeaux stayed true to his plan to remove himself from the area as quickly as possible.

(See photograph #11 taken from the old parade grounds at Camp Robinson circa 1897. Buildings left to right include 1874 Adjutant's Office, 1884 guard house then not existing, and 1874 guard house. Note that the covered porches were not present in 1877.)

Crazy Horse walked quietly with the Captain toward the guard house, his arms covered by the blanket draping over his shoulders and back. One of Red Cloud's Indians, Little Big Man, walked by his side. The soldiers of the guard, carrying bayoneted rifles and sidearms, followed immediately behind. Crazy Horse followed the Captain through the main door, and no sooner had he disappeared from view than he sprang back into the open howling with the desperation of an infuriated tiger, his arms flailing wildly with long, glittering stiletto-styled knives in both hands. I can only assume that Crazy Horse did not understand that he was to be placed into the jail overnight. Little Big Man grabbed his arms, attempting to pacify him, but Crazy Horse slashed the knife across the Indian's wrist to release his grasp. Crazy Horse then made a ferocious backward swipe with his left arm, Captain Kennington still in the doorway of the guard house, his intended target. The Captain called out, "Kill him! Kill him!" On command, the two guards lunged forward almost simultaneously with bayonets. The soldier's blade to Crazy Horse's left ripped through his buckskin shirt and lodged into the cabin's door frame, temporarily pinning Crazy Horse to the wooden structure. The second soldier struck from the right, with his blade finding its mark. Crazy Horse fell to his knees, dropped the knives, and placed his hand over the point of entry in his side, saying, "Let me go; you have hurt me enough!"

Seeing Crazy Horse fall, I hurried to him, finding blood seeping out from under the buckskin near his right hip. Confusion then ensued, and as the cowboys would say, "Hell was popping" The Indians milling around yelled at us. Even the friendlies, though they had supported the arrest, were not pleased with the result. One of Crazy Horse's warriors immediately sought revenge cocking his rifle and taking aim, but two of Red Cloud's Indians caught his arms and put him on the ground before he could fire. Hearing the cock of the rifle and seeing the ruckus, the guard of twenty soldiers raised their weapons and took aim at the one thousand Indians fronting them. Hundreds of rifles and pistols on the other side responded in kind. The Camp was a tinderbox ready to explode with the slightest further bit of instigation from either side. Apparently unaware of the severity of the situation, the Captain reaffirmed his orders and requested I help lift Crazy Horse onto his blanket and into the guard house. Knowing a more foolish decision could not have been made, I surveyed the scene to see Frank Grourard, the lying scoundrel largely responsible for the fateful events now befalling Crazy Horse, peering around the commissary building to my right. Wanting the ability to communicate with Crazy Horse and other Indians, I motioned for Grourard's assistance, which the cowardly whelp refused, electing instead to duck behind the building. The officers had fled to their quarters, orderlies had vanished, and no one could carry out orders, so I advised Kennington not to move Crazy Horse and wait while I ran to Clark to explain the situation.

Sprinting across the parade grounds, I saw Provost in front of my quarters, and I yelled for him to go to the guard house to interpret upon my return. I told Clark that he perhaps had enough men to put Crazy Horse in the guard house, but it would mean the death of a good many men and Indians, for the Indians were beyond ugly—war was about to break out. The Lieutenant became obviously distraught to learn of the debacle, but he was equally fearful of not following General Crook's order—that Crazy Horse be put in the guard house—to the tee. Clark hated to give in, but he finally agreed to my proposition to put Crazy Horse in the Adjutant's Office where I could care for him.

Touches the Clouds carried the now blood-soaked Crazy Horse to the Adjutant's Office and rested the greatest of Sioux warriors gently on the floor. It was dismal and lonely in that room, lit only by a kerosene lamp, with only me, Touches the Clouds, Provost, and Crazy Horse's father, at his side. I cared for my friend as best I could, administering morphine to ease his pain. At about 11:30 p.m. I pronounced him dead and drew a blanket over his face. But for the prominent scar creating his ever-present grimace, his face was at rest, his eyes peaceful. Touches the Clouds removed himself to announce to the people. Arms raised to the starlit heavens above, looking ever-taller than his full height of seven feet, he exclaimed, "The Chief has gone above!"

In the early morning hours, Crazy Horse's father claimed the body, it wrapped in blankets, and by travois moved it to a site on the Spotted Tail Agency for burial. The body was placed inside a government-provided coffin and placed on a low scaffold. For three days and nights, the father and mother mourned in Indian fashion by their son's body, from daylight to dark, to ensure the cattle and wolves would not disturb the body. On the third day, Lieutenant Lee brought them food and built a skeleton fence and box of sorts around the embalming platform. As soon as he completed the structure, he received word that Black Shawl Woman had succumbed to her illness, and the family wished her body placed by Crazy Horse. Lee complied. (See photograph #12 of the enclosed embalming platform on Spotted Tail Agency, September 10, 1877.)

Thus ends the historical record of Crazy Horse. It is my opinion that he had no intention of again going on the warpath and joining Sitting Bull as charged at the time of his arrest. A combination of treachery, jealousy, and unreliable reports resulted in a frame-up. He was simply railroaded to his death, but oh how preferable was death than loaded with chains and languishing away on the sands of the Dry Tortugas.

<hr>

I close the journal noting that I'm nearing its end. I flip through the few remaining yellowed pages. I think that, while it's all been quite interesting, and McGillycuddy has likely shed new light on events of historical significance, I certainly don't feel like he's revealed any huge secret. I remember his introductory letter and read it again.

You will soon understand that prudence dictated the need for an extended hiatus before its release to society.

I deliberated how best to bring the full extent of my experiences to light. In most instances, one would entrust the memoir to a university, historical society or museum. I elected to not do so, as first, the subject matter is highly sensitive, and secondly, doing so would not be very interesting. An initial revelation to an unknown descendant intrigues me far more. I hope that you feel you are being bestowed a gift and not a burden. One could simply read my private memoir to quickly uncover its secrets. I recommend resisting the temptation. From my experience, life on the move and in the open is vastly preferable to stagnation and closed quarters. In the event you have an adventurous spirit, like me, I encourage you to visit the places where these events occurred. No doubt much has changed since my days as topographer, contract surgeon, and Indian Agent, but any sights, sounds, and smells of Dakota Country still present will only embellish the experience.

Words of warning. Exposure of these writings will surely cause much consternation and debate between white and red men alike. My character, and likely yours, will be called into question, but know that all that I have written is true and accurate. My life was history and must be exact. I was deemed "the most investigated man of his age" by the papers, so I suspect my memoirs may also rekindle questions regarding my efforts to establish the Indians as citizens of this country. I, like all men, have regrets, but given a chance, there are few things I would change. I was young and full of courage. I was a clear thinker. I made decisions quickly, and I was always unswerving in my purpose. Let history judge me accordingly. Finally, if anyone expresses resentment in my actions or inactions to you, assure him that I was sincere in my judgments and that the responsibility rests solely with me and not with you, my Trusted Messenger.

Pretty dramatic, Valentine. If you have something to reveal, best get at it. The key hits the lock, and the door opens. It's always a soothing sound to me now, no matter the time. He's home. 11:17 p.m. "Glad you're home." Feeling somber after reading of Crazy Horse's death, I mean it. I'm glad he's home safely. "What did you do?"

"Nothin'. They was just wishin' me a happy birthday."

I instinctively observe his walk and talk. He might have had a shot or two, but it's all good. Brody tosses his cigarettes on the coffee table. He sits on the couch and leans forward, resting his elbows on his knees to look me squarely in the eyes, and with all seriousness says, "I know what I wanna do, Dad."

===

PART II

"Do not worry about your life, what you will eat or drink; or about your body, what you will wear. Look at the birds of the air; they do not sow or reap or stow away in barns, and yet your Heavenly Father feeds them. Are you not much more valuable than they? Can any one of you by worrying, add a single hour to your life?... Therefore, do not worry about tomorrow, for tomorrow will worry about itself. Each day has enough trouble on its own."

—Matthew 6:25-27

TWO YEARS DIGGING A HOLE. I'm still tired. I'm still broke. I'm still divorced. I'm a skeptic, but I don't want to become a pessimist. I don't want to give up. There's still some fight in me, but I'm filled with worry. Brody and I have started the climb and pulled ourselves from the bottom, but loose gravel sits over bedrock. The finger and toeholds we've established the past few months can easily crumble and give way at any time. Brody just told me he knows what he wants to do. Instead of feelings of excitement and optimism, I regretfully feel skepticism. I worry that we're about to tumble. I don't want to hear what he's about to reveal, especially since this revelation is coming on the heels of his conversation with Stripper Jasmine. That I've also just read about Crazy Horse getting stabbed to death doesn't help my disposition. If Brody's about to tell me he's had enough of this new life and he's moving back, I fear all the gains he's made will have been for naught. I don't have the energy to attempt a second climb. Brody looks at me intently, awaiting my response. Not wanting to hear the answer, I ask the question, "What do you want to do?"

"I wanna make music." My face must reveal my surprise because he dives into his reasoning. "Remember when you told me about… I think it was Charlie Daniels… he said he never worked a day in his life because he loved what he did?"

"I remember."

"Well, I love music."

Skepticism and worry reign. Pessimism lurks. An internal struggle of thoughts and emotion ensues; to support or not support, that's the question. The words "sex, drugs, and rock and roll" first run through my head. Without understanding in the least what he has in mind, I immediately question whether my encouragement to pursue a career in music would be the equivalent of buying him a van when he was sixteen. On the flipside, I've always told him to chase his dreams and that I would support him no matter what. Would discouraging him now make me a hypocrite and the equivalent of cutting his hair when he was fourteen?

"What do you mean, make music? Like play guitar?"

"Produce. Music producer. Nobody knows more music than me."

I can't disagree with what he just said. His interest in and knowledge of music is vast, running the spectrum from old country to heavy death metal. He always enjoys introducing me to a song from my era, something he can't fathom I wasn't into when I was his age, something I've never heard before. I know nothing about the music industry. I don't know what a music producer is or what they do, but I think it must involve more than just being able to name that tune. I'm aware that the pauses in this conversation—of my creation—are getting awkward. Then it strikes me. I have a mental conversation with myself: You didn't know how to hit or catch a baseball. You didn't know how to write a term paper. You didn't know how to build a house. You didn't know how to march. You didn't know how to give an order. You didn't know how to convince a jury. You didn't know how to close a deal. Throughout your life, you didn't know shit, but you weren't afraid to try because you had a loving mother who always supported you, no matter your immaturity, no matter your inexperience, no matter your previous bad decisions. A lot of words in my head that Brody would succinctly summarize in four. Be a fucking dad.

Do not worry about tomorrow, for tomorrow will worry about itself. Each day has enough trouble on its own.

I know how to respond. "That sounds amazing, Bro! You're right. Nobody knows more music than you. There has to be a good school here for that. We'll start looking tomorrow." Brody gives me the sincerest of smiles and responds with, "Bet!"

I climb into bed, and for the first time in a long time, I trust my fatherly instincts. I trust him to do what's right. I allow myself to believe that we're both going to keep climbing.

I search for "music production programs near me" and get three hits, one offered by a community college, one at a state university, and one private school that appears similar to a technical college. The community college offers a two-year program leading to an Associate's Degree. Required general education courses consume most of the first year with only two music courses—Introduction to Music and Music Theory. The university offers a four-year Bachelor of Arts program. It's expensive. Really expensive. The private school has an impressive website. Nice facility. Professional graphics. It's a six-month certificate program with a curriculum balanced between audio engineering and music production. Its motto: "We don't do homework, we work." I'm drawn to the third. Reassured that we have some options, I remove my glasses and turn off the reading light. From my bed, I can see the glow of his phone dimly lighting the walls in the other room. Engage Phase 2. I walk to the couch and bend down to kiss him on the forehead. "Good night, Son. I'm excited for you. Happy Birthday."

"Thanks, Dad. G'night."

━━━━

I slept like a rock. It's well past eight on a Sunday morning, and I'm glad Brody can sleep in before having to go to work in the afternoon. Feeling the need for coffee, I step out of my room to see Brody's head flopped back on the seat cushion and his legs hanging over the arm rest. Two eyes peek out from an opening under the blanket covering his bare chest. I stutter my step. "Oh. Hi, Ally."

"Hi."

I wasn't expecting this. I go about making my coffee and retreat to my room with journal in hand.

Pine Ridge Indian Reservation and Rapid City, South Dakota

In the spring of 1878, Chief Red Cloud, in conjunction with Indian Commissioners from Washington D.C., selected the site for Red Cloud's new Agency on the Pine Ridge in southwestern Dakota Territory. On January 29, 1879, I sailed through Senate confirmation to be appointed its first Indian Agent, one of the largest and potentially most volatile in the country. I was confident that neither the government nor the Indians would ever have cause to regret my appointment.

In my personal memoir transcribed to my second wife Julia, a copy of which is also in your possession, I elaborate in great detail of my time as Agent and interactions with Chief Red Cloud and the Sioux, the government, missionaries, and ranchers, but for purposes of posterity, I proceed now only to convey the reasons for my actions and some of the more interesting events of those days.

Having just marked my thirtieth birthday, I wasted no time in establishing my authority over the eight thousand Indians under my charge in a region encompassing about four thousand square miles. Such a Herculean task would first necessitate surrounding myself with men I could trust. I appointed William Allman to serve as blacksmith, earning sixty dollars per month. I appointed John Provost, my trusted servant, to continue in his service as Agency interpreter, for which he was to be paid six hundred dollars a year. The storekeeper, responsible for the intake and distribution of rations, was also a key position requiring a man of loyalty and honor. Despite having received guidance from the Office of Indian Affairs via telegram that "the rule in regard to the employment of relatives is applicable to all Agencies, i.e., that nepotism is disallowed," I easily circumvented the frivolousness appointing my older brother, Francis Stewart McGillycuddy to serve as the new storekeeper with pay of eight hundred forty dollars per annum. He became "Francis Stewart" and retained that name until his death many years later in Rapid City. In all other respects, I was determined to follow and enforce the policy dictated by the Office of Indian Affairs that the Indians under my charge be assimilated into white civilization and away from tribal traditions.

I imagined farms and homes covering the valleys, a new form of home government, and schoolhouses filled with happy red-skinned children. I conceived and embarked upon a three-prong plan to realize this vision. First, I would disperse the Indian camps away from the Agency office to plow the land and earn a living. Second, I would abolish the tribal system by realigning the power to deal with issues of order and law of the tribesmen away from the old chiefs to a police force. Third, I would build and staff schools teaching our language and values while continuing to encourage the Indians' intuitive appreciation of nature, but absent the ridiculous habits of savagery.

———

I hear Brody laugh and the front door close. "Brody... Come here." He pops his head into my room. "Ally gone?"

"Yeah."

"Is she going to get in trouble?"

"Na."

"I hope not... hope she told her parents. I don't want her lying to them. They'll blame you."

"I didn't know she was comin'."

"I don't care if she stays here. Just tell her to make sure her parents are OK with it."

"Aright."

"You know that's a hide-a-bed, right?"

"Ah, shit. I always forget that." Brody pulls his head back and starts to close the door. "Hey." He peeks back in. "I found a school that looks good." I give him the website.

"Right on."

My coffee is still warm, and speculating that he plans to get more sleep, maybe after a smoke, rather than wanting me to make breakfast, I continue reading.

———

While desiring to put all my plans into immediate practice, other matters, primarily finishing construction of the Agency buildings took precedence. Among them were the store, sawmill and gristmill, carpenter shop, barn, warehouse, black-smith shop, Agency office, council room, a hospital, and five sets of quarters for employees. All had only recently been built, and as I found them, all were of inferior character, poorly planned, and scarcely fit for anything more than temporary use. Almost all required outdoor battens, most needed chimneys, and some needed doors, besides work on walls and ceilings. Much was needed to make them serviceable for winter. The Agent's quarters, our intended home, was no exception. It was too small and so badly located that it actually stood in the water in rainy weather.

Despite these initial setbacks, Fanny and I remained optimistic and steadfast in our duties. Fanny demonstrated for our Indian friends the virtue of hard work from morning until night, tending to her garden yielding fresh vegetables, and caring for her turkeys, ducks, and chickens. Of course, all agricultural pursuits were in addition to her preparing meals, overseeing social activities, and keeping the quarters clean and presentable. Concerned so much had landed on her plate, I soon procured the services of one of the Agency wives and an Indian boy she called Tommy to assist.

I find it most appropriate here to expound on the virtues of my beloved, Fanny, best exhibited by a story of our early days at the Agency. I miss her so, and knowing she is waiting for me allows me to face the end of my days without fear or worry. One April Sunday, I sat in my office to welcome an uninvited Father McCarthy with news that he had come to the Pine Ridge Agency to establish a mission. I asked upon what authority to which he produced a letter from the Bishop of Omaha. To my explanation that the government demanded that only one denomination be represented on the Agency as not to confuse the infantile minds of the Sioux and the Secretary of the Interior had already authorized for the building of an Episcopal mission, the Priest responded, "The only authority I know is the Church of Rome!" I told Father McCarthy he was welcome to stay as long as he liked, but if he tried to build a mission, my only recourse was to remove him. He looked at me unwavering in his defiance. "Come to lunch with me, Father, and we can talk further, but there is no possibility of a change in the decision."

We entered the door of my humble abode to the tune of "I Dreamt I Dwelt in Marble Halls," for Fanny had wound up the music box upon our approach. I had purchased the music box on my most recent visit to Rapid City. While at two hundred fifty dollars it may seem an extravagant pleasure, it was well worth the price measured against my eclectic love of music, everything from the classical to the tom-tom of the Indian drum. Fanny greeted the Priest in her usual cordiality, taking his coat and saying, "Oh Gentlemen, your timing is impeccable, for I just made a batch of cookies." Father McCarthy, either hungry or fond of sweets, eagerly grabbed a warm treat from the plate offered him. "A lovely home," he commented. Indeed, while the exterior was horrid, Fanny had worked her magic to perfect the interior décor. A thick gray Brussels carpet with a flowered border covered the living room floor. In the corner sang the music box in its mahogany case, the size and shape of a coffin, from which protruded four large brass cylinders. Net curtains with a hand-darned, patterned border, edged with torchon lace, and lined with pale blue silk hung from iron rods, the curtains opened to allow the light to enter the room. Through double doors, the Priest could see into the bedroom, with its blue carpet bordered in pink. The bed was suspended from the ceiling by four iron rods attached to four large iron hooks. From the side, rods hung curtains matching those in the living room. A spread and pillow shams covered the swinging bed.

After lunch, as we sat at the dining room table over coffee, I remarked that personally, I would approve of the Catholic Church at all Agencies as it had an appeal to the Indian greater than all other forms of worship, the Sioux liking the chanting, the burning of incense, and the ringing of bells—all attributes similar to their medicine men.

"Then why not let them have it?" the Priest urged.

With a touch of humor, I explained that under the Grant Peace Policy, the government had preordained that the Red Cloud Indians should travel to heaven by the Episcopal route; the Catholics were detailed to save the souls of the Northern Cheyenne, the Presbyterian method was prescribed for the Yanktons; while the Congregationalists were assigned to save the Brules. I then completed my explanation by stating, "Even the white man often finds difficulty in deciding on which creed to base his hope of salvation." Father McCarthy replied confidently, "Not you. A McGillycuddy, an Irishman, a Catholic," to which I corrected him, "My father is a Protestant, my mother, an ardent Catholic." The Priest, fully intending the bite his next words would induce, said, "What a pity you did not follow the religion of your mother."

Fanny knowing my Irish temper, though never directed at her, intervened. "Gentlemen, I hope you found the meal agreeable and forgive my interruption, but there is the greatest of surprises awaiting us at the paddock." *She stood from the table.* "I will clean the table later. Shall we go?"

Father McCarthy, taking another cookie to nourish his short walk to the paddock, stood in agreement, saying, "Splendid idea." *Fanny, attempting to hide my consternation, carried the conversation, speaking of the sunshine on the cliffs to the south that morning, the spawning wild roses and clematis along the stream banks, and the plethora of species of birds in the area.*

We arrived to find two buffalo calves that had been captured earlier in the day during a buffalo hunt for which I had granted a permit. Fanny unhooked the barbed-wire fencing setting off the enclosure from the Agency and led us into the paddock, informing the Priest and me that the boys had presented the calves to her as a gift. The calves nuzzled her skirts, and she giggled in delight. Father McCarthy pet the animals in amusement. I proposed lending one of our cows to nurse them until old enough to wean. I soon returned with a cow to which the calves immediately dashed to her udder, butting it violently.

The Priest, out of my earshot, was not finished with his insults, saying to Fanny, "Ah, even wild animals know enough to latch themselves to a mother. Your husband's father may be responsible to Almighty God for the loss of his and your soul, and the government will be responsible for the loss of the souls of many Indians."

Fanny turned in anger. Her words were loud and clear. "Look here, Father. Mr. McGillycuddy has cordially explained the situation. Many of the older Indians, including Chief Red Cloud, have a leaning toward the Catholic Church on account of their friendship with Father de Smet. Were you to start building a mission here, the Indians would surely resist your removal, likely with violence. I can see it in the papers now, 'Father McCarthy, a priest of the Church of Rome, has caused an outbreak among the Sioux while opposing the government. Many souls lost.' I suggest you depart at once." Fanny, red-faced, marched past me. I said not a word. Father McCarthy said he would leave the next day. "A wife of noble character, who can find? She is worth far more than rubies" Indeed.

═══

I stop at an intersection of two gravel roads. I look curiously across the rolling countryside seeing plenty of old farm equipment, horses, cows, and silos, but nothing having the appearance of a music school, college, or studio. The GPS tells me I should take the road to the right guarded by a yellow sign, pocked with rusty bullet holes, reading "Private Drive."

"You think this is right?" I ask Brody.

"Listen to the phone lady."

"OK. A shotgun may be waiting for us."

After performing some cursory research and getting Brody's approval, I scheduled a tour of the music school. I drive the Kiva slowly down the narrow road lined by barbed wire fencing on both sides. We climb a rise and expect to find a farmhouse on the other side. Instead, we see a grove of massive pines, throughout which are scattered several wooden buildings—a compound of sorts. I recognize the largest of the buildings from the website and tell Brody we found our destination. In a clearing of well-manicured lawn stands a lodge, somewhat like a ski lodge, but one built by elves. The foundation walls, about ten feet in height, are of a reddish natural stone, protruding from which is a covered walkway with arches made of the same material. Upon this foundation is a strange menagerie of wooden structures, all clad in reclaimed barn wood, one built upon another, adorned with windows of different shapes and sizes—some square, some half-round, others octagonal. One end of the building appears almost like an ancient Scottish chapel. Two dormers, each about twenty feet tall, protect long narrow rectangular windows missing only the stained glass to complete the churchlike effect. At the other end stands a steeple made of three large gabled "bird houses" stacked one upon the other, each smaller than the one upon which it rests. Brody appreciates the folly of the architecture with a chuckle.

We walk up the drive, and I remind Brody to give a firm handshake and look his hosts in the eye.

"No shit, Dad." Brody leads us through the heavy door centered under a large, raised covered porch.

"You must be, Brody. Welcome. Nice to meet you." We exchange handshakes with our greeter, who informs us the school's owner and founder is on his way. Awaiting his arrival, we're guided to a display of framed gold and platinum records from bands and artists of every musical genre who have recorded in the studio.

Brody is impressed. He comments on some of his favorites. "Korn. No way."

"They finished their album here last month."

"Right on." Brody beams.

The owner and founder, about 65 years old, arrives and introduces himself with a friendly smile. Crow's feet spread from the corners of his bright eyes. He wears a charcoal gray turtleneck sweater that complements his full head of white-streaked gray hair, and his neatly trimmed beard and mustache, both white with patches of gray. He seems excited to show us his creation waving for us to follow like Willie Wonka showing his chocolate factory. We learn that we are at his recording studio that he started twenty-five years before. A musician and high school drop-out, he and his bandmates moved to California with dreams of becoming rock-n-roll stars. The band broke up, but he continued to perform and write music for the next ten years before moving back to the place of his childhood. His dream—to own a piece of land and build his home and a professional recording studio on it. While there was a whimsy to the studio's exterior, the interior is exquisitely done. Polished pine floors lead us from room to room of walls supported by post and beam supporting massive beamed ceilings above. A mix of stone and wood, rugs, and caramel-colored leather furniture exudes the feel of a mountain cabin. Brody and I are led into the studio that sits in the church-like section I had observed from the outside. The sunlight pours into the space from the large cathedral-like windows providing a 360-degree view of the surrounding treed land. A massive sound board with hundreds of different colored knobs, buttons, and lights fills the center of the room. Designated glass-enclosed areas for drums, piano, guitar and vocal recording surround. Brody's eyes light up in anticipation when he learns that he'd have six months of free use of the studio upon graduation.

The studio owner leads us to an outdoor patio to wrap up the tour. He gives Brody a signed copy of his book and tells a few humorous stories of recording sessions past. He then asks, "Why are you interested in coming here, Brody?"

Brody, suddenly put on the spot, sits in contemplation. He looks down and scratches at the corner of this thumbnail. Several seconds, uncomfortable perhaps only for me, pass in silence. Brody raises his gaze to meet that of the studio's founder. "Music is the only thing I've ever wanted to do. I wrote some songs with friends, and I knew what I wanted 'em to sound like in my head, but nobody could make 'em right. We couldn't pay for a good studio. I figure… cut out the middleman and learn how to do it yourself."

I'm certainly impressed with the school, the studio, and its owner, but nothing impressed me as much as Brody's answer. You're going to learn how to do it yourself, Son. We'll make it work.

———

Brody lets the last notes fade before resting his guitar on the floor, the neck leaning against the couch. "What ya' think?"

I'm shocked. "You wrote that?"

"Yeah. A long time ago."

"It's really good." It was good. I know nothing about music, but it doesn't take an expert to appreciate that it's original, interesting— certainly a catchy tune. "You have lyrics?"

"No."

"I'll write some tonight."

Brody gives me a gratuitous laugh and jumps up, grabbing his cigarettes and phone. He bounces toward the door.

"Got everything? I see the lighter on the coffee table. Lighter?"

Brody stops patting his pockets to make a one-handed catch of the lighter flying toward him. "I'm excited for you, Bro. Have a good shift. See you tonight."

"Bye, Dad." He starts to open the door.

"Ally coming over tonight?"

"Na."

I haven't seen Ally in several days. "Where's she been?"

"I'll tell ya 'bout it later."

"Ok. It's payday. Get your check."

"Shit yeah."

The door closes, and the apartment again goes quiet. I'm curious to know what's happened with Ally. Just days before, he sounded like he was falling in love. Just seconds ago, he sounded like it's over. C'est la vie, especially when the young are concerned. Whatever the issue, it certainly hasn't dampened Brody's mood. Feeling good about the day and hopeful for the future, I open the journal and read.

———

Having secured the fifty thousand dollar bond necessary for the procurement of farming materials, I placed the order for corn seed, one thousand horse-drawn wagons, twenty cases of axle grease, plows, shovels, spades, band saws, hay cutting machinery, and fencing materials to secure the cows and bulls that would be distributed. All were expected to arrive in the summer. On March 24, 1879, I held my first council with Chief Red Cloud and the other chiefs. We shared a pipe, and then I fastened a map of the reservation to the wall, showing the chiefs the Agency's location, near which most of the Indians had camped. I took great deliberation to show them the vast expanses of their land and told them to disperse throughout and await the coming of seed and tools necessary to plow the land and earn a living.

Red Cloud responded negatively, saying, "Little Beard, the Great Spirit did not make us to work. He made us to hunt and fish. He gave us the great prairies and hills and covered them with buffalo, deer, and antelope. He filled the streams and rivers with fish. The white man can work if he wants to, but the Great Spirit did not make us to work. The white man owes us a living for the lands he has taken from us."

Another chief added that if the Indians moved away from the Agency, they would be unable to obtain rations. Prepared for this line of inquiry, I responded that I would increase the amount of rations depending on the distance the Indians lived away from the Agency.

I trusted my tenacity and ambitious nature, but pragmatically I knew my sweeping reforms would take several years to realize. Still, the longer the non-progressive chiefs retained power, the longer the process of assimilation would take. Hence, the need for an Indian police force. Knowing the Indians despised any military presence on the Agency, I presented the concept as follows. "I, like you, want all the soldiers removed from the Agency. I trust you to keep order. Give me fifty of your best men, and we will have home government."

Again, Red Cloud protested, "This is my Agency! This is my land! I am Chief, and I keep the peace!" He then spewed a litany of grievances and demands, "Yes, remove the soldiers. Where is the twenty-five thousand dollars promised us for giving up our right to hunt on Republican Fork? Where are the wagons? When we went to see the Great Father, we asked him for three styles of wagons: heavy, medium, and buggies. We see none. Do not those wagons in part pay for our land? When we get wagons, Indians should move the freight from the Missouri River and take the money as the white men do now. What Indians receive, half-breeds and white men married to Indian women should also receive. This is Indian land, and I want the white man cutting down my timber and hay to pay for it!" I assured Red Cloud that all annuities would be disbursed, including the wagons, before winter. If he did not like the men cutting the timber and hay, it was within his power to "just stop them" I also agreed that half-breeds and whites married to Indians should receive the same annuities as the full-bloods, as they could teach the Sioux how to farm and care for their cattle. Red Cloud was unimpressed, saying, "We are here, and we have brains and hearts. We have eyes. When white men come among us, we can soon judge whether their work is for good or for evil. Your work is for evil."

Thus would begin an affair with Red Cloud that would rage from month to month, year to year, charges upon charges, councils upon councils, and investigation after investigation for the next seven years. No sooner would any conciliation on my part reestablish amicable relations than he would mourn at the loss of his power and resort to antagonism to civilization and the progress of his people. (See photograph #13 of Chief Red Cloud taken at Pine Ridge Agency, 1880.)

On September 26, 1879, word came that Sitting Bull was heading south from Canada to join the Agency. Nearly a month later, I was ordered by the Commissioner of Indian Affairs, Ezra Hayt, to "Require Sitting Bull's Indians to surrender their arms and ponies. Place them by themselves and feed them, but make no mistake, they are to be treated as prisoners of war. The idea must not be permitted that they can simply come back and be fed. Every one of them, if fed, must be made to earn his rations by work."

The idiocy of politicians confounded me then, more so now. I wrote to General Crook. "Is it to be wondered that these people who have been at times rebellious are not as yet self-supporting? The old maxim that a rolling stone gathers no moss was never more applicable. The failure in transforming these Indians in former years was due to the turning of the Agency into an asylum or rendezvous for rebellious members, like Sitting Bull's tribe. Yet, our leaders propose the same. The influence of turbulent outsiders and taking in of any more people of that class is to be protested. I suggest Sitting Bull be given an Agency of his own. The Indians of this Agency do not wish for them. The experience of locating the Crazy Horse band of fifteen hundred persons after the Custer Massacre of 1876 at the Agency, and the subsequent jealousies and troubles, finally resulting in his death, should be a sufficient test of the sordidness of this policy."

While I disagreed with allowing Sitting Bull to reside on the Agency, I used the pending threat of his arrival to advance my immediate objective of establishing a police force. Commissioner Hayt responded favorably to my request for accelerated funding and "to forming the force of fifty men and provide officer nominations and uniform sizes as soon as practicable. Secretary of War authorizes you to borrow, for a short time, fifty sharps rifles from Fort Robinson to be replaced with U.S. carbines the next fiscal year. General Sheridan is so informed." Over the constant protestations of Red Cloud, by early September 1879, the police force had thirty-seven members, and it was not difficult to fill the whole allowance early the next year. Over the next six years, the Agency police, under the leadership of George Sword, became a very reliable lot of young men who felt the importance of their position, ready at all times to obey orders given them. (See photograph #14, Pine Ridge Agency, 1880. I sit center, with left to right, Standing Soldier, a private of the police force, George Sword, police force Captain, interpreter Bill Garnett, and my staunch ally, Young Man Afraid of His Horses.)

As I recommend this photograph, I note the reference to Bill Garnett as interpreter, and find this an appropriate time to explain the unfortunate demise of John Provost. As you know, we first became acquainted during the Indian Expeditions in the north. He then served as my interpreter at Camp Robinson and had been by my side at Crazy Horse's death. For all his past loyalties, I had appointed him to continue as my interpreter at Pine Ridge. Provost was a half-breed, the son of "Old Man Provost," a French-Canadian trapper and an Oglala Sioux mother. John Provost was a white man in dress and appearance, but he also retained many of the Indian sympathies. He married a Sioux woman to become the son-in-law of Crazy Horse's uncle Black Elk. John had a brother, Charlie, two years his junior. While John had inherited the best qualities of both races, Charlie possessed the worst.

One day in July 1879, I summoned John and his younger brother Charlie, who spoke only the Sioux language, to my office to respond to a report by a Brule Sioux that Charlie had stolen his horses. I had Charlie wait while the Brule confirmed his horses were in Charlie's herd. I instructed the Brule to take back his horses. Tired of Charlie's trouble-making, I reprimanded him harshly, telling him to mend his ways or the next time he would be punished severely. Charlie wrapped his blanket around him and, without a word, left the office. I dispatched John to attend to other matters. No more than ten minutes after Charlie's departure, I heard a gunshot. Unbeknownst to me at the time, Charlie had gone to the blacksmith shop and asked William Allman, the blacksmith, to lend him a pistol so he could shoot a rabbit. Allman complied, and when the gun was in hand, Charlie told the blacksmith that Little Beard had scolded him and he was going to kill someone, maybe Little Beard, maybe himself. I ran outside my office to find Charlie's body face down, motionless on the ground. I rolled him over to see the mortal wound in his temple.

The blacksmith arrived shortly thereafter, stammering breathlessly, saying, "Charlie took my gun. He said he was going to shoot you or himself. Guess he's shot himself." Fanny next arrived, saying she had seen from the backyard Charlie throw off the blanket, put the gun to his head and fall.

John Provost and an innocent Clementi Bernard arrived next on the scene. Seeing the body of his lifeless brother on the ground, John drew a weapon from his belt and shot Bernard through the head. There had been no quarrel between them. They had been childhood friends. John's Indian blood, which had laid dormant in his veins until his brother's death, had awakened to its inherent traditions. Somewhere latent in his brain was the memory of a tribal custom. The dead must have company on the long journey to the happy hunting grounds. John, in muffled voice, said before the crowd that gathered and wrestled the pistol from his hand, "My brain whirled."

There being no court or guard house at Pine Ridge, I ordered a wagon team for John's transfer to Fort Sheridan. Upon its arrival, I took the reigns of the light buckboard and told John to get in. There was no need for shackles or sheriff, for we were friends, the friendship forged on the frontier through a sharing of common dangers. As we left the confines of the Agency, I told John I was sorry, but there was no other way. Lives could not be wiped out like that. With a heavy heart and no desire for sociability, I refused Captain Crawford's invitation to dinner that evening.

That winter, I was summoned to Deadwood by the prosecution for Provost's trial. I testified in favor of his defense as to his exemplary character, his assistance to the whites, and of the extenuating circumstances—John suffered the mental state of an Indian with a "bad heart," which was comparable to insanity. A verdict of manslaughter was rendered, and he was sentenced to a mere five years in the Detroit House of Correction. When I said goodbye to John, he thanked me for what I had said in his favor and conveyed that his head felt queer after killing his friend. I stated my intent to visit him in prison, but unfortunately, John died early in confinement, succumbing to consumption and before I could make the necessary arrangements.

═══

Something about McGillycuddy's story of the Provost brothers seems off, but I can't pinpoint it. It could be me. I'm having trouble concentrating because Brody's song keeps running through my head. That I can still hear it hours later, after only one playing, says something, I think. It's unique. I remove my glasses, setting them and the journal on the armrest. The curtain covering the sliding glass door not completely pulled closed allows the streetlight to illuminate the wall above Brody's couch in distinctive overlapping rectangular shapes. The ceiling fan spins slowly above my spot, giving off a steady cool breeze. It hums in beat with Brody's tune. I close my eyes.

I remember us as a family, father, mother, and son when Brody was three years old. We were still in the Air Force driving from Minot, North Dakota, to our next assignment in Biloxi, Mississippi, stopping en route in Branson for a two-day vacation. How happy we were. A magic show. A theater with at least 500 people. The flamboyant magician took the stage to amaze and thrill us. He walked into the audience, asking for a volunteer. Little Brody, blond curls, stood in his mother's lap, arm raised at length to gain the magician's attention. Selected, the patrons smiled and assisted his clumsy progress to the magician in the aisle. I see his little body walk up the steps holding the magician's hand. On stage, the magician asks, "What's your name?"

"Brody."

"What?" He holds the microphone to Brody's lips.

"Brody!" Seeing the lights and hundreds of faces looking at him, he does what any true entertainer would. He controls the stage. For the next three minutes, never was such a jig performed. Never was an audience so enthralled. A three-year-old imp of pure energy garnered the biggest applause of the night, by far. I smile in my sleep.

The door opening is always a soothing sound to me. He's home from work. 10:40 p.m. "Hey, buddy. How was it?"

"Good." He tosses his paycheck and some cash onto the coffee table. "Five hundred thirty-five. Can you take me to the bank tomorrow?"

"Sure. What's the cash?"

"I won my bet with Rafael. Fifty bucks."

I remember there was a bet, but the details allude me. I ask for clarification. Brody reminds me that Rafael had two months to date the new waitress. The grumpy Columbian cook had failed and apparently hadn't been too pleased about it, to Brody's delight. "Got this too." Brody reaches into his pocket and removes a scrap of paper upon which is a handwritten name "Bailey," a phone number, and a smiley face. With a devilish grin he says, "She said to call her if I ever needed anything. Girl's cute. Nice too. Call her Catholic-girl."

The revolving door of pretty girls continues. I don't ask about Ally. "Could your life get any better?"

"Hell, no. Love it."

━━━

Of the three prongs of my plan, the third, the building of schools and educating the children, I was most excited to engage. Unfortunately, the immediate demands of securing annuity funding and the chains for their supply, refurbishing and completing construction of buildings, creating a police force, and appeasing Chief Red Cloud to keep him and his governmental and religious cronies at bay delayed the advance of the project I held most dear. With the meager supplies I had initially been appropriated, I started construction of the first of five planned schoolhouses; its foundation laid the furthest from the Agency Office as an intended enticement for the Sioux to cover their land. By September 1879, it was still in unfinished condition, drawing the dismay of the two young Episcopalian clergymen sent by their Bishop, William H. Hare, to teach on the Agency. Learning upon their arrival that they would be living in tents temporarily as no teaching residences had yet been built, the soft-skinned lads' visit was short-lived but not ended before they complained to their superior.

I shortly thereafter received a letter from Indian Commissioner Hayt stating, "I understand the school is still in unfinished condition and, in large part, unfit for use. I suggest you make great haste to finish the building as best you can, perhaps erecting two temporary partitions on the south end of the schoolhouse, one running east and west and the other north and south, so that clergy can have one room for a school room and one for a bedroom. If temporary benches are also made, a school can begin at once."

This correspondence was immediately followed by instruction dated September 7, 1879, stating I must "get ready immediately for departure to the Carlisle Indian School in Pennsylvania twenty-four boys and twelve girls from each of the main camps, totaling seventy-two in all, to be examined by the post surgeon. None but the absolutely sound and healthy should be sent. Children of chiefs preferred." An army officer, Lieutenant Pratt, who had opened the Carlisle Indian School, arrived on September 21ˢᵗ to escort the selected children to Carlisle, but there was opposition from some of the chiefs—Chief Red Cloud being the most vocal. Offered as a show of support of the policy and personal sacrifice, I loaded our Indian boy Tommy, Fanny's helper, onto a wagon, promising a visit in the near future. The faithful 'reliables' followed in kind.

The following winter, Fanny and I went to Washington, stopping at Carlisle, Pennsylvania, curious to see how the Indian children were faring. Pratt escorted us around the buildings before taking us to see Tommy and the other Indian children. All appeared in fine condition, although their cropped hair was startling; Fanny and I were so used to seeing its length flowing in the winds of the plains. Tommy was overjoyed to see us, nuzzling Fanny's skirts like one of her buffalo calves. He was homesick and wanted to go back to the Agency, but I assured him it was much to his advantage to remain at the school. Upon returning to Captain Pratt's office, he informed me that Tommy had voluntarily taken the surname of Tommy McGillycuddy. Tommy continued his studies at Carlisle for another six years.

Several Commissioners of the Quaker City Indian Peace Commission, a group with great influence in Indian matters, had accompanied us on our tour. After the tour, one of the Commissioners asked why it was so much more difficult to civilize the Indian compared to the Negro. I chose my response carefully. "There is much difference between the two," I said, "as the bear and the eagle to buffalo and the goose. A wild goose hatched as a domestic bird becomes a barnyard fowl. A buffalo raised among cows becomes as gentle as they. Not so with the bear and the eagle. You cannot tame an eagle into a domestic bird nor make a pet of a grizzly bear. Only hunger can but for a time tame the untamable. Hunger alone had forced the Indian to surrender, and though they had been subdued, they were never conquered."

Urged to elaborate, I continued relating a story of a nestling eagle that had been brought to me as a gift by the Indian boys the previous summer, about one month after Fanny was given the buffalo calves. I chastised the boys for removing the bird from its nest, knowing they had come a long way. I told them it was unlikely the mother bird would again accept it now having the scent of human hands. I did not insist on it being taken back. Instead, I took it upon myself to feed the eaglet and attempt to train it. I made it a massive netted cage, a poor substitute for the native crags, no doubt, but not cramped in the least. I hand-fed it chunks of fresh meat every day. I spoke softly and never looked it directly in the eyes. Despite my efforts, its wild look never softened. It never showed any sign of loyalty or friendliness, only screeching with raucous voice as it grabbed its food. Months later, discouraged but knowing what needed to be done, I released the full-grown bird. Days passed into months, snows fell unceasingly, and temperatures dropped. Walking to my quarters one snowy afternoon, I saw high in the air and circling lower and lower the great bird. The circles grew smaller and smaller until, at last, the eagle settled on the snow-covered ground. The bird willingly allowed a blanket to be thrown over its body, and unresisting in any way, allowed me to carry it back to its netted cage. I removed the blanket, hoping for signs of affection to the one who had *fed him, but I was sorely disappointed. There were none. Nor in his cold hard stare was there any indication of submission. I dared not try to touch it. The land was filled with snow; nothing was moving on the plains, the rodents hidden, the fish under ice. The eagle was hungry. It was the same with the Indian. The white man, the railroads and corporations, as well as the government, had systematically removed all subsistence on the plains, largely for the intended purpose of forcing the Indians to surrender. They had done so. Like the eagle, they had come in to be fed, but they were not conquered. (See photograph #15. It speaks for itself.)*

As the weather turned colder in November 1880, I received an additional two thousand five hundred dollars to complete the schoolhouses at the cost of five hundred dollars each, in addition to receipt of five heavy iron box stoves for use in heating the schools. Dissatisfied with progress to date and under heavy political pressure, I appointed a new superintendent of schools, a person of virtue and trust, my beloved Fanny.

Despite previous governmental admonishments of hiring those of family relationship, the Acting Superintendent of Indian Affairs, E.M. Marble, supported the recommendation stating, "Mrs. McGillycuddy, having taught school before her marriage, is highly qualified for the post and most deserving of this most important of positions. I trust she will tend to the promotion with the best interest of the service, with pay of eight hundred dollars per annum." As I knew she would, Fanny took to the task of completing and getting the schools up and running with vigor. The final inspection of the schools was carried out in February 1881.

━━━

So much more I could tell of those exciting times, but that is not now my purpose, so I summarize my days as Indian Agent at Pine Ridge as follows: If I wished to continue the Sioux as savages and feed them until they finally died out, I would have recommended the continuance of the tribal system as the most feasible one. My only desire for this noble people was to advance them toward civilization. I was young in those days, and I had to come down pretty hard on the Sioux at times, and some never did understand what I was trying to get at; chief among them was Red Cloud.

To be eternally harassed by the old man became somewhat monotonous. With an Indian of that background, the end justifies the means. Like the lesson learned from my eagle, food and hunger were often the only practical means to weaken his power and enforce my policies. Red Cloud refused to have his people take to the land. He refused to send his children to the schools. My threat to discontinue the distribution of supplies, beef and rations to Red Cloud until he complied met tepid response in Washington.

What earthly reason or inducement can be advanced why an Indian should go to work and earn his own living by the sweat of his brow when an indulgent government furnishes him more than he wants to eat and clothes him for nothing? Select eight thousand whites of the pauper class to the reservation, feed them as you do the Indians, and they would hold a caucus and vote to assassinate the first one of their number who attempted to become self-supporting. In a partial measure, I informed Red Cloud's Indians that they could draw their annuity goods independently of their chief if they desired, which a good number did. This change in distribution took power from Red Cloud, and resulted in him becoming my everlasting enemy and my being investigated on two occasions by the Department and brought before the Dakota grand jury on trumped up charges that I had stolen flannel, brass kettles, and corn. While I have largely been endowed with Christian virtues of meekness, humility, and forbearance, I have not where smitten on the one cheek, turned the other to Red Cloud.

On March 18, 1886, Red Cloud obtained an audience with the newly-elected President Grover Cleveland and told him, "Our Agent is a bad man. He steals from us and abuses us, and he has sent all the good white men out of our country and put bad men in their places." In my closing statement to the resulting investigatory committee, I stated, "It has been my policy and instructions that it is the duty of the Agent in every way possible to break up the authority of the chiefs, and I have endeavored in every way possible to break up the authority of the chiefs where that authority tended to work against civilization."

In the end, I accomplished much of what I set out to do, despite the continuous counter-efforts of Red Cloud and his Democratic cronies. Farms and ranches spread across the Agency. An influential police force was established. Children were educated in schools, and at the end of my tenure, Red Cloud's band had been reduced to a meager three hundred. His influence greatly diminished among the other Sioux. My final words to the Congressional investigatory committee were in the third person, "If McGillycuddy is not the proper man for Agent, recommend his removal, for the world is wide. He is still comparatively a young man, and time will vindicate him if he needs vindication." I was removed from office in May 1886.

I was glad to be freed of government service and appreciative of the many opportunities subsequently offered me. I accepted the presidency of the Lakota Banking and Investment Company and the vice-presidency of the Black Hills National Bank. I was also appointed Surgeon General on the Governor's staff. I, a frugal man and having few living expenses on the Agency, saved practically all I had earned as Agent. I applied a portion of our significant nest egg to construct a house on a slope north of Rapid City. The residents watched with interest as we set the red sandstone foundation, upon which were laid walls of red and white sandstone bricks. The second story was painted olive green. The local paper commented that I was building a house *the likes of which had never been seen before. While many found the architecture outlandish, I liked the color and the way the red Jurassic sandstone harmonized with the landscape. (See photograph #16 of the house, Rapid City, South Dakota, 1888.)*

It was a time of great prosperity, and Fanny and I enjoyed our evenings sitting next to the fireplace talking of our many happy days on the plains without regret. Many of our Indians would come to visit us and share coffee, slices of bread, and fresh-baked cookies and doughnuts. On one such visit, our buffalo calves, now full-grown and the female now having a calf of her own, were returned to us. I released them in a valley near town.

Fanny's degrading health was the only thing that troubled me. She had gained weight alarmingly, and she suffered from frequent headaches. Her face would often flush. One Sunday morning, she dressed for church and went into the yard to look at the fresh blossoms on her plants. I found her fallen among the flowers, for she had had a stroke. She lay in bed for many weeks, unable to speak but could communicate Indian signs with her left hand. While frustrated with her loss of utility, her spirit was not broken. After many months she was able to walk around the house with assistance. In warm weather, she rode with a hired driver in the fresh air of the countryside in a low phaeton with a fringed top. Her soft smile never left her. (See photograph #17 taken in Rapid City, 1887.)

======

"I'm pleased to congratulate you on your acceptance. I was very impressed with your ability to communicate the passion and desire you have to succeed in the industry and believe that you will prove that our confidence in you is not unfounded… I welcome you and feel you will make a great addition to our student body."

Over my shoulder, Brody reads the letter from the music institute he handed me moments before. He anxiously waits for me to finish. I do and look up to see him smiling. "Never thought I'd go to college."

"Congratulations, Bro." I stand and pull him in for a hug. I feel small next to him. He towers over me but bends at the waist, allowing me to embrace around his shoulders. "I'm proud of you, man. You excited?"

"Hell, yeah."

"You're going to kill it. You have a couple of months until you start. Keep doing what you're doing. Save a little money."

"I have a good job. I can pay for it."

I appreciate the offer, but I know he hasn't the faintest idea of how much money I have left, our monthly expenses, or the amount of his tuition. "We're good. Just save a little of each paycheck. Maybe half. You'll probably need a laptop." I've looked at the tuition payment plans and selected the least onerous—half of the full tuition paid by the end of the first three months, and then $233.33 per month for the next 36 months. I can get us to the mid-point, then he'll have to cover.

Brody steps onto the balcony for a self-congratulatory smoke, and I settle back into my spot to finish McGillycuddy's journal. The last page is in the form of a letter.

Dear Trusted Messenger,

I hope this writing has been of interest and provided some insight into Crazy Horse, the Sioux, and my early days on the plains. I finish this volume writing of a place that profoundly affected me as a young man. In 1875, I was invited on the Newton-Jenny Party as surveyor for the Black Hills Expedition to map the topography and geology of the region, while the Expedition, led by George Custer, assessed the area for major gold deposits. On June 25th, I set out to explore the highest point in the hills, Harney Peak, from which I intended, by means of triangulation and astronomical observations, to determine the distances between the tallest peaks, i.e., Harney's Peak, Custer's Peak, Terry's Peak, and Bear Butte. The year before, Custer had attempted to reach the summit, a pugnosed butte of perpendicular granite rock, forty feet in height, to no avail. I had a tree cut at the base of the rocky outcrop and wedged it into a crevice leading to the peak. My back against the tree and my feet against each side of the crevice, I shimmied upward to be the first-ever to reach the top. (See photograph #18.)

From this peak, I took in the sweeping vistas of the Black Hills, my love for which has never diminished and upon which I shall eternally gaze. I have left detailed instructions for the burial of my cremated remains. My ashes shall be placed in a brass safe, which shall be interred in a small crypt hollowed from a gigantic boulder located on the summit of Harney's Peak. A simple metal plaque will cover the front of the entombed box, the removal of which will reveal a keyhole. The box's lock is a specialized lever tumbler lock of Chubb detector design. I spared no expense in its making, commissioning a young gentleman named Glenn Hall in Paramount, California, to perfect its construction. The only key to this lock is in your possession, contained within the front center pouch of the satchel gifted to you.

Further revelations await you, my Trusted Messenger. Be mindful of my earlier words of advice and warning, but upon discovery, do with it as you see fit.

V.T. M'Gillycuddy

Brody sidesteps into the room from the balcony, and I give him the journal. "Read this." I go to the closet to retrieve the satchel that I haven't looked at since the day after its arrival. Pulling it from the top shelf, I examine its front to confirm the presence of the middle pouch McGillycuddy referenced.

I hurry to our living area to see Brody looking at me, confused. "What the fuck?"

"Don't know." I sit in my spot and lay the satchel in my lap. I pinch the pouch's tarnished brass buckle and pull the cinched strap to release it from the buckle's prong. I pause. Brody stands over me anxiously. I give him the satchel. "Open it." He takes the satchel to his couch to continue the process. I lean forward in anticipation as he pulls the strap through the buckle and, without hesitation, digs into the pouch. His eyes widen as he simultaneously removes his hand to reveal an ornate skeleton key.

"No way!" He raises the key and presents it for my viewing, allowing me to see the key's detail. It's about 4 inches long. Made of brass. The head is sculpted into the shape of a heart, contained within is an intricate design appearing similar to Celtic knots I'd seen in Ireland. Fitting for a "Valentine McGillycuddy," I think. The bit is large, extending over half of the shaft and having six or seven distinct notches. A heart shape pierces the bit's center. Brody brings the key to his face for closer examination and then tosses it into the air. My heart stops. He catches it with one hand and says with vigor, "Let's get this shit!" I appreciate his enthusiasm, and I'm excited too, but I counter his free spirit with my innate skepticism. Brody means let's get in the Kiva **NOW** and "get this shit." I need more information.

"Hang on. Let me see that." I take the key and give it a closer look. "Look up, McGillycuddy plaque Harney Peak. Images." Brody grabs his phone, complies with my search request, and scrolls for a few seconds.

"Dude. This shit real." He gets up to show me the screen of his phone. Wow. It is real. As described, there is a plaque made of what appears to be bronze. His name, "Valentine T. McGillycuddy," in scripted letters, runs across the top. Beneath, in quotes, is his nickname given to him by the Sioux "Wasicu Wakan" and the dates "1849-1939." I notice there are scratch marks on the plaque across the word "Wakan."

If I remember correctly, McGillycuddy wrote that he was given this nickname after he saved the Indian girl's life in childbirth. It meant "white miracle man" or words to that effect. It appears by the scratches that at least one person has taken exception to the moniker.

My initial skepticism is now replaced with belief. I contemplate us making a trip to the Black Hills in South Dakota. I ask Brody, "Could you get a week off work?"

"Yeah. It's been slow. I can find someone to cover for me."

I search the current temperature at Harney Peak. The high today will be 38 degrees with snow. Forty degrees is the warmest it'll get in the next ten days. Most of the roads in the Hills are closed until March 31st. I share my findings with Brody. "It'll be at least a month until we can go. Gives us time to plan things. What do you think's in there?"

"Treasure."

I know that's not likely, but McGillycuddy did go to great lengths to secure something that was important to him. He was wealthy. I suppose there's a chance that whatever he's gifted us has some monetary value. I show Brody the photographs of the mansion and Valentine and Fanny posing in the library and give him an abridged version of McGillycuddy's story from Crazy Horse's death to his time as Indian Agent, and then becoming a man of means in Rapid City society. Brody concludes my summary with, "Told you we're rich."

"How hard do you think it'll be to get that plaque off?"

Brody looks at the picture still on his phone. "Easy. Crowbar and hammer. I can get into anything. One time I… "

"I don't want to know."

"It's not bad."

"Good. I don't want to know."

———

Brody rolls the window down. "South Dakota, here we come!" He pulls a cigarette from the pack and puts it between his lips.

"You can't smoke that." Brody's initial excitement turns to dismay when he learns that he can't smoke in the SUV we've rented for the trip. Not confident that the Kiva can make such a journey and not wanting to spend money on motels, I elected to rent something big enough for us to sleep in.

"How far is it?"

"Twenty hours. You can smoke when we stop for gas."

"Damn, Dude."

"You'll be all right." The plan for the road trip is simple. Drive two days sleeping the first night in a parking lot. Open the lockbox on Harney Peak, which I've learned has been renamed to Black Elk Peak, and drive back. The roads in the Black Hills have been open for about a month, but the hiking trail to the summit has only been open for a week. Temperatures are still cool there, downright cold at night, but I figure it's best to make the ascent before the start of tourist season. I'm hoping we'll have the trail and summit to ourselves and can remove the plaque and open the box without interruption or incident. With sandwiches, chips, a full cooler, McGillycuddy's journal and photographs for Brody's reading and viewing pleasure, coats, blankets and pillows, key, crowbar, and hammer in tow, we hit the road.

Brody's read the journal on and off since our departure, occasionally stopping to look at one of the photographs, change the music (selected largely to accommodate my music tastes), to eat a sandwich, or smoke a cig at a gas stop. "Look at that." I point to the west, where the first glimpses of the Gateway Arch in St. Louis are visible. It's early afternoon on a clear day, and the sunlight bounces off the metallic structure dramatically.

"That's cool. What is it?"

"The St. Louis Arch. Gateway to the West. Once the pioneers crossed the Mississippi, they were in the West. There's an elevator that takes you to the top." I proceed to tell Brody about when his mother and I rode in the claustrophobic capsule and how it slows down and clanks as it makes its way through the arch. "Nice view once you get up there."

"Fuck that… "

"Hey. Watch the language."

"Since when you care about that?"

"I don't know. Maybe it's because you're twenty now. A guy I knew… a guy I respected a lot once told me that cursing was a cover for lack of intelligence. People swear because they aren't smart enough to use an intelligent word. That always stuck with me... and you're smart."

"Or they want to get their point across."

"Just be aware of your words. Cut down on the swearing." We ride for a few minutes in silence. Brody speaks.

"What you think of McGillycuddy?"

"Where you at?"

"He's teachin' Crazy Horse to use a fork."

"I think he liked Crazy Horse... maybe fascinated by him. Guy had guts. Think about it... he saw Crazy Horse the first time at Rosebud... guy got shot in the arm... then the Indians wiped Custer out... then a few months later... he wasn't much older than you. He goes to Crazy Horse's camp the day after he surrendered. You know he was nervous riding in the first time."

"I can see that."

"What you thinking?"

"He acts like he likes the Indians... "

I interrupt. "He saved the girl... and took care of Crazy Horse's wife."

"Yeah. He got pissed... **mad**... at that soldier too when he gave the Indian a morphine shot. But... somethin' off about that dude. Tryin' too hard to make himself sound good."

"A little self-serving. I agree. He had a big ego. Probably had to. Keep reading and let me know what you think. Give me a sandwich. We'll stop in Omaha... six, seven hours. OK?"

"I'm good."

══════

We pull into a parking lot in Council Bluffs, Iowa, sided by two large RVs. I'm tired and ready to stop for the night. Brody jumps out and lights a cigarette. I reach into the glove box where I've prepositioned two zip-lock baggies, each containing a toothbrush and travel-size tube of paste. Mine also contains my contact case, solution, and cholesterol pills. I check the fuel gauge. I'll gas up first thing in the morning at the station across the road. I open the door to feel a cool, stiff breeze blowing from the north. I grab Brody's coat and then exit, moving toward the smoldering tip in the distance.

"Freezin' here." I give Brody his coat and baggy.

"We'll brush in the bathroom." Feeling the cold, I start walking briskly toward the store. Brody stubs his cigarette and runs up from behind, grabbing me around the shoulder. "We on an adventure, Pops."

I appreciate the moment. "We are.

We climb into the back of the SUV, where I have the seats laid down and blankets and pillows making a bed. We settle in. Our teeth are clean. We're tired, warm, and happy, which minimizes the annoyance of the parking lot lights flooding through the windows. Brody plays a song on his phone I haven't heard before. There's a line about "singing loud" that triggers a memory. I wait until the song ends and say, "Remember when you were in that play in middle school. You were a fish."

Brody chuckles. "Yeah. *Little Mermaid*. I was Flounder."

"You were so good." As I remember the performance, Brody wore a yellow jumpsuit with a green fin on his back. He had a dance routine with two of the prettiest girls in the school. He danced and spun them around while singing a song. The girls had put his hair, well below shoulder-length, into a ponytail exposing his face. He never wore his hair back, and it took me off guard.

"I was horrible. That was so embarrassing."

"No, you weren't. I was proud of you." I'd been to several of his choir concerts and was each time frustrated with not being able to hear the words, the kids too nervous to cut loose and sing with gusto. Heading into the play, I told Brody, "I don't care how you sound, but sing loud." I then shared my distaste for young muted voices and proceeded to simulate, in mocking fashion, past concerts with elementary and middle school performers singing so quietly you had to read their lips. Brody got my point and didn't disappoint. "You sang loud, Bro." I, half-speaking, half-singing aggressively, almost like a punk rocker, repeat what I can remember of the lyrics to his song, "She's in looove... She's in looooove... See how she **shimmers**, see how she **shakes**!"

Brody laughs. "Stop."

"You belted it, Bro. Loud... really loud. Everybody could hear every word... probably in the parking lot." Brody busts out in laughter, I think replaying that moment from his childhood in his mind. Tired and excited to be doing something new, we almost get the giggles. Normalcy returns. "Seriously, Bro... that meant a lot... I knew you listened to me."

It's sunny, partly cloudy, and I'm enjoying letting my mind wander numbly. Since turning west onto I-90, a headwind with 30 to 40 mph gusts has tormented our progress and cut into my fuel efficiency, requiring me to stop in Chamberlain, South Dakota, to gas up. "We're stopping."

"Good." Brody looks up and scans the horizon. The terrain across Eastern South Dakota is largely unremarkable farmland. Brody has found entertainment in McGillycuddy's journal the past two hours. The interstate immediately before us makes a steady, gradual descent to a river basin. The river spanned by a four-lane bridge before making a sharper ascent to bluffs on the far side. A cloud's shadow pushed by the winds races towards us center-lane. "What's this river?"

"The Missouri… the same Missouri we followed for two hours this morning."

"I read about it. They wanted to move the Indians to the Missouri."

"That's right… I don't know if it was here though… they were in northern Nebraska… about 60, 70 miles south… could've been. Where you at in the book?"

"They tryin' to arrest Crazy Horse, but he bolted. Dude got framed."

I smile, amused by Brody's characterization and that he's interested enough to pick up the finer details. "Yeah. Sounds like it… you liking it? Pretty interesting."

"Hell, yeah. History."

"Keep reading. Gets good." We've cleared the river, and I pull onto the exit ramp. "No arches here."

"Ain't got McDonald's?"

"What?" I make the connection. "No. There's McDonald's. No arches like St. Louis. You're in the real West now, Boy."

Brody, using his money, made carefully selected purchases of Corn Nuts, Slim Jims, licorice, and Mountain Dew. Perfect road food. I make an additional purchase of a fresh bag of ice that goes into the cooler.

"How much further?"

"About 3 hours to Rapid City. Another hour into the Black Hills."

Brody assesses the landscape and, unimpressed with his first views of the "real West," which doesn't look much different from the east of the river, takes a bite of his beef stick, and keeps reading McGillycuddy's journal.

I've driven an hour since our last stop. Brody's been engulfed in his reading. The change in terrain is becoming noticeable—rolling hills now, less agriculture, larger plots of grazing land and the incessant gusts blowing the green, tallish grasses in waves. Brody's voice breaks the steady hum of the wind pushing through the windows.

"They gutted him!" Brody looks at me with a slight side-to-side shake in his head. "That so wrong."

"I agree."

"That interpreter… "

"Grourard."

"Yeah." Brody flips through the photographs and pulls the one of Frank Grourard and the two Indians on horseback from the pile. He looks at it intently for several seconds. "Lyin' bitch."

"Hey, watch it." I correct his choice of words, but I'd had a similar non-favorable reaction to Grourard, as did others at his time referring to him as a liar and coward. By McGillycuddy's account, Grourard intentionally misinterpreted Crazy Horse at the council with Crook after Crazy Horse agreed to fight the Nez Perce, ultimately leading to his arrest, stabbing, and death. I imagine the gigantic Touches the Clouds shouting his contempt and scrambling with ill-intent to get Grourard in his grasp, the points of bayonets keeping him at bay. "Lying bitch" would probably have been a fair interpretation of Touches the Clouds' words that day. I extend my hand. "Corn Nuts." Brody pours a handful of the salted kernels of granite into my palm. "Check it out." I nod toward the outdoors. "It's starting to look different… finish the book… almost there."

━━━━

"Done." Brody closes the journal. He's finished just in time to enjoy the scenery of the Black Hills. A wet spring, every hue of green is represented in the landscape, emerald the predominant color of the grasses, the shrubby spruces evergreen, the pines a slightly darker green, the higher hills in the distance a darker shade yet. The streams bubble with the first run-offs of melting snow from the higher elevations. Sporadic waterfalls trickle down the steeper embankments. Protected by the heavily treed hillsides, the wind is now surprisingly almost nonexistent. There's little traffic, and I drive slowly on the winding road allowing us to take it all in. Brody describes the scenery and moment succinctly, "Nice."

"It is. What did you think of the journal?"

"Liked it. Liked him even less at the end, though."

"McGillycuddy?"

"Yeah."

"Why?"

"He's a hypocrite. Talked how the Indian boys had such a good life, just hangin' out, no school, then as soon as he's in charge he throws 'em in school… and Tommy… "

"Who?"

"Tommy. The Indian boy worked for him."

"Oh, right."

"Sent him to Pennsylvania… kid takes his name and wants to go back, and McGillycuddy leaves him there. Cold as fuck."

Not liking his choice of language, I shoot him a disdainful look with a furrowed brow. I consider Brody's analysis and can understand his dislike of the Indian Agent. I find it interesting that Brody's empathies lie with the Indian boys, while mine have always been with McGillycuddy's challenge of trying to enforce policy in the face of intense political pressures. "He had a tough job."

"Made a ton of money too. I'll take it if he wants to give it, though."

"Don't get your hopes up. I don't think it's money."

"What else could it be?"

"I don't know… might be, but if it were an inheritance, like from a trust or something, we probably would've just gotten a check. His letters call me 'Trusted Messenger'… he has a message… a secret he wanted hidden for eighty years. We'll find out tomorrow."

"Tomorrow? We're almost there. Let's get it."

"It's a four-hour hike. Will be dark before we get to the top. We'll go in the morning."

After meandering our way through the Hills for another half hour or so and intent on putting eyes on tomorrow's point of embarkation, I turn onto a gravel road and roll around a bend following the signs to "Campground" and "Black Elk Peak Trailhead." Then it appears. Sylvan Lake. A more beautiful scene I can't imagine. A smooth body of clear mountain water with protruding islands, contained on its far end by a massive natural dam of white granite. Lodgepole pines and cathedralic stone spires surround. I turn onto another road bringing us close to the water and in the direction of the trailhead. A mother goose and five goslings swim close to the shore, their wake the only apparent disruption to the lake's surface. Awestruck, Brody and I don't speak until moving into a grove of pines blocking the lake's view.

Brody asks, "What's this place?"

Sylvan Lake."

"We stayin' here?"

"We are now. Wasn't planning on it."

"Right on."

The sounds of birds and the first rays of sunlight pierce the SUV's shell. A gentle alarm. My dreamy thoughts focus on one song coming from directly overhead replicated over and over, five notes consistent in pitch, low to high and finishing low again. So consistent in tempo, each call is precisely three seconds apart. "Hear what I'm saying... Hear what I'm saying." I'm not yet fully awake, but the bird sounds like it's talking. No joke. "Hear what I'm saying... Hear what I'm saying." I start to anticipate the next call as I subtly return to consciousness. I open my eyes. "Hear what I'm saying."

I remember a drizzling rain falling just after sunset and that the night got cold, but not unbearably so. The heater running for a short time took the edge off, and we slept peacefully after that. I anticipate the next series of notes. This time the call is delayed by a half-second with an added note at the end. Consistency broken, I sit up. It's chilly. I see my breath. I wipe the condensation from the window. A layer of frost blocks the view. Brody is curled in fetal position wrapped in double blankets pulled to the top of his hoody-covered head. I climb to the driver's seat. Not wanting the immediate hassle of contacts, I put on the prescription glasses I've stowed in the door's cubby and step outside. The ground crunches beneath me. I survey my surroundings. No wisp of wind. Droplets flash-frozen after the drizzling rain hang from every bough and needle refracting and displaying in sparkling fashion the rays of the rising sun like millions of the tiniest of white bulbs hung through the forest. I take in the silence, crisp air, the smell of the morning pines and admire the flickering diamonds in the trees. I knock on the window above Brody's head. I want to know McGillycuddy's secret or get rich… whatever he's hidden for us.

The trail is well maintained, and the steady, gradual ascent meandering between exposed granite pinnacles hasn't been difficult to hike. We aren't necessarily above the treeline, but the pines have thinned out considerably, lumped together now only in small groves allowing us to see our destination, the summit of Black Elk Peak. Rain below had turned to snow at this elevation overnight. A light dusting still covers the ground to reveal that we aren't the first hikers on the trail this morning. Two sets of footprints precede us, potentially dashing my hope that we'll have the summit to ourselves for the extraction.

Not more than fifty yards further up the trail, I see another set of tracks, animal tracks, and bend down for a closer look. Brody does the same. "What is it?"

"Mountain lion, probably." I tell Brody about seeing a mountain lion in California and watching news stories of how they had pounced, and in some cases, killed unsuspecting joggers. I follow the tracks with my eyes. They disappear into a rocky area to our left. I'm not concerned as the remaining part of the trail covers wide open ground. Brody and I scan the rocks and cliffs, hoping to catch a glimpse of the cat without success. We share a drink from a water bottle, and despite Brody's initial protests to a sandwich that's been in the cooler for a day and a half, we eat. "Probably another hour. Want me to carry for a while?"

"I'm good." Brody pulls the hammer from the backpack.

"What you doin'?"

"Fucker ain't eatin' me."

———

The last mile has been a steeper climb, and I'm a trifle winded when I catch up to a waiting Brody smoking a cigarette. "Look." Brody points to a winding staircase of hundreds of steps carved into the mountain, leading to the summit. We haven't met the two hikers, so I suspect they'll be waiting for us at the top.

"There's people up there. Put the hammer away."

Brody complies, throws the pack onto his back and leaps forward, bouncing two steps at a time, cigarette in hand. He disappears around the first bend. Knowing my limitations, I make a conscious decision to take the stairs slowly, one step at a time. My head down focused on each step, I nearly bump into the leader of two young hikers descending the spiraling staircase—a man and woman in their mid-20s. He put—his hand on my shoulder to prevent a collision. It startles me. "Whoa. Sorry about that." I observe that they are wearing matching sets of expensive-looking hiking gear—jackets and pants of water-resistant material, fine leather boots, packs with built-in hydration systems, sunglasses, logoed hats, hiking poles, etc. Real hikers. Quite a contrast to my hiking apparel—jeans, light jacket over a flannel shirt, the combat boots I wore in the Air Force and knitted winter cap.

"It's all good. Beautiful morning."

"It is. You guys made good time. Heading down?"

"Yeah."

It's a dumb question, but it's intentional. I want to make sure they aren't planning on hanging around. "Have a good hike."

"You too, man."

I climb a few steps and stop to confirm their intended departure and that nobody else is en route. Satisfied we'll be alone for the immediate future, and adrenaline now pumping, I start-double stepping until I reach a small viewing platform. Above me is a fire lookout station, no longer in service, made of stone blocks probably quarried from the mountain as they match the color of the naturally existing stone perfectly. I catch my breath and admire the beauty of the entirety of the Black Hills. I pick up a cigarette butt from the stone pavers and follow the path upward.

"Over here." Brody is kneeling and appears to be digging his fingertips into the side of a boulder. He drops the pack from his back, drags it by a strap to his immediate right and unzips the main pouch to remove the crowbar. I scan the area for unexpected company, and seeing none; I climb the remaining few steps.

Not that I have any reason to think any plaques other than McGillycuddy's would be on the top of this mountain, I confirm he's found the correct target. It's much smaller than I expected. Brody positions the crowbar's claw at the plaque's top center and slowly slides it to the right. He stops. "Hell, yeah." In an instant, he stands and, with full swing, slams the hammer's face into the crowbar's neck. Chips of granite fly, and the sound of metal striking metal first pierces my eardrums before echoing off the stone surroundings. My ears ring. Damn. That was loud. I blink my eyes.

Brody flips the bar and slides the chiseled edge of the shaft into the gap he's exposed. Realizing he's going to take another swing, I turn my back. Another metallic gunshot rings through the Hills. Brody sinks the bar deeper into the void and wraps both hands around its neck. He plants one foot firmly against the boulder and leans back, the bar supporting his full weight. He jerks. The plaque flies off and hits the ground with a clang. Brody's fall is slower but more dramatic. He swings his arms frantically, trying to regain balance, but on his heels, gravity prevails. His rear end hits, and he slides into the stone wall behind him, defending against the 100-foot drop on the other side. Brody smiles.

"Told you I could get it off."

I look to where the plaque had been, and as McGillycuddy promised, see a keyhole centered in the face of an entombed lockbox that is perfectly square at its front, six inches high by six inches wide. Protected from the elements for eighty years, it shines like a new penny in the sun. The sounds of Brody's efforts still ringing in my head, and realizing anybody within a five-mile radius heard the same, I hurriedly scramble to remove the key from the backpack's zippered front pouch. Brody crouches next to me, positioning himself for a clear view of the box's interior once opened. I insert the key and attempt to turn it counter-clockwise without success before trying the other direction. A distinctive click. We look at each other with excitement.

"This is nuts. Open it."

Using the key as a handle, I pull toward me, expecting the front to swing open. It doesn't. Instead, the box on a roller or slide system of sorts, separates itself slightly from the face of the boulder, allowing me to grip around its edges. I pull and slide it out. It's shaped like a safety deposit box about twelve inches long. I set it on the pavers, and we inspect it. It appears designed to open from the top, but it's such a tight fit that a sheet of paper couldn't fit in the microscopic gap between lid and box.

Undeterred by the obvious, Brody slides the crowbar's chiseled claw along the lid's edge. "Hang on." Brody continues to examine the box and contemplate how he can use his tools to gain access. The key's ornate head still protrudes from the keyhole a quarter turn to the right of vertical center. I try turning it again. "Awwwwwwww!!!!" The hinged lid springs open with force like a jack in the box without the clown, causing us to jump back in surprise. The shock subsides, and we release our nervous energy with subtle laughter.

Brody leans forward to peek inside. "'Bout took my head off."

I look also. My initial reaction is that of disappointment. The contents are sparse. The predominant feature, McGillycuddy's metallic urn, laid on its side, is what Brody removes first.

"What is it?"

"His ashes." I extract the rest of our bounty—a cinched small white leather pouch decorated with a beaded Indian design and another leather-bound journal, this one looking more like a ledger book. Confirming the box is indeed empty, I look down the path expecting someone to come around the corner of the stairs at any moment. Brody, unimpressed, returns his attention to the urn. "Put that back."

"What if it's diamonds and shit."

"It's not." I pause and consider his words. "Shake it." Internal sounds like sand in a jar confirm the absence of jewels.

"Put it back." McGillycuddy again interred. I act quickly, closing the box, lifting and sliding it back into its hallowed chamber. I turn the key counter-clockwise to its vertical position as mechanized clicks confirm it is again locked. I put the key into my pocket. "Get the plaque." I reach into the backpack and remove a utility knife and large tube of fast-drying, construction-grade glue.

"What's that for?"

I reach for the plaque in Brody's hand. "Putting this back." I slice through and remove the top half of the tube's tip, that I recover and secure in my shirt pocket, and proceed to squeeze generous amounts of the glue along the backside edges of the plaque and on the granite around the lockbox. I set the plaque into position, ensure level, and press it against the granite, causing the excess glue to ooze out on all sides except for a 2-inch section along the top that Brody bent with the crowbar. Not having a rag, I remove my knitted hat intending to use it to remove the waste. I instead create a gummy, smeared mess around the perimeter, both on and off the bronze face. The hat sticks to my fingers. Intending to fold it inside out to expose clean cloth, I remove my left hand that's been holding the plaque in position. The plaque starts a slow downward slide. I push it upward and press harder. What a cluster.

"Go watch for people. If you see someone coming up the steps, run back here." I turn my attention to the beaded pouch and journal still on the ground, and not wanting to get the glue on the items, I switch hands and use my clean left to secure them in the backpack. I need ten more minutes for the glue to set.

━━━━

A whistle. I look toward the fire lookout to see Brody waving vigorously for me to come. I hoped for ten minutes. I got about seven or eight. I ease my pressure before completely removing my fingers but keeping them hovered in front of the plaque should I need to stop another downward slide. To my delight, it stays in place, then to my dismay, I notice a circular pattern of five distinct fingerprints I've glued onto the plaque's center. I'd be a horrible criminal. I grab the backpack and give the area a quick scan to ensure I'm not leaving any additional incriminating evidence behind. I step in Brody's direction with a strange mix of feelings—pride and frustration, excitement and disappointment, anxiety and relief. A Forest Ranger appears to Brody's left. Shit. Add fear of arrest to the mix.

Brody's lit another cigarette and engaged in conversation as I approach. He laughs—cool as a cucumber. Me, not so much. I haven't done anything illegal, at least I don't think so, but my naturally guilty conscience makes me feel like I have. I suspect my countenance and demeanor convey the same. Stay calm.

"Howdy."

"Mornin.'" I glance at the Ranger's holstered sidearm.

"You guys been up here before?

As a former prosecutor, I know the police routine for voluntary contacts. Engage, ask questions, keep them engaged, ask for identification, look for strange behavior, find reasonable suspicion to detain. I suspect Federal Forest Rangers are trained the same.

"No. First time. Beautiful."

"Where you staying?"

"Stayed in the campground last night. Sylvan Lake."

"Silver SUV?"

"That's the one. It's a rental." Early season and the only vehicle in the campground without a camper or any camping gear has obviously drawn his attention. Knowing he's about to ask for identification, I beat him to the punch. I reach for my back pocket. "Let me get my I.D., Ranger... I was an Air Force JAG... I get it." I hand him my driver's license with a clean left hand. "Was stationed in Minot and drove through here once. Always wanted to come back and explore the area. Any recommendations?" The Ranger looks my license over. Brody takes the last pull from his cigarette and turns his head away from the Ranger to blow out a cloud of blue smoke. I mentally tell him not to toss the butt. The Ranger has ignored my last question. Brody returns to the conversation.

"You see those mountain lion tracks?" Head tilted downward, the Ranger looks at Brody through the tops of his eyes and returns my license without making eye contact.

"Yeah. We call her Sally." He stares at Brody. Too intently. Intimidation tactic. Brody returns his gaze without speaking. Several seconds pass until the Ranger breaks the silence, "The reason I'm up here is because you didn't stop at the station for a wilderness permit." Brody laughs.

"A permit? Didn't know I needed one."

"How long you staying?"

Brody chimes in. "A week."

"In the campground?"

Brody extinguishes the cigarette with his fingers and puts the butt in his pocket. "Maybe. Why you give a fuck?"

The Ranger immediately takes an aggressive stance, hands on hips, his right thumb tucked into his belt with fingers hovering over his weapon.

I snap at Brody, "Stop!" I focus on the Ranger. "Listen. I apologize. I didn't know. If there's a fee, I'll pay it."

Still staring Brody down, the Ranger takes a deep breath through his mouth and exhales through his nose, nostrils flaring. "Stop at the station and fill out the form if you're staying."

"We free to go?"

"Not stopping you."

I shove Brody's shoulder, encouraging him to walk away.

He does, and I follow him down the stone stairway. We don't speak for the first mile of descent. I stop to see if the Ranger is following us. He's not. "That guy has anger issues."

"Asshole."

"With a gun. You shouldn't have antagonized him."

"Whatever. I was bein' nice as hell to that guy. He was bein' a dick just 'cause the way I look."

I know Brody's probably correct in his assessment.

"Think he'll notice the plaque?"

"Na... so what if he does? It's our shit. We can prove it."

"Yeah. We can... but if he takes permits that seriously, I don't want to find out how he handles vandalism." I reach into my pocket to confirm I still have the key to produce as exculpatory evidence if necessary. The cigarette butt I'd put in the same pocket sticks to my middle finger. I raise it for Brody's viewing as if flipping him off. "Picked this up for you."

"Not mine."

"I picked it up at the top of the steps."

"Not mine... nasty... better wash your hands." Brody digs into his pockets and extracts two cigarette butts, and says sarcastically, "I don't litter, Dad."

We've made the descent and can see the station where our "friendly" Ranger instructed us to stop and fill out a form if we planned on staying in the campground. My gut tells me we should move on, but Brody wants to stay at least another day to explore around the lake and take in some of the other attractions of the Black Hills.

"C'mon. We're here. Got nothin' else to do. Don't stress over that dude."

The words of McGillycuddy's first letter come to me. I've read it so many times I nearly have it memorized and can now almost visualize each handwritten word.

> *I hope that you feel you are being bestowed a gift and not a burden. From my experience, life on the move and in the open is vastly preferable to stagnation and closed quarters. In the event you have an adventurous spirit, like me, I encourage you to visit the places where these events occurred. No doubt much has changed since my days as topographer, contract surgeon, and Indian Agent, but any sights, sounds, and smells of Dakota Country still present will only embellish the experience.*

"You're right. We'll stay a bit longer." I finish filling out the form for the wilderness permit and slide the government's copy through the slot in the dropbox. "All set. Want a fire tonight?"

"Hell yeah." Brody's again in cellular range. "Check this out."

I accept his phone, expecting a funny video or picture of one of his friends. The screen is all text. I read:

"Crazy Horse's father Waglula took him to what today is Sylvan Lake, South Dakota, where they both sat to do a hemblecha or vision quest. A red-tailed hawk led them to their respective spots in the hills; as the trees are tall in the Black Hills, they could not always see where they were going. Crazy Horse sat between two humps at the top of a hill north and to the east of the lake. Waglula sat south of Black Elk Peak, believed by the Sioux to be the home of the Thunder Beings, but north of his son."

"Sylvan Lake. Black Elk Peak. Here, right?"

"Yeah."

Brody reaches for his phone. "Hang on. I'll find the spot." He types and taps into it. "What direction is northeast?"

"We're northeast of the lake now. Should be straight up the trail."

Brody looks up the trail, back to his phone, and back up the trail as he gives me his phone. "Top of the screen. Has to be it."

"I think you found it."

"Let's check it out."

"We will… tomorrow. I'm spent. Let's go to the store and get firewood and hotdogs or something… need more ice."

"That'll take ten minutes… when we get back. We got time."

I look up the valley and can see the granite-crowned hill Brody's found in satellite imaging. I calculate the distance and travel time. My best guess is that it's about a mile, maybe a little more as the crow flies. Will probably take about an hour to get there, around 5:30, maybe 6. It gets dark around 7:30. McGillycuddy speaks to me. "*If you have an adventurous spirit like me… man up.*" I look at Brody. "Got our wilderness permit. Let's do it."

Brody smiles. "On an adventure, Pops."

Brody remains fresh and leads us to where we believe is the site of Crazy Horse's vision quest. I'm keeping pace, but I can tell I'll feel the effects of ten miles of mountain hiking tomorrow. We're over halfway to our destination when I try to spark up a conversation to take my mind off my burning glutes and calves. "Did what you read tell you about Crazy Horse's vision?"

"Yeah… said he went to a spirit world and saw a warrior and horse on a lake. The horse floated and danced around in a weird way. That's how he got his name. The warrior didn't dress fancy and only wore one feather hanging upside down… and a white stone behind his ear. Crazy Horse's dad told him that if he dressed like the warrior, he'd have special powers, and he had to always use those powers to help his people… never for himself."

"That's how McGillycuddy described him… but I think Crazy Horse told him the medicine man gave him the stone."

"To make him bulletproof. He did."

"I'm impressed."

"Told you I'm into it. I think we need to get off here." We've reached the point where the trail makes a 90-degree bend to our right. Brody's saved a screenshot of the satellite image he showed me earlier. We confirm his initial assessment that we need to go off the path and head uphill toward the granite towers peaking over the top of the pine grove before us.

"Lead the way, Bro."

It's been less than half a mile to reach our destination since leaving the trail, but the terrain has forced us to weave between and around trees and boulders, making it seem much further. Now I'm truly spent. "We should sit up there." Brody points to the top of two massive boulders nestled tightly together, so large that I can't begin to estimate how much they weigh. I nod and psych myself up for one more small climb. Brody's selection of resting spots is perfect. From this high vantage, we gain a clear view of our newly found magical environment. We're surrounded on three sides by walls of white granite. Thousands of years of water erosion has dug deep vertical crevices into the stone, separating the walls into distinct sections, each shooting up a hundred or more feet from the forest floor—a horseshoe-shaped stadium of stone in which we're almost perfectly centered. The setting sun casts shadows from our left, across the field, and halfway up the façade to our right, the top of which gleams as if capturing all possible remaining sunlight. Down the treelined valley, a ribbon of emerald green meanders following the creek's path running to the glistening Sylvan Lake below. Brody speaks. "Crazy Horse was here. Can feel it."

"It's amazing. You're joking, but I wouldn't be surprised if this *is* the spot."

"I'm not joking. We found it. This is where I'd look for a vision."

I take a seat and reach for my toes, stretching my legs. I pat the ground to my right, encouraging him to sit. "I'm glad we came. Great idea. Let's see what we got."

Brody slides the straps off his shoulders, sits, and tosses the backpack between his legs. I suspect he'll remove the beaded pouch first, which he does. "Give me the journal." Brody gives the pouch a gentle shake before untying the leather strap cinching its top closed. He reaches in and furrows his brow slightly as if he can't make out what he's feeling. Between the tips of his fingers and thumb, he holds the end of a strand of sinew that he slowly lifts away from the pouch, from which hangs, once revealed, a small white stone. We both instantly know what we have.

"No way." Brody wraps the string around his left ear and looks down the valley allowing me to see the dangling stone. I lean toward him and take it between my fingers for closer examination. It's agate. The sinew is wrapped tightly around its bubbly exterior. "Keep tellin' you… we're loaded. Has to be worth a fortune." I've heard Brody's proclamations of instant wealth several times since first introduced to Valentine McGillycuddy. This time I don't dismiss the idea. Still enthralled and in disbelief, a slurry of thoughts run through my head. Crazy Horse is probably the most famous Indian ever—they're carving a monument of the guy into a mountain about ten miles away. I can prove it's real. Maybe we could get a lot of money at one of those expensive auctions. Christie's, maybe?

Suddenly aware of the stone's potential value, I release my grip. "Take it off... carefully... don't break the string... put it away."

Brody, sensing the tension in my voice, turns his smiling face toward me. The scar in his cheek dimples. "I like it. It's a good look."

"Take it off, Bro... carefully."

Brody chuckles. Under my watchful eye, he untwines the chord from his ear and returns the stone to the pouch. "It's a rock, Dad... but it's cool as hell we got it... especially here."

Satisfied the white stone is secure, I assess how much time we have left before dusk. The valley below remains well lit, but the wall to our right is now almost entirely engulfed in shadow. I open the journal. A neatly folded piece of cream-colored paper is tucked against the spine between the cover and the journal's first page. I carefully release the folds. It's on letterhead.

Hotel Claremont

Berkeley, California

It's dated April 25, 1938. Like previous letters, it's handwritten in cursive black ink. I anticipate it will confirm that Valentine has given me a sacred stone received from Crazy Horse as his final act of appreciation of Little Beard's friendship before his death at Camp Robinson. I read it out loud for Brody's consumption.

Dear Trusted Messenger,

If reading this, your journey has been successful. You, too, have appreciated the views from the summit of Harney's Peak and the beauties of the lands under. You now possess the last pieces necessary to complete the puzzle of my creation and thus know the secrets I have hidden, buried deep within me for so long. It is my hope that those secrets will remain in this world upon my passing, and my soul, then cleansed, will fly over the divide and through the heavens to be with Fanny and my Creator in pure and holy state. What we can perceive from the other side I do not feign to know, but as I bring this letter to close, it is my hope that at a minimum, I am aware of your existence on some level and that what I offer brings a sense of excitement and only other good things. Perhaps we too someday shall meet and together share our now common experiences.

Sincerely,

V.T. M'Gillycuddy

We sit silently for several seconds. I refold the letter. Brody speaks. "Dude wasn't all bad, I guess… could sure write a good letter."

"Yes, he could. We should head back." The diminishing light will make it difficult to read further. I give Brody the journal to return to the backpack.

"Let's hang for a bit. This place is cool… may never get back here."

Something about his words strike me. I wasn't much older than him when I had similar feelings of wanting to stop to take in a view, absorb a feeling, and capture a moment. I was new to the Air Force stationed in England for my first assignment and still a newlywed. My mother-in-law came for a visit, and we planned a weekend trip to Bath. I always got along with Adele. We had a splendid day touristing, exploring the city, and making our best efforts to contain our laughter like gigglish children in church as three Jewish women from New York praised the "butta" while eating their Sally Lund's buns. That afternoon we checked into a countryside bed and breakfast, and I inquired as to the nearest pub where we could get an evening meal.

"Ahhh, Hun. Ain't nothing but a jaunt over the hill and down the road." Having completed the transaction for the room, our caretaker took us outside the cottage and pointed through the fields of the property and up the hill. "You'll see the road up there. Go left. You'll see the pub." We followed our lady's instructions, commenting on the ducks, chickens, and the largest pig we'd ever seen as we moved to the base of the hill. I opened the gate to the first enclosure, and we started our climb in drizzling rain.

We reached the next fence and walked its length, looking for an entrance. There was none, at least none I could find. Climb or go back were our options. The consensus was to climb and continue. My now ex-wife climbed over the fence first to help her mother from the other side. Adele, a small woman in stature but not light in weight at the time, planted her foot on the bottom plank. Her daughter pulled her arms from the other side. Seeing her struggle, I gave fair warning and shyly planted my hands into her rear end and lifted. She cleared the fence and grounded herself on the other side. We repeated the process three more times before reaching the top of the hill in laughter. It was a rare moment where nobody complained about the inconvenience, the awkwardness of the situation, or the drizzling rain. We were together on a hillside in England. We enjoyed the comedy of it all.

Now on high ground, I looked back toward the City of Bath tucked into a sunken river valley surrounded by higher ground left and right. The sun hit the city's highest points perfectly framed by a full rainbow, fronting a backdrop of dark gray storm clouds.

I'd never done it before and hadn't done it since, but I knew the moment was special—I made a conscious decision to remember. I scanned my eyes from left to right, up and down. I repeated the process. Remember this, I told myself. I close my eyes and see it again. It works. I open my eyes and convey the story to Brody.

"Take it all in. Burn the image into your brain." He realizes, as did I as a young man in England, that this is a special moment. It's not corny to him in the least, and I appreciate it. We don't speak. The image of the granite walls and boulders, trees, distant mountains, valley and lake below shimmering in the dwindling sunlight, conjoined with the feelings of togetherness and contentment, will be with us forever ingrained in our minds.

A loud screech echoes off the walls of our stadium, bringing us back to reality. We have nature's front row, 50-yard line seats. The mountain lion enters the field cautiously from the left and into center position. Sally. She hunches her shoulders to the ground, waits, and stalks a few steps before completely freezing. She bolts. Her prey bounces off the top of a boulder and jumps. Sally leaps and, with a flaring paw, cuts the rabbit down mid-flight. She meows, and two cubs present themselves from where their mother first appeared. The mountain lion takes the carcass in her mouth and proceeds to cross the stadium floor, exiting to the right, her crying cubs following. We remain oblivious to her attention. The field of play now clear, Brody whispers in my ear. "Got my spirit animal. Next tat."

I whisper back. "That was cool. Me too… maybe."

The dry split logs I purchased from the General Store up the road after our return spark to emanate warm light and cook the hot dogs impaled on the end of our homemade spits, two each. I sit on the cooler and Brody on the ground. The soothing radiant heat heavies my eyelids but the sounds of slowly turning tires on gravel entering our enclave gets my attention and prevents my sleep. The vehicle producing the sound follows shortly after, its headlights passing over us as it turns the bend. I inspect my hotdogs that are bubbling on the underside. I spin my spit. The truck slows and creeps by our site. I can't see the driver, but I suspect I know who's behind the wheel.

"Wave." I wave as if to a passing friend. Brody stands and waves like a boy to his parents in the stands after winning the Special Olympics. He's instigating again, but I'm too tired to care. After a full day trekking the mountains and hills, the hot dogs taste better than the most expensive filet mignon. We plan to hike to the top of the Crazy Horse Memorial tomorrow.

Tucked under two layers of blankets in the SUV, Brody snores next to me. I now somewhat wired by the thought of the public servant patrolling our grounds, I prop my pillows, sit up and open our newly-acquired McGillycuddy journal to read by flashlight for a while.

In November 1890, I returned to public service at the request of the Governor of South Dakota, Arthur C. Mellette, with whom I was well acquainted as I had served as surgeon general on his staff. He enlisted my assistance appointing me a commander in the National Guard and charging me with the responsibility to investigate the rise of a new messianic religion among the Sioux. I was informed that a Paiute Indian in Nevada by the name of Wovoka had started the new religion that prophesized that a time would come when the whole Indian race, living and dead, would be reunited on a rejuvenated earth. The white man would disappear, and the Indians would once again live in happiness, free from death, disease, and misery. All the Indians had to do to bring about this new paradise was to perform a circle dance that the whites dubiously named the Ghost Dance. The new religion of the so-called Ghost Dance had spread quickly throughout the Indians of the West, in my opinion, driven by the fact the government had again reduced the amount of annual beef appropriations, this time by an additional thirty percent. Some estimated that between fifty and one hundred thousand Indians across Nevada, Utah, Idaho, Colorado, Wyoming, Montana, Texas, Kansas, Nebraska, and of course, the Sioux in the Dakotas, were participating. The return of Indian dancing was perceived as an immediate threat and cause of great concern among the settlers in those areas. It was believed the Indians intended to go on the war path again.

Having experienced the spectacle and delight of Indian dances, I continued to encourage them for as long as I could. The government did not feel the same. While I was Indian Agent, I received a letter from the Indian Commissioner stating, "As the sun dance is a relic of barbarism and tends to retard and destroy all efforts made to promote the welfare and civilizing influences of the Indians, you will immediately take measures to prevent your Indians from attending it and also induce the leading members of the tribe to cooperate with you in discouraging such heathenish practices." I ignored the demand from the ivory-towered bureaucrat who had hardly ventured west of the Appalachians, and obeyance of which would have resulted in hostility and further delay of my objectives. Days later, I accompanied a Chicago Tribune reporter to Spotted Tail's camp where the

Sun Dance commenced. All passed smoothly, except few Indians reported for beef issue day, as most were still participating in the dance.

Political pressures eventually forced me to enforce the policy of no more Indian dances, the last Sun Dance being held in June 1883.

I shared my experience and belief with the Governor that I saw no great danger in allowing the Indians to dance. I should let them continue. If the Seventh-Day Adventists prepare their ascension robes for the second coming of the Savior, the U.S. Army is not put in motion to prevent them. Why should not the Indians have the same privilege? If the government would but increase the beef rations to previous levels, this likely ends now, but if that is not possible, let them dance through the winter. When the green grass comes, and with it no messiah, it ends then.

Matters were already beyond the Governor's control as the settlers were demanding military involvement and the issuance of weapons to the civilian population. As was usually the case, the Sioux garnered the most government attention, especially now that Sitting Bull, the traditionalist, now on the reservation at Standing Rock, was believed to be encouraging the Ghost Dances and instigating another Sioux outbreak. To thwart any such attempt, over one thousand soldiers from Companies A, B, I, and K of the Seventh Cavalry, each with thirty days rations and two hundred rounds of carbine ammunition, were dispatched to Pine Ridge to prepare for a serious campaign. The Governor requested I go to Pine Ridge and assess the potential dangers to the settlers of the area, which I did.

———

The birds and sun have little impact on me this morning. I sleep through my gentle alarm and fall into one of those deep morning sleeps, causing us to get off to a slow start. I'm sore, as expected, but

I feel surprisingly rested. I need coffee, though, to get me moving at full speed. Brody skips rocks into the lake as I buy a cup to-go from the General Store. There's a slight breeze, but it's supposed to warm up throughout the day. Overall, another pleasant morning in the Black Hills. There's a chance of rain later. I drive slowly to the Crazy Horse Memorial, taking in the views, while Brody reads about the rise of the new Ghost-Dance religion 130 years before. He soon finishes the section and asks if I want him to keep reading. I do.

I left the Governor and arrived at my old Agency the next day to find soldiers on the ground. Word of my arrival spread quickly, and Red Cloud formed a council to which I was invited to discuss the presence of troops. Red Cloud gave my introduction.

This is Little Beard, who was our Agent winters ago when he was a boy. There was bad feeling between us, but when he went away, he said someday I would say that his way was best for the Indian. I will tell him now that he spoke the truth. Little Beard, we have not behaved half as badly as we did in your day, but you never sent for troops. We settled our troubles among ourselves. It looks as though the soldiers are here to fight. We do not want to fight. Can you not send these soldiers away? If you will, we give you twenty-five of our young men you can take as hostages, and everything will be settled in one sleep.

I informed the council that I no longer had the authority to make any deals with the Indians, and that I was there only to represent the Governor but promised I would take their words to the soldier chief at the Agency. Then Little Wound spoke,

Porcupine has come to us with this story of the Ghost Dance and the coming messiah. Whether it is true or not, I do not know, but it is the same story the white missionaries told us that the messiah will come again. I gathered my people and told them that if it is a good thing, we shall have it. If it is not a good thing, it will fall to the earth of itself, but we should learn the signs and dances that if the messiah comes in the spring, he will not pass us by. But I ask you, why have the white soldiers been brought here to stop the dance unless it is true?

As promised, later that day I did speak to the soldier chief, General Brooke. In a very pompous manner, the General asked if I thought I could settle this matter. I replied confidently that I thought I could, as I had ten years of experience with these Indians, that they had my confidence and vice versa. The presence of troops had frightened the Indians, and it was fostering the belief that it was a sign that the prophecy would come to pass. Simply move the troops over the Nebraska line and let the dances continue through the winter. The Indians would not go to war in winter, and when the messiah did not return in the spring, the movement would fizzle. But if the troops remained, trouble was sure to come—not through the old warriors, but through the men too young to have felt the power of the army during the Indian Wars. General Brooke did not heed my advice, instead ordering for the arrival of howitzers, Hotchkiss guns, and additional troops.

We pull into the parking area at the Crazy Horse Memorial, and Brody asks, "Why you think the General didn't listen to McGillycuddy?"

I think before responding. "May have wanted a fight. I think it happened a lot back then. They were trained to lead men in battle and believed that was their sole purpose. If you didn't experience war, you didn't get promoted… never became a war hero. That's what got Custer. Wanted the glory so bad he made a bad decision."

Brody points at the massive unfinished monument carved into the mountain above us. "Got everybody killed by him."

We walk across the nearly empty parking lot, still looking at the unfinished monument above, before reaching the entrance. The nice lady at the booth answers my questions. "Twenty-four dollars for two people."

"How far is it to the top?"

"Just over 3 miles."

I look at Brody. "Have your heart set on going up there?"

"Not me. Thought you wanted to."

A six-mile hike today would probably do me in. Paying for more pain makes the prospect of doing so even less attractive. "Rather go hang out around the lake?"

"Definitely."

It was a good decision to have a day of rest and save 24 bucks in the process. On the ride back to Sylvan Lake, Brody pulled up some images of the memorial on his phone. From the parking area, we could see that the face appeared completed. Beyond that, the rest of the gigantic sculpture was designed to include his arm pointing into the distance. His torso and the head of his horse required imagination. Brody shows me a closeup of the face and comments, "I don't know… looks like George Washington… and where's his scar?" Reading McGillycuddy's journal, we've both formed our own mental images of Crazy Horse's appearance, and I have to agree, the carving doesn't jibe.

We soon return to the lake and walk around its backside next to the natural dam holding in the mountain waters. Brody's wandered off to explore, and I've found a comfortable place to read. Rainclouds are developing in the west, but I'm in the sun now with a clear view of the water. We have the area to ourselves. I open the journal.

My attempts to sway General Brooke proving futile, I turned my attention to speaking with the delegation of Northern Cheyennes, led by Porcupine, a surprisingly young man sent West to learn if the messiah was real, and if so, bring back his message to the tribes. As discussed at the council, he had recently returned from a personal encounter with the leader of the new religion. Having the full authority of the Governor's Office at my disposal, I was able to quickly arrange the meeting. Below is a summarized version of Porcupine's statement given to me that day. I elect to exclude introductory portions pertaining primarily to his travels to Pyramid and Walker Lakes in western Nevada; this location is known from diagrams drawn and explanations given.

What I am going to say is the truth. The two men sitting near me were with me and will bear witness that I speak the truth. The fish-eaters told me that Christ had appeared on earth again. They told me Christ had summoned us and others from fifteen or sixteen other tribes. There were more different languages than I ever heard before, and I didn't understand any of them. They called a council and told me to remain fourteen days in camp, and then Christ would come to see us. They fed us all. Then they said the Christ would be there in two days. Hundreds of people gathered at this place. They cleared off a place of all grass in the form of a ring. We waited all day, anxious to see the Christ.

Just before sundown, I saw a great many people, mostly Indians, coming dressed in white man's clothing. The Christ was with them. They all sat in the ring. They put up shoots all around the circle, as they had no tents. Just after dark, some of the Indians told me that Christ had arrived. I looked around to find him and finally saw him sitting on one side of the ring. They all started toward him to see him. They made a big fire to throw light on him. I never looked around but went forward, and when I saw him, I bent my head. I had always thought the Christ was a white man, but this man looked like an Indian. He sat with his head bowed all the time. After a while, he rose and said he was very glad to see his children.

He spoke in Lakota."I have sent for you and am glad to see you. I am going to talk to you after a while about your relatives who are dead and gone. My children, I want you to listen to all I have to say to you. I will teach you, too, how to dance a dance and I want you to dance it. Get ready for your dance, and then when the dance is over, I will talk to you." He was dressed in a white coat with stripes, and he wore moccasins. We danced until late into the night until he told us we had danced enough.

The next morning after breakfast was over, we went into the circle and spread canvas over it on the ground. The Christ appeared again. We were crowded in very close. We had been told that nobody was to talk, and even if we whispered, the Christ would know. He was not so dark as an Indian nor so light as a white man. He had no beard or whiskers. He was a good-looking man. I had heard the Christ had been crucified, and I looked to see. I saw a scar on his face and his wrist, and he seemed to be the man. I could not see his feet. He then opened his coat and showed us another scar on his side.

He spoke again to us."I have been to heaven and seen your dead friends. When I came back on earth, the white people were afraid and treated me badly. This is what they have done to me. They killed me, and now there are many holes in me.

"Brody!!!!"

Not believing what I've just read, I continue.

Porcupine continued talking, but I heard not another word, for my head went light and my breathing became labored such that I feared I too would befall a tragedy like my beloved Fanny. It had been over thirteen years since I had pronounced him dead at Camp Robinson, but the truth was self-evident—Crazy Horse was alive, and he was the messiah of the Ghost Dance craze.

"Brody!!!!!"

PART III

"When a vision comes from the thunder beings of the
West, it comes with terror like a thunderstorm; but when
the storm of vision has passed, the world is greener and
happier; for wherever the truth of vision comes upon the
world, it is like a rain. The world, you see, is happier
after the terror of the storm."

—Black Elk

I've called twice for Brody. He now appears on top of a giant slab of rock composing a portion of the granite dam standing within feet of the vertical face dropping to the water below.

Brody yells, "All good?"

I motion for him, and he disappears from his roost. It must have taken some effort to reach that spot and to climb down from it because it takes longer than expected for him to reach me. He eventually does, looking concerned. "You OK? What's up?"

"Sit. Read this." I hand him the journal. "Tell me when you get to the part where the Indian says they sat in a circle the next morning after breakfast."

Brody reads a few sentences. "You gotta come climb over here."

"I will. Read."

"OK. I'm there. Sounds like a cult."

"Keep reading." I watch for a change in expression. His eyes widen.

"Scar on his face and side... holy shit... it's Crazy Horse."

I smile and nod. "Read the next paragraph."

"No way!" Without a request to do so, Brody continues reading out loud.

I must explain how this could be possible by elaborating on what took place within the dreary confines of the Adjutant's Office at Camp Robinson that September night of 1877. We, being myself, Touches the Clouds, Crazy Horse's father, and my interpreter, John Provost, laid the wounded warrior on his blanket on the office floor. Touches the Clouds leaned over him, almost whispering in his ear, offering words of encouragement while his father laid his hand on Crazy Horse's chest, singing mournful songs of his son's certain death. I had Provost light the kerosene lamp as I lifted Crazy Horse's blood-stained shirt to examine his wounds. The blade from the first bayonet strike left only a surface wound running under Crazy Horse's ribs. The second wound was severe, the bayonet having pierced him above the right hip bone and penetrating deep into his abdomen. There was no exit wound. Knowing there was little I could do medically, I poured alcohol into the wound and closed it with stitches. Crazy Horse's pupils contracted into two pinpoints; he clearly was in shock. His eyes were darting back and forth, stopping to look briefly at his father, then his friend, the ceiling, and then to repeat the process. I held the lamp close to his face and then covered his eyes with no change in dilation. When Crazy Horse's pain became obviously unbearable, I gave him an injection of morphine. I resigned myself to wait until my friend's passing. The warrior slipped into a deep sleep. Around 8 o'clock, I believed his death was soon imminent, as his breathing had slowed to one shallow breath every ten seconds, and his pulse dipped to approximately 40 beats per minute.

A clap of thunder echoes through the Hills. I look up. The clouds that have been building from the west throughout the day have blown in quickly. They have an eerie greenish-blue tint, and they're on us now. "Stop. We need to go."

Our return to the vehicle starts as a casual walk until a wind gust hits us so fiercely from behind that I think we've been thrown into a tornado. The trees bend, and a mix of dust, needles, and shards of graphite sandblast our backsides. On the water, whitecaps appear where glass was just moments before. A trunk of lightning jumps from the center of the lake that branches into individual bolts striking the surrounding treetops. Boom!!!!! We run for cover. Hail starts to fall and bounces in our path. Small frozen granules, at first the size of peas turn into ever-larger spheroids—marbles next; and as we reach the safe confines of the SUV with covered heads—golf balls.

The falling ice beats into the metal hull with a deafening roar, and the windshield succumbs to the pounding. Cracks radiate from the point of impact, and, believing it will shatter, I put my hands against the glass to provide additional support. Brody raises his un-inked arm to me in wonderment. All the hairs are standing perfectly upright. A sizzling sound precedes the brightest flash of white light imaginable, joined by a simultaneous deafening boom that rocks us. The pounding gets harder. I yell, "Do it!"

Brody provides additional support until the gusts lessen, his arm hairs flatten, and the stones transition from golf balls to marbles, then peas and then silence returns. The threat of losing the windshield now removed, I run my hand over the spiderweb pattern. The innermost layer of glass is still smooth. A single raindrop splashes, and then another, and another, and then as if sitting directly under a waterfall, the rain is torrential.

The sandy soils of the campground are quickly eroded, forged into fast-flowing streams, one of which runs directly beneath us.

A large branch caught in the current is pinned between our front and back tires, partially blocking the flow and causing muddy waters to spray up the driver's side of the vehicle. We slide sideways down the slope several feet, and for a moment, I have thoughts of us being swept away in the flash flood.

And like that... with zero transition... it's over. The clouds pass, and the afternoon sun returns as if nothing happened but for a sparkling layer of hailstones, several inches deep, and the weakening runoff that continues to flow from higher ground. Brody and I look at each other, trying to comprehend what just happened. I speak first. "That was interesting."

"Interesting?" Whether it's a release of nervous energy or residual excitement from experiencing something new, Brody's adrenaline is pumping. "That was insane!" He laughs and hits me on the arm. "Dude, we barely made it back before the big shit hit! Would've killed us... and you see my arm?... that lighting hit the truck... had to. Thunder Beings are pissed!"

"Thunder Beings?"

"They live on Black Elk Peak. Come back every spring."

"Glad we were here for that."

"Need to learn your Sioux culture, Dad."

I start the SUV and run the wipers. The hood is dimpled like a giant golf ball. I question whether my insurance covers rental vehicles, and thinking it does, I assess the campground. It's a muddy mess. "Let's head out. Maybe we stop at Fort Robinson. Two hours straight south. We'll take I-80 back."

The General Store took a beating, and the owner is already on the roof inspecting the damage, which is significant. At the same time, his wife graciously handles the purchase of our fuel and road food needs. We take a last look at Sylvan Lake before our departure, it again in its full glory—its waters returning to a glassy surface that reflects the clouds above and its granite outcroppings.

Brody wraps up our stay with three simple words, "Love this place."

A half-hour into the drive, I ask Brody to read from the journal, and he does.

With Crazy Horse's death seemingly near, my immediate concern was how the hostile northern Indians would respond to the news. Matters indeed looked quite dubious in the aftermath of the failed arrest, both sides heavily armed, weapons drawn and pointed at the other; but fortunately, few Sioux had witnessed the stabbing, as Crazy Horse had been surrounded by the soldiers of the guard. The stories among the Indians ran the gamut from Crazy Horse being stabbed by a guard to being stabbed by Little Big Man, to he had fallen on his own knife trying to fight, to he was only "possuming" and playing a trick on the white man, to he had been ill and died of natural causes.

Of these possibilities, the first and actual cause, that a soldier's bayonet was the source of the injury, was the most dangerous if learned by the Indians to be true, for it would surely spark an uprising and result in many unnecessary deaths. To thwart any kind of retaliatory attack, I devised a simple disinformation campaign starting first with Touches the Clouds and Crazy Horse's father. I showed them, using my fingers, the size of the entry wound. Now stitched closed, it appeared much smaller than when first incised. I then took one of Crazy Horse's knives that had been recovered by Touches the Clouds, it originally being a butcher's knife that had been ground to a very slender and pointed blade like a stiletto, the blade six inches long. For demonstrative purposes, I stabbed the knife through a sheet of paper. I did the same with a bayonet and compared the size of the incisions to that of the entry wound, going to great pains to convince the Indians that Crazy Horse must have either accidentally stabbed himself or fallen on his knife. Had the wound been created by a bayonet, the puncture wound would be much larger. Neither seemed entirely convinced, but I gave the sheet of paper and Crazy Horse's knife to Touches the Clouds and encouraged him to inform the other Indian leaders what he had learned from Little Beard and to do so quickly—before Crazy Horse died, as to avoid any further bloodshed.

I continued to monitor Crazy Horse's vital signs that changed little over the next hour. Then to my surprise, slightly after nine o'clock, his heartbeat and breathing started to normalize. Medically I have no explanation for his improved condition. From all experience, a piercing of the bowels, while a slow process, always resulted in death. I attributed his turn for the better to a momentary surge of energy, a final triumphant stand before the inevitable fall. But a fall there was none, and Crazy Horse remained stable, forcing me to consider the possibility, though slight, that he may survive. This created a new dilemma. If he were to live, unfair as it was, a prison in the Dry Tortugas awaited him, the order already having been issued. This assumed that he would live long enough to complete the journey; it was more likely that he would die en route enchained within a locked boxcar.

As I carefully considered all possible options, Touches the Clouds returned to report he had conveyed my message, but there was still no consensus among the Indians with some believing what he had shown them, some choosing to believe what they think they saw, some believing what they heard from others. At a minimum, I had further laid the seeds of doubt, and that doubt was ultimately proven enough to ward off a fight. Then to my further amazement, the color returned to Crazy Horse's face, and he opened his eyes. Seeing me, he spoke, "Hau kola." He raised his hand to his head and confirming the presence of the white stone there found behind his ear; his hand dropped, and he fell back into sleep. I felt for a pulse. The old man, now believing his son had finally passed to the spirit world, took my hand, and with tears streaming down his weathered cheeks, looked me squarely in the eyes. He spoke between mournful gasps.

> *We were not Agency Indians, we preferred the buffalo to the white man's beef, but the Gray Fox kept sending his messengers up north saying, "Come in, come in." We came in, and now they have killed my boy. Hard times had come upon us, but we were tired of fighting. Red Cloud was jealous of my boy. He was afraid the Gray Fox would make him head chief. Our enemies here at the Agency were trying to force us away. We only wanted to go back to our hunting grounds in the North.*

Feeling the father's pain, I prayed for Divine guidance, but I already knew what I had to do. I motioned for Provost and Touches the Clouds to come closer and then rested my hand on the old man's shoulder, and the other hand remained in his grasp. I told him, "Your son is not dead. He may live. He may die. I do not know." Hearing my words through Provost, the old man's expression changed to excitement and then joy. "Pilamaya, Pilamaya. Wasicu Wakan." Having heard this Lakota phrasing after saving the Indian girl's life during childbirth, I needed no interpretation. I removed my hand from his shoulder and held it up to stop him.

"No Wasicu Wakan. I am not a miracle medicine man. I am Crazy Horse's friend, and I agree with all you have said. If Crazy Horse lives, the soldiers will take him to a prison far away. I do not want that. Listen now to all I say." I looked at Touches the Cloud to reinforce the need for strict attention. I paused before continuing because what I was about to suggest amounted to treason. If exposed, I would be the one imprisoned, but death by noose or firing squad was more likely. "I want to help my friend. I want to help you. I will tell the soldiers that he is dead, but he is not. You will tell all the Indians he is dead, but he is not. You will act as if he died, but he did not. Cover him and take him away and care for him in secret. He may die soon. I do not know, but if he dies, he dies with you, and it is better. If he lives, I will be happy, but nobody other than you, you, you and I can ever know he lives." I pointed at each man and then myself as Provost translated.

"If Crazy Horse lives, he can never show himself again to his people. He must go away. If the soldiers learn he is alive, they will kill him and many Indians. They will kill me too. If we had a pipe, we would smoke on these things, but we do not. You must promise me you will not tell anybody." I put my fist onto my heart and waited for them to do the same as the Lakota sign for a promise that can never be broken. "I trust you all. If Crazy Horse lives, you will tell him the same."

Receiving "haus" from all, I gave Crazy Horse another small dose of morphine to ensure his continued sleep and comfort during the move and called for additional blankets to cover the body. At about 11:30 p.m. I pronounced Crazy Horse dead and drew a blanket over his face. But for the prominent scar creating his ever-present grimace, his face was at rest, his eyes peaceful. Touches the Clouds removed himself to make the announcement to the people. Arms raised to the starlit heavens above, looking ever-taller than his full height of seven feet, he exclaimed, "The Chief has gone above!"

Word of Crazy Horse's death spread quickly through the Indian camps, and the situation remained tenuous. I appreciated and readily accepted Touches the Clouds's offer to sleep on the porch outside my quarters to ensure no harm would befall us. While some of the younger hostiles took to their horses and charged and yelped around and through the Camp, in the end, as hoped, there was no violent response. Several days later, I spoke with Touches the Clouds. He informed me that the body wrapped in blankets and resting in a coffin on the embalming scaffold at the Spotted Tail Agency was actually a deer carcass. I expressed my concern that Lieutenant Lee had conveyed his bewilderment that Crazy Horse had not been laid to rest in traditional Sioux fashion. The embalming platform was unusually low, it elevating the body only three feet off the ground. Traditionally, most Sioux sleep their last sleep in the tops of trees or upon upright pine stations fifteen feet or more above the ground. (See Photograph #19 of a traditional Sioux burial scaffold and compare with Photograph #12.)

Touches the Clouds assured me that my secret was safe. After that conversation with Touches the Clouds, the last I would ever have with him, I did not ask about Crazy Horse, nor was I ever informed as to his status. It was always my hidden hope that he had survived, disappeared and flourished, but until my investigation of the Ghost Dance thirteen years later, I had no idea whether that be the case or whether he perished the next day or sometime later. To the best of my knowledge, all of the men in the Adjutant's Office that night stayed true to their oath to never again speak of the matter, except one.

It's been a pleasant drive, the first half through the southern portion of the Black Hills and the second half largely through the Oglala National Grassland in northern Nebraska. The conversation has been sparse, but I don't think either of us has felt uncomfortable with that. I certainly haven't. Rather, listening to Brody read has been soothing, the story thought-provoking, our snacks tasty, and the scenery stunning, making further conversation seeming unnecessary. Driving across the rolling hills of the grasslands, green with spring grasses and speckled with yellow prairie flowers, we saw a small herd of buffalo in the distance. Brody commented on imagining what it was like when millions of them were out there, and we did. We also made a slight detour to look at a reconstructed sod house to note that its grass and cactus-covered turf roof, two feet thick, could probably much better handle a hailstorm like we just experienced than modern construction.

It's early evening when we enter Fort Robinson State Park. I follow the signs to "1874 Adjutant's Office" and "1874 Guard House," our intended destination. Having just read about the events occurring in and around these buildings, we're eager to see them up-close and firsthand. A thought runs through my head that McGillycuddy would be proud. I too hope he now has a sense of what we're doing.

Brody sets up our arrival with a special lyric, "Walkin' again where Crazy Horse tread. Valentine saved him, he not dead."

It's a short walk from the small roadside parking lot, across a portion of the old parade grounds, and to the reconstructed log cabins replicating the original guardhouse and Adjutant's Office.

A stone monument with a plaque commemorating this location's unique history stands in front of the guardhouse. The plaque reads,

ON THIS SITE

CRAZY HORSE OGALLALA CHIEF

WAS KILLED SEPT. 5, 1877

I point out the inscription is not entirely accurate, at least according to McGillycuddy's historical account, in that Crazy Horse was stabbed at the guardhouse, but he "died" in the Adjutant's Office about forty yards to our left.

Brody elaborates further, "Shouldn't even be here. He didn't die... how many people you think know that?"

It's a question the answer to which I'd yet to ponder. "I don't know. Not many... I don't think McGillycuddy told anybody else. He said everybody kept the promise not to tell except one guy... and that was over 100 years ago... we might be the only ones." We walk to the guardhouse to learn the reconstructed cabin sits on the original foundation. The structure and its interior are historically accurate. I stand near the entrance and imagine the moment when Crazy Horse, realizing he was being arrested, drew knives, attempted escape, and had a bayonet thrust through his gut. He fell right here. I imagine McGillycuddy kneeling over him and Frank Grourard ducking behind the commissary that once stood to my right.

We continue our walking tour visiting the Adjutant's Office. I see four men inside lit by a kerosene lamp. One a giant. All kneel over a motionless Crazy Horse on the floor. The old man grieves. We proceed across the parade grounds, a surprisingly large area, with a white-painted pine pole standing erect at its center. One thousand whooping Sioux on horseback, armed and prepared to go to war race about.

Reaching the far side, we retrace the steps of husband and wife, arm in arm, walking down officer's row on a moonlit night and hear Fanny's pleas to accompany her husband to Crazy Horse's camp. *"Oh, Valentine. So dreary and lonesome is camp life. It is no wonder men do go so mad."* I stop in front of their former quarters and imagine Crazy Horse riding between houses to enter the stirring parade ground before him. McGillycuddy's writings and photographs have allowed me to create mental pictures of his story—like individual frames in a comic book, but now, having stood on the actual grounds he described, the still frames have transcended into vivid, colorful moving scenes. *"No doubt much has changed since my days as topographer, contract surgeon, and Indian Agent, but any sights, sounds, and smells of Dakota Country still present will only embellish the experience."* So true, McGillycuddy. So true.

———

At first, I worried, sometimes to the point of paranoia, that my act of insubordination would be discovered, but as days turned into weeks and weeks into months without incident, my concerns lessened until they were no more.

A coyote yelps just outside the campground, getting my attention. I throw another chunk of wood into the dying flames and stoke the coals. The log ignites to increase my reading light, and I return to the journal.

From my experience, it is at those times when we let down our guard, as I had, that our good fortunes change. Such it was that day in June 1897, when, as the newly appointed Indian Agent at Pine Ridge, I had to deal with the horse thievery of Charlie Provost, brother of my interpreter, John Provost. Much of what I previously disclosed about that encounter is true. Indeed, it corresponds precisely with the official reporting of events, but a lie of omission therein I committed that I will now amend.

As noted, Charlie was a bad seed and prone to doing no good. Tired of Charlie's trouble-making, I reprimanded him harshly, telling him to mend his ways or the next time he would be punished severely. Clearly upset that I should scold him, Charlie wrapped himself in his blanket and left my office without speaking. His temper was boiling. Knowing his dubious reputation, which included never backing down from a fight, I anticipated his return. I did not anticipate what would happen when he did.

Having dispatched John to attend to other matters, I looked out the window, waiting for Charlie. Seeing his approach, I exited to meet him outside. His face red, stopping but inches from mine, the veins in his forehead bulging, he spoke, "Thasunke Witko. Wiconi." I was not yet fluid in Lakota, but I certainly understood the name of Crazy Horse, the first words. I had also heard the last word, although it took a moment to recall its meaning. I then remembered Crazy Horse using the word when he gave his pot of stew to the old hungry squaws outside his tipi and Provost telling me on the ride back it meant "life."

Charlie's true intentions at that moment I did not know, but I did know, to my core, that Charlie knew my secret and that his brother, my trusted interpreter, John was the source of betrayal. As Indian Agent responsible for over eight thousand Indians, many of whom still considered the white man their enemy, I was never without a concealed sidearm, a trusty .45 caliber Colt pistol, and I was not afraid to use it. I did that day putting a bullet through Charlie's head. John, with his best friend as his side, Clementi Bernard, soon came running. John, seeing the lifeless body of his brother on the ground, was visibly upset. I told him, "He threatened me, John. It was self-defense." I then asked, "Who else did you tell?"

John feigned ignorance at first, but true to his betraying nature now revealed, looked at Clementi, who facing the end of my barrel, quickly divulged what he knew, and he too received the same fate.

Seeing a number of men approaching in the distance, one of whom was the blacksmith, William Allman, I dropped the pistol and wrestled John to the ground. The men separated us upon arrival, and I told them what had happened. Charlie had killed himself. Seeing his dead brother, John's "brain whirled" and, using Charlie's pistol, shot his best friend to accompany Charlie on the journey to the spirit world. Fanny corroborated my version of events to say that from the backyard, she saw Charlie put the pistol to his own head and fall. In hindsight, the story that William Allman gave Charlie a gun so he could shoot a rabbit was ludicrous, for no white man would ever have given Charlie Provost a gun, but such were those days on the plains where investigations were modest, and justice was swift. John made no attempt to save himself, as first, he knew his disloyalty was responsible for all that had happened, and secondly, his word bore no weight to that of me, Fanny, and William Allman, who was my dear friend, and as Agent my second official appointment to the Agency, after only my brother. John Provost was my third appointment.

Taken aback, I close the journal for the night. Brody asks, "We goin' back tomorrow?"

"You want to?"

"I'm in no rush."

The coyote lets his presence be known again. "Let's check out Pine Ridge first. You can read on the way... McGillycuddy will surprise you." Brody looking into the dark for the coyote nearby, tosses his cigarette butt into the fire. "Sounds good to me."

═══

It's a misty morning, and with visibility low, there isn't much to look at on this portion of the drive. Brody breaks the silence. "Damn! McGillycuddy's not playin'!" He continues reading aloud, and I slip back to imagining life on these plains over a century before.

After John's arrest and his subsequent passing in prison, I was confident my secret was once again safe. Weeks again turned into months and months into years, this time ten, without any further mention of Crazy Horse. Enjoying my life of affluence and prosperity in Rapid City, I again let my guard down, and once again, the trickster spirit from Sioux folklore, Iktomi, played his malicious trick, this time through the words of Porcupine just days before. My initial reaction to the new Ghost Dance religion was that it was but a passing Indian craze that would falter as soon as the messiah did not appear in the spring. Now I knew that not to be correct. Absent divine intervention, the messiah would indeed appear, and the potential ramifications were dire.

I contemplated how best to proceed. From all accounts, Sitting Bull was sponsoring the Ghost Dances at the Standing Rock Agency, and many believed he was responsible for fueling the enthusiasm for the new religion in the region. *This seemed entirely plausible based on my previous conversations with Crazy Horse discussing the Sioux holy man, a traditionalist, who had always garnered the admiration of the younger hostiles still attracted to a life of warriorhood. I returned to Rapid City that day, arriving late in the evening to inform Fanny, to her dismay, of my intended travel plans and to secure supplies for the upcoming three-day ride to Standing Rock on the northern border of South Dakota.*

I arrived at the lodge of Sitting Bull at night. Alone again on the opens of the plains and riding under the starlit skies, I was at times able to shed my troubles. Riding up the last hill to the sounds of Indian song and glow from a smoky, hidden fire, those troubles returned. Cresting the hilltop, from my vantage, I saw approximately one hundred Indians, men and women, all dressed in white shirts, standing in a circle and pointing their arms to the west. Another one hundred, sitting, surrounded them. A massive bonfire lit the area casting shadows of the Indians and the sacred tree in the center. Unlike the Sun Dance, there was no drumming to accompany the singing. A woman stood next to the sacred tree, pointing a pipe to the west.

The song soon ended, and all the Indians cried together, joined hands and sang a new song. They moved slowly in a circle-dance from left to right. All of the dancers wore one feather, either of eagle or crow, including the women, which is something I had never witnessed before. Gradually one of the song leaders quickened the pace, ultimately leading to a great crescendo. The dancers shared the leader's excitement, and the dance grew ever intense. They cried sounds of grief into the night and threw dirt over themselves. *Increasingly more and more leaped away from the circle and fell to the ground with trembling limbs, but otherwise laying motionless, seemingly dead. When most of the dancers had fallen, an old Indian, I assumed to be Sitting Bull, emerged from a tipi located on the east end of the dance circle and proceeded to kneel next to each dancer, putting his ear to their mouth. I waited until Sitting Bull tended to all the fallen dancers and then rode slowly down the hill, consumed with feelings of anxiety not felt since that first time I rode into Crazy Horse's camp.*

Entering the light at the base of the hill, I raised my hand in salutation to indicate that I came in peace. This action was not enough to avert two breech-loaders pointed and aimed in my direction. I informed the two young men forming my greeting party, best I could, that I was Little Beard who had been the white father of the Oglala at Pine Ridge, that I was a friend of the Sioux, and that I wanted to speak to Sitting Bull. Still at gunpoint, one of the men departed to relay my message.

As I waited, I observed the woman who had been holding the pipe to the west throughout the dance. Now, as the fallen started to recover, she walked slowly in my direction to exit the circle. The fire lit her face to reveal Black Shawl Woman, Crazy Horse's wife. She did not look at me. When first told of her death but a few days after that of her husband, it seemed odd to me, for although still quite ill, she did not appear when last seen to be at death's door. Still, her passing was not out of the question. Sorrow could have quickly worsened her condition. My feelings were mixed seeing her. I was glad she was alive. I was at the same time disappointed. Her manufactured "death" proved that either Touches the Clouds or Crazy Horse's father, or both, had also forsaken their oaths.

I waited for nearly a half-hour until the messenger returned indicating that I was to follow him, which I did to a cabin of large hand-hewn logs with but one window on its end and a door centered in its front. Several Indian women of differing ages, in long skirts and wrapped in blankets, stood outside lit by a fire from a makeshift stone pit about fifteen feet from the door's center.

My guide motioned for me to dismount, and the women furthered their distance as I approached. He opened the door to reveal a single room dimly lit by kerosene lamps to which I entered. There before me, sitting next to a pot-belly stove, was Sitting Bull with legs crossed. His braided hair, parted down the center, framed his wide, leathery face. The thinning braids laid over his also-wide shoulders and rested on his chest. A medallion received from the President during his visit to Washington and a crucifix hung by chains from his neck. A single eagle feather standing upright from the rear of his head was his only other adornment.

Frowning and with eyes glaring, he motioned for the young man to leave and for me to sit on the blanket before him, saying, "I have been waiting, Little Beard, and now we meet." Sitting Bull spoke surprisingly good English, which I suspect largely developed during his time traveling and performing with Buffalo Bill Cody's Wild West Show. The conversation that followed was spoken in both English and Lakota, but being one of the most intense of my life, I remember it word for word and therefore find it best to convey it in dialogue fashion with interjections of thought throughout.

"I am here at the request of the Governor of South Dakota to investigate this new religion and determine whether or not it poses a threat... is danger... to the people of the State."

Sitting Bull nodded. "The whites call it the Ghost Dance Religion, no?"

"They do."

"Little Beard, you have lived among us and know our ways more than other white men. You have lived in two worlds, as have I. I have tried to know the white man's world and their ways, but I... spin." Sitting Bull put his hands to both sides of his head and moved them in a circular motion as his lips turned upward in a faint smile, his head shaking in frustration. "That is not the word." He continued. "Ghosts scare white people. There is nothing to fear. We pray to the spirits. Our mothers and fathers, and elders passed. There is nothing to fear. There is no danger. Tell the Governor so."

"Do you believe a messiah, the new Christ, will return if the Sioux do this dance?"

"My people hope it is true. They did not hope before."

"Sitting Bull, I sat with Crazy Horse many times. He was my friend. He spoke of you often. He said you had a 'big brain,' but you are not sharing it with me. You know more than you say."

"As do you, Little Beard. Tell me what you know, and I may tell you too."

A game of cat and mouse ensued, both suspecting the other of knowing more than willing to divulge. I suspected Sitting Bull was the founder and sponsor of the new religion that had excited tens of thousands of Indians across the West. He suspected I was aware it was so, along with Crazy Horse's important messianic role therein. I sat in contemplation when Sitting Bull broke the silence.

"Little Beard, it is late, and you have come many miles to get here. We will speak the truth in the open; then, we can eat and sleep. I am not afraid to tell you. I know you are trapped and can tell no other man. If the white man learns what you have done, you too are the enemy. We are the same." He laughed and then called loudly, to which one of the women from outside soon responded. He spoke to her in Lakota. We sat in silence, looking into the fire of the open pot-belly stove. The squaw returned with a plate of steaming venison. It placed before us, Sitting Bull encouraged me to partake, which I hungrily accepted.

Then he continued speaking, "Crazy Horse came to me. I thought he was dead. But there he was." Sitting Bull pointed to the center of the room. "He told me all that happened. He stayed in my camp for many days, and we talked. I prayed for a vision, and on the bank of a river, it came to me. It was the strongest vision I ever had, stronger than before the Greasy Grass. The winds blew the grass a different way. It pushed a warrior to the West until he landed between two lakes under the mountains. At that place, the warrior became powerful. A man and spirit one." Sitting Bull interlaced his fingers in demonstration. "Then the winds blew the warrior spirit back here. He had holes in his body. He shined like the sun. He raised his arms to the sky, and the winds blew in every direction. All the white men were pushed into the oceans or carried away by a whirlwind, but the Indians remained. The winds stopped, and the buffalo and our ancestors came out of a hole in the earth."

Sitting Bull took a piece of meat and ate. After swallowing, he asked, "What do you want to know, Little Beard?"

I pointed at the crucifix hanging from his neck and asked, "Are you a Christian?" Lifting the crucifix from his chest, he said, "This was *a gift from Father DeSmet. He was a good man. He taught me his religion, and it is good, but it is not good that the whites do not obey the Christ's teachings. If they did, they would not treat the Indians bad. If they do not do what the white Christ tells them, it must not be true, so I do not believe."*

"So you are familiar with the resurrection. After Christ died on the cross, he came back to life."

Sitting Bull glared at me intently but then smiled. "I am. On Easter Sunday. It is a strong story."

"And you think the Indians will believe that Crazy Horse is the new Christ coming back from the dead?"

"Ahhh. I do not think. I know this. Many Indians from many tribes already believe the messiah is coming. They will dance, and when Crazy Horse appears in the spring, all Indians will believe and follow him as one powerful tribe. He will teach them to return to the old ways, and they will follow. The words that Crazy Horse is the messiah and that he has come back from the dead will spread in every direction faster than the winds... and when the white men read it in their newspapers, many whites will believe too."

"How will the whites read of the second coming if they all suddenly die?"

"I did not say this. That was not my vision."

"You said they will be pushed into the oceans or swallowed by a tornado."

"They may die, I do not know. I only know the white man will no more live on our lands. After they are gone and the Indians return

to the old ways, they will see and hear the spirits again." Sitting Bull shook his head again and chuckled to himself. "This is why the whites call it the Ghost Dance, but like you, they do not understand. The spirits will not return like ghosts. They never left. They have always been here, but the Indians' eyes have been closed and their ears covered until now. There are no Indians left. But when the white man is gone and the Indians no longer want the white man's things, their eyes and ears will open to the spirits, and the Indians will again live a good life."

I looked at the pot-belly stove, and kerosene lamps warming and lighting the room but let the hypocrisy of Sitting Bull's last statement pass without comment. Sitting Bull pointed at the plate of venison, now half full. "Eat. I have a lodge for you to sleep." Sitting Bull paused. "Little Beard, you have done some good things and some bad things. We did not ask you white men to come here. The Great Spirit gave us this country as a home. You had yours. We did not interfere with you. The Great Spirit gave us plenty of land to live on and buffalo, deer, antelope and other animals. But you came here and took our land and killed our game. It was hard for us to live, so we tried living as you wanted. We stopped fighting. We stopped hunting. We farmed. We went to your churches. Our children went to schools. You wanted the Indians to do these things, and now we are hungry and poor. Still, you say, why do the Indians not become civilized? We do not want your civilization! We want to live as our fathers did, and their fathers before them!"

Sitting Bull lowered his arms he had raised to emphasize his final point. He continued speaking more softly, "But you did a good thing for Crazy Horse, and now good things happen for the Indians. They dance and pray and are returning to the old ways. They hope. It is good. You should not want to change this, so do not try."

I considered expressing my opinion on the matter, but Sitting Bull saw that I was attempting to speak, and raised his hand and continued without providing any opportunity for response. The conversation was no longer an open dialogue. "Little Beard, Crazy Horse will appear in the spring, and all will believe he is the new Christ, risen from the dead. This is good, but the Great Father and his soldiers will then know your lie, and they will do bad things to you. You know this. You are not a bad man. I do not want bad things to happen to you. Tell the Governor there is no danger. Then you must go far away and never speak of these things. This is all you can do if you want to live. This is all you can do if you want good things for the Indians."

—————

Whiteclay, Nebraska, population 12, famous for selling more cans of beer to the Oglala than McDonald's has sold hamburgers to the entire country. The demarcation zone separating two very different worlds. The streets are littered and pocked with potholes, and most of the buildings have been vandalized with graffiti, much of which is militant propaganda. The black image of the grim reaper with scythe is painted onto the side of an old house, standing alone, on the far side of town. The heading "Lakota Death" warns us as to which side we are about to enter. We drive onto the Pine Ridge Reservation, greeted by a wooden sign reading:

The hillsides on the short drive to the town of Pine Ridge are dotted with old, run-down mobile homes and the remnants of past government housing projects. Many windows are boarded shut, blue tarps wave from the roofs, and each commune seems to have two or three junked vehicles. We enter the town of Pine Ridge and pass a Pizza Hut. So much for not wanting the white man's things.

Coming off our visit to Fort Robinson, where many of the buildings from McGillycuddy's time had been renovated or reconstructed, I expected a similar experience at Pine Ridge. Far from it. We drive first down the main strip looking for signs indicating places and events of historical significance. There are none. At the edge of town, I turn onto Sitting Bull Road, go around the block to return to the main drive. I see a white bell tower peeking over the top of an abandoned building advertising "Chinese, Fried Rice, Pepper Steak" on a spray-painted wall. Nearing the church, I can see that it's old, and while the front doors have recently received a coat of red paint, the church appears no longer in use. A tall chain-linked fence topped with barbed wire surrounds the severely overgrown, weed-infested grounds. The brass bell that once called the faithful to worship still hangs in the deteriorating tower. The stucco at its top fell away some time ago, exposing the mud-brick beneath.

The sign out front reads, "Holy Cross Episcopal Church." A quick search discloses that it was built in 1880, the first church established on the Pine Ridge Agency. The historical summary makes no mention of Valentine McGillycuddy, but no doubt it was constructed during his tenure as Indian Agent and where he and Fanny attended Sunday services. I suspect there may have been a few uncomfortable moments of soul-searching in the pews after the Provost affair. I feel modest satisfaction in finding at least one relic of the Agency's past, but thinking there has to be more, I ask Brody, "Where is everything? Was hoping we could see his house at least. From there, we'd have an idea of where his office was, the corral where they kept the buffalo calves, the blacksmith shop. Had to have been close to the church." I look at the vacant two-acre lot to our right, wondering if it once housed the now missing buildings.

"None of that's gonna be here anymore."

"Why not?"

"Why would the Indians keep it? Bet they tore that shit down first chance they got."

Brody's made a valid point. I remember McGillycuddy's frustration with Red Cloud, he challenging the Agent tooth and nail every step of the way as McGillycuddy tried to implement his plan to civilize the Sioux. *"This is my Agency! This is my land! I am Chief, and I keep the peace!"*

"I saw a Chamber of Commerce office back there. I'll ask."

Brody stays outside to smoke. My business inside done, and now with several pamphlets promoting the Reservation's tourist attractions in hand, I exit the Chamber to find that within five minutes, Brody has found his own attractions. Surrounded by three girls, he's in his element.

He smiles and laughs, and seeing my approach stubs his cigarette and ends the conversation with, "Right on." The girls walk away before I reach the sidewalk, their long, straight, jet-black hair swaying behind them. The faintest scent of perfume mixed with cigarette smoke lingers. Brody asks, "What'ya find out?"

"He thought I was nuts. Said they tore that shit down 100 years ago."

Brody laughs. "Could go to a party on the rez tonight."

"I'll pass. How about Pizza Hut?"

"Bet."

The Pizza Hut is unremarkable and, like any other, to include other white patrons. Our waitress, a Lakota girl about seventeen years old, is lovely. She wears the expected uniform, but a delicate red, white, and black beaded necklace adds flavor to her look. Her hair is parted down the center and hangs in a long ponytail down her back. I observe that her thick eyebrows are perfectly shaped. She flashes us… flashes Brody really… a friendly smile, her white teeth standing out against her tanned skin. She pours our water and tells us she'll be right back to take our order. Brody subtly monitors her departure. "These girls cute as hell." We haven't been around many people the past several days, certainly not any attractive girls, and Brody is enjoying the improved scenery. We decide on a medium regular crust three-meat pizza, an order of cheese bread, and salad bars, the last selection at my suggestion that we need to get "some ruffage."

Eating my salad, I start shuffling through the pamphlets. "Not much here to see." Brody probably disagrees. He glances every now and then to inspect the wait staff. I half expect him to suggest the "party on the rez again" as an option. He doesn't. I open a pamphlet celebrating the wonders of the Badlands National Park and toss the remainder of tri-folds his way for perusal. Our pretty waitress soon returns to serve our pizza and bread, and we dive in hungrily. In between bites, I read the pamphlet. Interesting geological formations, buffalo, bighorn sheep, and several campgrounds to choose from. Fossilized remains of ancient rhinos, horses, and saber-toothed tigers. They don't permit open fires, but each site has a charcoal grill. One hour away. Sounds good to me. I make a mental note to buy charcoal, tin foil, and a bit more food and ice before we leave town.

"How about the Badlands?" Brody, holding a slice of pizza in one hand and a pamphlet in the other, reads intently and doesn't respond.

I knew I shouldn't have had that last slice, but I couldn't resist. I'm now uncomfortably full and feeling the onset of heartburn. Brody's eaten heartily as well. He's been quiet, but unusually so. He eventually confirms his agreement that the Badlands should be our next stop, but that's it. We receive the bill on which our waitress has written, "Thank you!" and drawn a smiley face. She flashes Brody another smile. I calculate 20% and leave a cash tip on the table. Brody looks, pulls his wallet from his back pocket, and sweetens the pot by another $5.

"Trying to impress?" I ask.

"Na. Not that... just... she could probably use it."

We're restocked and back on the road. "You've been quiet. What you thinking about?"

"Nothin'… these people got it rough."

"Why's that?"

Brody removes the folded pamphlet he'd read in the restaurant from his pocket. He scans it, looking for the desired content. He then reads: "The Pine Ridge Reservation is home to the lowest life expectancy in the United States. Life expectancy for men is forty-seven years. Women fare slightly better, with an average life expectancy of fifty-five years. The Reservation has the lowest per capita income in the United States. American Indians living on Pine Ridge average an annual income of $7,773. The Reservation ranks as the "poorest" county in the nation. It ranks last in the nation for quality of life. Alcohol and drug addiction. There is an 89% unemployment rate. The school dropout rate is over 70%. One in four children born on Pine Ridge is diagnosed with Fetal Alcohol Syndrome. Tuberculosis is 800% higher than America as a whole. Infant mortality is 300% higher than America as a whole. Teen suicide is 150% higher than America as a whole. Approximately 58% of children are being raised by their grandparents.'

"It keeps goin… you get the idea."

We drive in silence and with a new understanding. Within the old, run-down mobile homes and remnants of government housing projects dotting the hillsides around us, many with windows boarded shut and blue tarps waving from the roofs, are people suffering.

It's been a somber drive, and I'm glad we're stopping to find a campground for the night so I can walk off some of the pizza. I pull into the White River Visitor Center on the southernmost part of the Badlands. The pamphlet made promises of bighorn sheep and we aren't disappointed. Five sheep are at the edge of the parking lot, all with full rounded horns, to greet our arrival and improve our moods. They seem so tame moving towards us that I consider getting some bread from the cooler to feed them, but being unsure of the rules on "feeding the animals," along with our last experience with a Park Ranger still fresh in my mind, I quash the idea.

I enter the Visitor Center to ask about the nearby campgrounds and soon learn several are just up the road. I exit the metal-sided building and look to where I left Brody. A bighorn sheep, a ram, is within inches of his outstretched hand. It turns its head sideways with open mouth to accept his gift and then bolts backward to separate himself. Brody wipes his hand on his jeans and looks to see if I saw what just happened. Seeing me, he gives a thumbs-up signal. I scan the parking lot for witnesses. There are none, and then a feeling of pride comes over me. He just hand-fed that thing. Had it been left to me, acting out of concern of disobeying rules that may or may not exist, he wouldn't have had that experience. Brody seized the moment and acted out of a sense of adventure. Thumbs up, My Boy.

We've selected our camping spot for the night and walked about a half-mile up one of the trailheads to rest on a plateau overlooking the Badlands stretching into the distance. It's an interesting landscape like nothing we've seen before. There are thousands of dulled peaks as far as the eye can see. All are similarly shaped like gigantic chocolate drops, each between 200 and 300 feet high. Their bases melt into a common layer of harder earth below. A labyrinth of green valley floor twists and turns throughout to create a natural maze. Horizontal striations of red, white and tan earth exposed by thousands of years of erosion tie each peak to the next. Only the highest points are lit in the fading sun, leaving the mazelike valleys below in the shadows. A strip of lavender on the horizon with pinkish hues above creates a colorful backdrop.

Brody points to a small herd of Bighorns in the valley below. "That was cool feeding that sheep today."

"That was cool."

"He was lookin' right at me… big brown eyes. Reminded me of giving Jake a treat. I miss that dog."

"I miss him too." I haven't thought about Jake in a long time, by intention. "Were you there when he was put to sleep?"

Brody waits before answering; I think questioning if he wants to open the doors of discussion to a painful topic. I'm also now wondering why I asked the question and whether I should have. Brody responds before I can change the subject. "No. Mom called and told me it was time, but I didn't go… I couldn't… I was fucked up."

"I should've been there. I feel guilty about it."

"Shit. Nothin' you could have done."

I know that I couldn't have changed the outcome, but I still harbor feelings of guilt that I wasn't there at the end. He was my dog. He hated going to the vet. It pains me to think he was probably shaking, looking for me, wanting me to hold him, and after 17 years of loyal, unconditional love, I wasn't there. Tears well up in my eyes, and though I'm trying to hide my emotion, it's noticeable. I let it go.

"I'm sorry for a lot of things, Brody. I'm sorry I left you when I did… things were… it was… I'm sorry." I tell myself to hold it together to no avail. I'm tired. For reasons I can't explain, I've opened the emotional floodgates. Perhaps subconsciously, I wanted this to happen… or needed it to happen. We sit side by side, both feeling the discomfort of emotion. We look at our phones out of habit. No service.

Brody speaks. "I didn't help. I'm sorry too, Dad. I fucked my brain up."

"What?" I wipe my tears and look at him.

"I have. I was smart… I took so many drugs, man." I see that now the tears are welling in my son's eyes. He, too, succumbs to the weight of bad memories rising from a past hell and breaks down, dropping his head between his knees, his back heaving in sobs.

I slide closer and put my arm around him. "You're fine, Brody."

"I'm not. I can tell I'm messed up. Can't even get a full sentence out anymore."

He weeps. He weeps hard. I want all his pain to leave him. I want to take it from him. Please, God, give it to me. I want it to end. I pull his head onto my chest and hold him tightly with both arms. I rock him gently. Please give it to me. All of it. Please. We weep together. My tears fall into his curls, wetting the back of his head; his soak into my flannel. Embraced, we let the wounds reopen. We feel and regret, both sorry for ourselves, our mistakes, and the pain we caused the other and those we love and who love us. Slowly it subsides. Deep breath. Slowly it subsides. Our breathing normalizes.

Be a "fuckin' dad," I tell myself. I speak, "You're fine, Brody. It's coming back. I see it all the time. You can still play the guitar... I heard you... you played that song perfect. It'll all come back. Just takes time."

Brody releases his hold, sits up and wipes his face with his sleeve. I do the same. "Shit. Sorry 'bout that. Stupid."

"Nothing to apologize about. I mean it... it hasn't been that long... even on this trip... you just read all of that journal. You found where Crazy Horse had his vision quest and took us there. C'mon. Nothing's wrong with your brain. You may not see it or feel it yet, but it's all coming back."

"Just mad at myself. I always liked being smarter than everybody else."

"Like when we were in Canada... you were three... and you told the kid in the playground, 'I'm more 'telligent than you.'" Brody's heard the story many times. I immediately question my attempt to add some levity, but he chuckles and wipes his face again.

"Yeah. But I became a clown. Always showin' I could drink more, do more drugs, act crazier. I don't wanna be stupid anymore."

"You aren't. That's over. Hey." I wait for him to look at me. "I'm so proud of you. You impress me. There are great things in your future. I know it. Not many people could turn things around like you have. Took a lot of willpower... a lot of... gumption."

Brody sniffles, then smiles. "Gumption?"

"Gumption… and now you're going to school. It's all good. You'll see." I put my arm around him, and we look over the Badlands, now turned fully pink in the fading light. We sit for several minutes in silence. I search for what I want to say next. "It's OK to think about our mistakes sometimes, so we don't make 'em again… but we shouldn't dwell on 'em. You're doing great. We need to stop beating ourselves up so much… both of us… should treat ourselves… how about a motel and shower?"

"Hell yeah. You gettin' ripe."

======

It's been an emotional day. After several days of hiking and sleeping in the back of the SUV, the hot shower rejuvenates our spirits, and we're grateful to lay in the beds of a three-star motel room in Rapid City. Brody rummages through our bags looking for a snack, and removes the journal, "Want this?"

"Yeah." I pat my chest looking for my reading glasses. I normally slide one of the temples under my collar. Not feeling them, I scan the nightstand. I think I must have left them in the SUV, but then remember using them to sign the paperwork at the front desk. "I lost my glasses."

"They're on your head."

I shake my head and smile in appreciation that the search for my reading paraphernalia is ended. I settle under the blankets with pillows propped against the headrest and open the journal. Brody finds a bag of jerky that he rips open with his teeth. He speaks, "Bein' on the rez we kinda know it doesn't end well, but I'm still rooting for the Indians."

I reread the last paragraph describing McGillycuddy's encounter with Sitting Bull. I turn the page to see the heading, "The Badlands of South Dakota." "Brody, you won't believe it. McGillycuddy goes to the Badlands next."

"Bet he don't feed a bighorn."

———

The Badlands of South Dakota

Sitting Bull had confirmed my suspicions that Crazy Horse was indeed the messiah of the Ghost Dance Craze. I did not minimize Sitting Bull's prophesy nor his plan of implementation. Although misplaced, it was ingenious. As War Chief during the Indian Wars, he consolidated all the Sioux tribes into a unified fighting force for the first time, that for a brief period, outnumbered the army and allowed them to defeat Custer and the Seventh Cavalry at the Little Big Horn. Sitting Bull now sought to implement a similar unification strategy on a grander scale by means of a simple dance. It was working.

Tens of thousands of Indians across the West, without common language, now shared an ever-growing belief that a new messiah would soon resurrect. Upon his return, the days of Indian prosperity would return. The potential for a second Indian War, one that would dwarf the first in lives, years, and expense, was well within the realm of possibility. For left to its own devices, when the messiah appeared, the already smoldering flames of tens of thousands of radicalized Indians would ignite into a roaring blaze of tens of thousands more. And while the tenets of the new religion were framed in terms of peace, the founders were warriors at heart. The new Christ would not hesitate to incite the masses to war if believed necessary for the Indians' ultimate success.

A telegram from the Governor awaited my return to Rapid City, dashing any hope of enjoying an evening meal with Fanny. The Governor was concerned that a number of Sioux leaders, primary among them Short Bull and Kicking Bear, had removed their three hundred lodges from their Agencies and into the unforgiving vastness of the Badlands. Two weeks earlier, General Miles visited the White House to confer with President Harrison over the Indian crisis.

The President looked to Miles to take every possible precaution to prevent an Indian outbreak and to suppress it promptly should one come. General Miles had been tasked to organize the army's preparations "to anticipate the movements of the hostile Indians and arrest and overpower them in detail before they had time to concentrate in one large body," but as was often the case, the arrival of necessary troops, ammunition, food and supplies took longer than desired and a significant number of Indians, approximately two thousand in number had escaped and were now congregated in the Badlands.

The settlers were already frightened. They were more so now. En route to the Badlands, Short Bull's nephew, Circle Elk, a graduate of the Carlisle School in Pennsylvania, was shot and killed by white ranchers while seeking sugar and other items from a nearby settlement. The homesteaders surrounding the Badlands feared Indian retribution. Based on these events, the Governor approved distributing guns to a home guard unit in Rapid City, and he requested my assistance to ease tensions with the hostiles if possible. I knew the Indian leaders well, but I suspected that finding them in the Badlands would not be an easy task. To Fanny's dismay, I informed her I was leaving the next morning. I provided no details other than stating I would likely be away for several weeks as my investigatory duties for the Governor were proving more consuming than expected.

Rest assured, given my predicament, I fully considered Sitting Bull's advice to simply "go away and speak of the matter no more." I foolishly harbored a sliver of belief that I may be able to dissuade Crazy Horse if presented the opportunity. Rationally, I knew that was not possible. Despite saving him from a life of imprisonment, he would show me no loyalty, grateful only that he had been given another opportunity to help his people. He was like my eagle. Easter but four months away, and me without any semblance of a plan to thwart the messiah's return, I prepared to move us to Bolivia when the time came. In the meantime, the Governor requested that I attempt to ease tensions with the Ghost Dancers in the Badlands, and so I did.

The next day, I entered the Badlands from the north. The Badlands extend over a broad area covering roughly three thousand square miles in southwestern South Dakota, a dreaded yet majestically eroded and scarred terrain. Isolated and remote, it promised the Sioux a measure of security from the soldiers. I crossed the Cheyenne River, and it grew dark and began to snow, forcing me to make camp. It was an unpleasant night on the periphery of the Badlands with little food and no fire. Early the next morning, Sioux warriors armed with Winchesters found me and, in due course, ushered me to the Ghost Dancers' camp. We weaved through the valley bottoms for several hours before reaching a broad, flat-topped escarpment rising three hundred feet from the surrounding floor. The women had set up camp on this plateau with tipis facing east in the traditional circular arrangement. Sentries watched in all directions from points on the southern perimeter. Cedar and juniper groves dotting the fringes of the grounds provided firewood. My escorts led me through the camp and over a narrow land bridge leading to another, but smaller, elevated plain the Sioux called Maka Nawchizin, meaning "Ground that Defends Us." It became known to the army as the "Stronghold." The height and precipitous slopes on all sides made the Stronghold formidable to army incursion. A military assault would prove costly.

In all, I estimated approximately three thousand Indians had taken to the Badlands to partake in the dancing. Of the total, one thousand were young warriors manning the Stronghold and all appearing well-armed. It was not lost on me that this was the largest gathering of Sioux since the Little Big Horn fourteen years earlier. Foraging parties had for some time augmented food supplies by killing cattle and capturing horses pastured by the government and local ranchers. Significant quantities of dried beef were on hand. At my request, a council was formed attended by Short Bull and Kicking Bear as leaders with approximately fifty followers of lower standing. The Indians reiterated their grievances of short rations and concern over punishment of their recent pillaging. I countered that I had come to rescue them from their sorry plight, for even if the army did not attack, they were waiting on the periphery and no longer would they be able to steal cattle. Eventually, their food supply would run out, likely before the messiah's return in the spring.

I provided assurance that the soldiers did not want war, and if they would simply return with me to Pine Ridge, General Miles would treat them kindly and allow them to return to their respective Agencies *without retribution. I would then personally do what I could to convince the Great Father to increase the beef rations to previous levels if the Indians promised to give up the Ghost Dance. Some level of discussion ensued, and it was apparent that, to some extent, a fissure had formed between the more progressive, mostly older, and the younger radicals. I fully intended to exploit this apparent rift if possible.*

Short Bull rejoined by stating, "It is better to die here as brave men than to live like cowards at the Agency on scanty rations, disarmed, without horses or guns. It is better to dance here. If we do not, the messiah will not come. We will not return."

Short Bull's call for bravery struck me. Taking a different tack, I inquired into some of the specifics of the new religion, namely the purpose of the shirts the men wore and that the whites were calling the Ghost Shirts. Kicking Bear elaborated, stating the Lakota referred to the shirts as the Sacred Shirts, and that the messiah had told him that the shirts should be made of cloth and decorated with symbols of the sun, moon, stars, eagles, crows, and buffalo. No metal objects were to be used as these things came from the whites. The messiah had told him that the bullets would not harm them if they wore the sacred shirts. The shirts were so powerful the whites could now be destroyed altogether. This, of course, all made perfect sense to me. Crazy Horse believed he was bulletproof due to his rituals and the sacred symbols he wore, i.e., his lightning and hail face paint, one eagle feather worn upside down, and the white stone he wore behind his left ear. The materials were not important. The inherent power in the sacred symbols was.

Understanding the shirt's protective nature made it easier for the Indians to maintain their belief in the Ghost Dance and ultimately defy even the U.S. Army; I elected to test the Indians' strength of conviction in their newly acquired power. I recalled my electric machine at Camp Robinson and how I never witnessed a warrior, they then fresh off the warpath, shy from the challenge of trying to grab the coins through the electrified water. Although the stakes I would propose would be more severe than an electric shock, I suspected this new herd of young bucks would respond in similar fashion if challenged to prove their courage.

I spoke to the council, "This is a strong power. Crazy Horse was my friend, and he was the only Indian who had this power. Now you all have it. He was the bravest of all the Lakota." I then related my first-hand account of his bravery at the Battle of the Rosebud when Crazy Horse rode up and down our pickets. Bullets filled the air, but he was never hit. Some of the older Indians grunted as confirmation of the truth of my story. "Now you have this power," I pointed at the group of instigating young men, "but I do not know if you are brave like Crazy Horse. When the soldiers come, you may run away, making the power useless. If you are brave, you should show me this power, and I will go back to the soldiers and tell them to go away, for their bullets will only fall to the ground when they touch the sacred shirts."

As expected, eventually there was one courageous sacrificial buck willing to prove his mettle. Finding a willing shooter was harder. After several minutes of discussion with no takers, a nervous Kicking Bear countered my challenge with a cunning move of his own, announcing that his vision told him that the sacred shirts' powers were limited to the white man's bullets. If there were to be any such test, the bullet would have to come from my gun.

The tables had turned, and it was now my mettle being called into question. I pondered how best to proceed. If I refused Kicking Bear's challenge, it would only bolster the Indian's belief in the Ghost Shirts and likely ensure the majority would hold out until the messiah's return. If I accepted, I would surely end the young man's life, but the Indians would see the folly of their ways and that they had been misled. Many would secede.

The council had formed around a large fire surrounded by a wall of cypress boughs set up in lean-to fashion as a wind block on the west and northern sides. I motioned for the warrior to move to the open area to the south. He walked confidently to where instructed, his unbraided black hair wrapping around his head as he exited the confines of the wind shelter. He turned to face me, pressed his chest forward and extended his arms shoulder height and parallel to the ground. I stood and withdrew my trusty Colt, it retrieved after and not fired since the Charlie Provost incident. His eyes glared. His composure did not waver. Sitting Bull would have been proud, for there was at least one Indian left.

Reaching acceptable firing range, I turned to address the council. "This man has proven his bravery and should be respected by all. If the sacred shirt has the powers you say, it will protect him, and I will tell the soldiers to go away." All were silent in anticipation. The end, while honorable, would not justify the means, certainly not for this brave warrior. I found an acceptable middle ground. I had him remove his Ghost Shirt, wrap it around his left hand and raise his arm to its previous position. Ensuring his fingers were fully extended, I aimed and fired a slug through the center of his palm. The force threw his arm back, but there was no other immediate reaction.

In a state of wonderment, the warrior calmly brought his hand forward, rolling its backside upward for viewing. There were no signs of blood, but the bullet had clearly ripped through the bundle of white cloth in dramatic fashion. Then a drip, slow at first, became progressively faster, turning into a steady trickle. A puddle of blood soon formed on the snow-dusted soil below.

The council erupted into a fractious dispute. Two Strike and Crow Dog immediately declared their resolve to return with their one hundred and forty-five lodges, whereupon Short Bull's impassioned followers leveled their guns at the dissenters, now believing based on their leader's own words that the sacred shirts would only stop white man's bullets.

Short Bull, feeling the immediate threat of losing control of his congregation raised his arms and shouted dramatically, "Listen, my friends! Listen! I have words from the messiah! I was to wait, but now is the time. The messiah is with us. He said the white man is interfering too much. He will come after one more moon instead of the spring. We must dance!"

━━━━

I slept in. Brody's sleep continues. The modest motel on the outskirts of Rapid City has a surprisingly good breakfast bar, serving fresh fruits and juices, a choice of cereals, oatmeal, eggs (hard-boiled and scrambled), bacon, bread for toast, bagels and muffins, and a waffle machine using packaged batter. The selection is plentiful, the food is hot, the bacon is crisp, and the counters and tables are clean. The price is certainly right.

I contemplate making Brody waffles but elect not to, knowing he prefers morning sleep over morning food. I share the dining room with a handful of older couples. The kids still in school, the retirees are on the front end of the hordes of tourists that will soon swarm the Black Hills. I suspect many of them were already aware of the "good breakfast" here. The barkeeper exits the kitchen pushing a cart through swinging doors. She's Lakota, about forty years old, short and portly. Her black hair is tightly bunned and pulled away from her face making its round shape appear even rounder. She wears the company uniform of black pants and a tan shirt, both one size too small. A black apron covers her front. Using my plastic cutlery, I cut a piece of bacon against the styrofoam plate and put it on top of the scrambled eggs already on the end of a piece of toast. I take a bite and observe. She resupplies the warming trays and examines her work domain. She replaces an empty pot of coffee with another that's full. Satisfied, she starts to wipe down the far end of the counter, and not in a cursory fashion.

I prepare another bite when from my periphery, I see the arrival of new patrons. A family of three. The mother, in her early thirties, holding a baby, leads the way examining the buffet. The father of about the same age follows. Mom wears a sundress and flip-flops. Dad is in T-shirt and shorts with the same footwear. Both wear expensive-looking sunglasses hooked around their ears but resting on top of their heads. I do a quick pat for my reading glasses and feel them on my chest. I think their dress is odd given the current temperature is about fifty degrees, and today's high will be sixty-five. I take another bite.

"This is disgusting." I look up. Mom paces the counter. Lakota woman continues wiping. Dad stands back indifferently. "I'm not eating here." Dad moves forward to inspect, and a quiet discussion ensues. Lakota woman steps back, looking at Mom and then her buffet. I stand with a coffee cup in hand and approach.

Speaking loud enough for Mom and Dad to hear, I address Lakota woman, "Thank you for breakfast." I glance at her name tag, "Grace. Everything is great." I glare at Mom as I walk past to refill my cup, but she isn't finished.

She questions Grace, "How long has this been sitting out?"

It may not have been my place, but I chime in. "She just put a new batch in. It's good." I proceed to my table, walking past Mom.

She mumbles, "I didn't ask you."

I stop and turn to address her. "No, you didn't, but if this isn't good enough for you, stay in the fuckin' Ritz next time." Grace goes back to wiping the counter, and Mom marches out of the dining room. Dad turns and follows, void of any emotion. I finish the remainder of my breakfast in peace, wave at Grace, and receive a subtle smile in return.

Brody is still sleeping soundly. I set a warm go-cup of coffee on the nightstand and contemplate whether we should head home. We've been on the road for just under a week, and there's no immediate need to get back, other than Brody's employer would probably like him back soon. His classes don't start for another three weeks. We've visited all the locations McGillycuddy's identified in his journal except for the Rosebud Battlefield in Montana. I'd considered making the trip, but as it would lengthen our return by another four to six hours, I elected not to.

I look through the old photographs looking for anything else we should see before leaving the Black Hills. Photograph #16—the McGillycuddy mansion in Rapid City. Brody can sleep for another hour, I'll read, and then we'll see if the mansion is still standing.

━━━━

Short Bull's revelation that the messiah had amended the timeline for his return, such that now it was but one month away instead of the spring, was offsetting. Time was now truly of the essence. My demonstration proving the Ghost Shirts were not impervious to bullets did convince Two Strike and Crow Dog to return their lodges to Pine Ridge. The next morning I served as escort to ensure their safe passage, and, as promised, as envoy to request an increase in beef rations. Soon after exiting the Badlands we were met by a group of scouts no doubt dispatched to patrol Indian movements beyond the Agency. I rode forward and waved as the men approached. The head scout waved back. It was none other than the weasel, Frank Grourard. I last saw him at Camp Robinson peaking around a nearby building as Crazy Horse lay wounded on the ground. A wave of anger came over me. But for this coward and his lies, none of the tragedies of the past fourteen years would have been. The order to arrest Crazy Horse would not have been issued, and he would not have been stabbed, I would not have been forced into committing treason, Charlie Provost and Clementi Bernard would live, John would not have died in a prison cell, and a young warrior would still have his hand. The ramifications of the evils of Frank Grourard, the cur, continued.

Seeing it was me, he halted his horse at a safe distance. No pleasantries were exchanged. I stared him down, he knowing that if we had met alone on those frozen plains, things would now be much different. I said only this, "Go back and tell the General to have rations ready."

General Brooke received the arriving Indian bands warmly and told them they had nothing to fear and that they should return to their camps, where he would furnish them with supplies and give them everything they needed. The Indians were pleased. After the meeting was dissolved, I met with the General.

He brimmed with optimism stating, "I will furnish them food and give as many employment and rations as I can. There is little to do now but to wait and see how this Sioux cat is going to jump."

I informed the General that indeed Sitting Bull had inaugurated the messiah craze and that the Indians remaining in the Stronghold, true believers, were better equipped for war than ever, having ample food, weapons and ammunition. I also relayed that the hostiles now believed the messiah would return in the next thirty days. The General responded, "Sitting Bull requested permission to take his people, and several other bands, to join the others in the Badlands. Of course, McGlaughlin (the Agent at Standing Rock) denied it, but he believes Sitting Bull will try to slip out in the night at some point. The Indian Police are watching him." The General paused. I contemplated my response. He continued, "Why so morose, McGillycuddy? When nothing happens, the cold will cool the ardor of the young bucks, and this will soon be over. You said so yourself. Perhaps by the new year if we get a good blizzard."

Indeed, such had been my initial advice to handle the messianic craze, but now for obvious reasons, a policy of simply "wait and see" was no longer acceptable. I contemplated leaving right then and starting my life of exile. I spoke. "I fear the army waits to its detriment, General. An outbreak is at hand, and immediate action is necessary to suppress it. There is only one prudent course of action, and frankly, I am shocked at the army's acquiescence. No messiah is necessary. Only the prophet. Sitting Bull plans to distribute fifteen hundred stands of concealed weapons to the Lakota, and then he can spark the next Indian War with but one word. You must cut the head off this snake. Take him entirely out of the reach of his followers. Arrest him now. Use the Indian Police. They will have a more salutary effect on the Indians there. Surround the Badlands. Let nobody in nor out. A direct attack would prove too costly but tighten the cordon every day, and there is a chance this can be resolved peacefully. I am sending the Governor a wire now that I met with Sitting Bull and the Ghost Dancers remaining in the Stronghold, that you have been advised on the proper course of action, and that any further delay should be viewed as incompetence. I suggest you make haste to inform General Miles."

I had no information to suggest that Sitting Bull planned to distribute fifteen hundred stands of concealed weapons. It was a necessary fabrication.

The next morning, December 14, 1890, the arrest order for Sitting Bull was issued to the Lieutenant of the Indian Police at Standing Rock. General Miles' military response was swift, first to prevent an outbreak and second to bring to bear upon the disaffected Indians such military force as would compel prompt submission to the authority of the government. He dispatched twelve troops of the Seventh and Ninth Cavalry, altogether eight hundred men, with three Hotchkiss cannons and a 3.2-inch gun of Battery E, First Artillery to surround the Badlands on three sides and eliminate any Indian threat attempting to enter or leave the area.

He told the press, "Sitting Bull is high priest and leading apostle of this latest Indian absurdity. No Indian has the power of drawing to him so large a following of his race and molding and wielding it against the United States or of inspiring it with greater animosity against the white race and civilization. It is a more comprehensive plot than anything ever inspired by the prophet Tecumseh or even Pontiac. I hope the problem may be solved without bloodshed, but such a happy ending to the trouble seems improbable."

Miles did not understand how truly correct he was in his words. This was already the largest military operation in the United States since the Civil War but had Miles known the full extent of Sitting Bull's plot, the response would have been ten times greater and its restraint against the Sioux, nil.

Wounded Knee, South Dakota

It's time to wake Brody so we can make checkout. I put my hand on his shoulder coax him back into consciousness. One eye opens. "Mornin'. Sleep well?"

"Hell yeah."

"Brought you some apple juice."

"Right on."

"Get up. It's 10:30… checkout's at 11." Brody sits up and twists his torso from side to side, cracking what sounds like every vertebra in his back. I wish I could still do that. I think that mine have all fused together. I attempt to find out if that's the case planting my elbow into the mattress and twisting especially hard to produce one dull "pop" from my lower back.

Brody nods disingenuously. "There you go." He throws his head from shoulder to shoulder to complete his self-realignment.

"I thought we'd check out McGillycuddy's house. It's downtown." I show Brody the photograph. "Then we should probably head back."

"Right on."

I stand with Brody while he smokes a cigarette in the parking lot. The family from breakfast exits the motel with Mom and baby leading the way to the family vehicle. She drops her sunglasses onto her face, and Dad, two steps behind, does the same. I subtlely point them out and tell Brody about that morning's encounter.

"You really say that?"

"I did."

"No way."

"I did." I slap Brody on the back. "A wise man told me sometimes you have to swear to make a point."

"It's true."

We're pleased to find the McGillycuddy mansion still standing at 727 South Street, on the corner of Mount Rushmore Road. It appears surprisingly well-maintained, and it's just as McGillycuddy described in his journal. I have to agree with his color choices, considered unusual by the local residents at the time—the upper olive green exterior contrasts nicely with the lower sandstone walls of scarlet and cream. A sign near the front porch informs us the mansion is the completion of a restoration project started in 2011. A historical society in Rapid City purchased the landmark with the intent to return it to its original design and into a museum and research center. We enter the ornate doors and stand on the original wood floors. The wall inside the entry displays a photograph of the mansion dated 1888. It's almost identical to what we received from McGillycuddy, except our photograph shows the owner and his dog pictured on the walk leading to the porch. A second photograph, this one in color, shows people posing on the porch. A sign underneath states, "Descendants of Valentine McGillycuddy visit and celebrate the completion of the historic home." Descendants? I read the smaller print to learn they are three of Valentine's great-great-grandchildren and three of his great-great-great-grandchildren. Last name: Gorenflo.

I show Brody, and he verbalizes what I'm wondering, "We related to them?"

"Not that I'm aware of." I hadn't considered the possibility of other heirs. It seems odd that I, rather than one of them, would inherit access to his personal tomb.

A friendly old gentleman appears from one of the back rooms and shuffles towards us with the assistance of a cane. He's bald but for a strip of white hair that encircles his shiny pink dome above. He wears khaki jean-styled pants of a heavy polyester blend, a plaid brown long-sleeved dress shirt, buttoned to the top with turquoise bolo tie, and cowboy boots. He talks like a cowboy. "Hello, Gentlemen. Welcome. I'm Denny. I'm the curator." He cleans his thin-wired round spectacles. "Did you sign our guest book?" I make our introduction and sign for both of us. He asks, "Have any questions for me?"

Brody takes advantage of Denny's offer. "What's the coolest thing you have of his?"

"Well, we have a lot of Dr. McGillycuddy's things. Much of his correspondence. How much do you know about Valentine McGillycuddy?"

"Quite a bit."

"Do you know he was friends with Crazy Horse?"

"Yes."

"You might find this interesting."

We follow the curator to a row of showcases located along the study's inside wall. Denny leads us to the second case and directs our attention to a photograph of an Indian.

Denny speaks, "A lot of people think this is a picture of Crazy Horse."

Brody is ready to respond and show his knowledge of the subject, "But it's not. McGillycuddy didn't think he ever had his picture taken."

"That's right. That's what he says in those letters with William Garnett… you know your stuff, young man."

I look at the letter to William Garnett, dated October 25, 1927. I note it is on the same letterhead as the last letter McGillycuddy gifted me—Hotel Claremont, Berkeley, California. Garnett's response, dated December 14, 1927, is also encased, and it confirms the tintype photograph is not of Crazy Horse, but a Rosebud Indian named Goes to War. I comment to Denny, "That's great you have these. Interesting."

Brody moves forward, scanning the other items. "No way. Is this his gun?"

Denny responds, "It is. He had that most of his life, from when he was a doctor with Crook during the Indian Wars, and when he was an Agent at Pine Ridge."

Brody and I lean over the glass case staring at the ivory-gripped Colt .45. The ivory has darkened, and the barrel once silver is now gray with the patina of age. Brody asks, "Did he ever use it?" I snap my head to look at Brody, whose head is already turned in my direction, revealing a devilish grin.

"Oh. I don't know. I suspect he had the need to use it from time to time."

Brody stands upright. "Bet he did."

Denny, perhaps somewhat motivated by our knowledge and interest, leads us around the exhibit with gusto, conveying McGillycuddy's history and pointing out other items of interest, including Fanny's fox-furred pillbox hat that I was thrilled to see. Brody and I listen intently, and both of us are tempted at times to correct him or elaborate on his presentation based on our special knowledge, but we don't. I stop to look at a framed photograph on the wall of a beautiful woman wearing a long, silken, Victorian dress. Exposed shoulders reveal her youthful skin. A swatch of fine white lace covers her bosom. An ostrich feather adorns her elegant hat. She holds hands with, and gazes fondly at a little girl standing on a chair of exquisite design. The eyes of woman and child are locked on the other. A placard below reads, "Julia McGillycuddy and daughter, Valentine McGillycuddy, in San Francisco, California, 1909."

I find it interesting, but not surprising that he named his daughter after himself. Intrigued by the subject matter, I call for Denny's assistance, and he shuffles forward to oblige me. "Did he have any other children?"

"No. One daughter from his second marriage. His first wife, Fanny, couldn't have kids."

"I saw the picture of his grandchildren up front. Did you meet them?"

"I did. Nice folks. Very appreciative of what we've done here. They donated most of this."

"Are they from California?"

"No. East coast."

We thank Denny for the personal tour, and I ask where the stables would have been and if Brody and I can walk around the lot before leaving. I leave a $10 donation, and Brody and I exit onto the porch.

The front door closes, and Brody bursts out, "That was cool… but Dude… was hard not to say anything. Bitin' my tongue the whole time."

"I know. I was too. Even the small stuff…"

"Oh, shit… can you imagine showing Denny the journals… the key… and then Crazy Horse's stone! Instant coronary."

Brody and I share a good laugh, and not out of disrespect to Denny, who's been delightful all afternoon, but out of a realization that we are sharing the discovery of a hidden history that is known to no other people in the world—check that—except perhaps the grandkids that until now I didn't know existed. We meander casually around the lot of the McGillycuddy mansion. I imagine a time when this was still the frontier, and no other buildings were surrounding it. He and Fanny would have had a remarkable view of the Black Hills. It's been such an enjoyable day, I'm hesitant to do anything to change it, but I know it's time. "Hey, Bro. We need to head back."

"Yeah."

I look at the mansion, the topmost crests of the Hills peeking over, and the flowers in the beds forming buds in the warming air. Beautiful. I remember Valentine's last entry. He was at Pine Ridge stressed over what would happen next, worried that he would be forced to abandon his intended sanctuary built at the foot of the mountains. It was winter. Snow covered the ground. The vibrant colors surrounding now disappear, and the snow-covered Hills reappear unobstructed. I imagine light coming from the upper-level window of Fanny's bedroom and her sitting nervously inside. I look to where the stables would have been and imagine his horses warm and fed and ready should he and Fanny need them for a long southward journey. I remember Wounded Knee. "McGillycuddy said we should go to Wounded Knee next. Saw the sign on the way up. We'll take I-80 back."

"Hasn't let us down yet."

━━━━

We left Rapid City about thirty minutes ago, and we're once again entering the eroded landscape of the Badlands. Brody has been reading the journals since our departure, and he's caught up to where I left off. Brody summarizes McGillycuddy's predicament with, "Not looking good. Should bolt."

"Keep reading."

The date of Sitting Bull's arrest was set for December 15, 1890. Agent McLaughlin ordered Lieutenant Bull Head, the head of the Indian Police at Standing Rock, to make the arrest as follows: "The time has arrived for the arrest of Sitting Bull and that it can be made by the Indian Police without much risk. I, therefore, want you to make the arrest before daylight tomorrow morning and try to get back to the Sitting Bull road crossing of Oak Creek by daylight or as soon after as possible. The Cavalry will leave here tonight and will reach the Sitting Bull crossing on Oak Creek before daylight tomorrow, where they will remain until they hear from you. I want you to send a messenger to the Cavalry command as soon as you can after you arrest him, so they may know how to act in aiding you or preventing any attempt at his rescue. I have ordered all the Police at Oak Creek to proceed to Carrignans School to await your orders. This gives you a force of forty-two policemen for use in the arrest. P.S. You must not let him escape under any circumstances."

Through my connections within the Indian Police, the organization of my making and design, including my former trusted Lieutenant, George Sword, I was able to reconstruct with a high level of certainty the events surrounding the arrest.

At five-thirty o'clock in the morning, a mile from their objective, the policemen broke into a gallop, dismounted and surrounded Sitting Bull's cabin. The ever-present packs of dogs greeted them, and no doubt aroused and awakened the Ghost Dancers camped nearby. Eight officers banged, pushed the door open, and burst inside to find a naked Sitting Bull wrapped in his blankets, sitting upright next to a floor mattress with a wife and one of his children. Elsewhere in the room were two older men, visitors who had stayed the night after the Ghost Dance.

Sitting Bull was told he was under arrest, to which he replied, "This is a great way to do things. All right. I will go with you. I will put on my clothes." Sitting Bull requested that his preferred horse, a gray mount given to him by Buffalo Bill in St. Louis, be saddled and brought from the stable. The police obliged, and Sitting Bull dressed, pulling on his breechclout, leggings, and moccasins. Between the commotion inside, frenzied dogs, and his wailing wife, Sitting Bull's Indians now gathered, pressed closer and called out against the police. When Sitting Bull was within a matter of feet from his horse, his son appeared from the cabin. He began chiding his father for cooperating with the arrest, calling him a "fool" and "crazy."

Sitting Bull became agitated, pronouncing, "Then I will not go." Seeing his followers, he called on the assembly to attack the police and save him. He became steadily more non-compliant and thus created a commotion of women and children crying and more and more men gathering around the arresting party. Two policemen took Sitting Bull by the arms. One positioned himself to his rear, pointing his revolver at the back of Sitting Bull's head. Matters escalated quickly. One of Sitting Bull's followers pushed his way through the crowd, threw off his blanket and fired his Winchester, its bullet striking Lieutenant Bull Head in the side. The Lieutenant, still holding Sitting Bull's arm, wheeled and discharged a round into Sitting Bull's chest. From behind, Sitting Bull was shot through the head. I waited at Pine Ridge as the reports of the arrest started to trickle in. The first from Agent McLaughlin later that day was as follows:

> Indian police arrested Sitting Bull at his camp forty miles southwest of the Agency this morning at daylight. His followers attempted rescue, and fighting commenced. Four policemen killed and three wounded. Eight Indians killed, including Sitting Bull and his son, Crow Foot, and several others wounded. Police were surrounded for some time but maintained their ground until relieved by United States troops, who now have possession of Sitting Bull's camp and all women, children, and property. Sitting Bull's followers, probably one hundred men, deserted their families and fled west up the Grand River. Police behaved nobly, and great credit is due them.

Army reports from the field started arriving shortly thereafter. The cavalry had positioned themselves on the crest of the heights a few miles to the southeast during the arrest. Hearing the shooting, they responded and engaged in a two-hour firefight with Sitting Bull's warriors who had taken refuge in a thicket on the Grand River. The cavalry had dismounted and were lying on the brow of the hill firing at them with their carbines until the Gatling gun was positioned and opened on the warriors in the brush. They were then seen scurrying up the bluffs on the other side of the river. Of particular interest to me was this report:

> We heard a shout, and as we looked up, there directly in front of us, about one hundred yards away, sat a naked painted Indian on a white horse with the sun just rising, shining directly on him. He made quite a picture. We jumped for our guns. The Indian shouted, "Father, you said we were going to live!" and he turned his horse and disappeared into the thicket out of which he had appeared. We began firing into the thicket. The Indian emerged about one-quarter of a mile away. We opened fire on him. He charged into the open and ran his horse the length of the valley. Once more, he dashed into the open and once more, the bullets turned him back to the timber. A third time he dashed into the valley, this time passing between two cavalrymen sent out as pickets. Both fired at close range but missed. This time the Indian continued up the valley and out of sight. Hundreds of bullets were fired at him, but it was little short of a miracle that one of those bullets did not hit him. We made no attempt to follow him, as our horses were tired after an all-night run, and his was fresh.

═══

"Both of 'em pushin' their luck." Brody drops his bare feet from the dash, sits up and looks outside at the surrounding Badlands. He opens the glove box and removes the white leather pouch. He jostles it against his hand and peers at the white stone inside. "Think there's somethin' to this? Never gets hit."

"Don't know… maybe their guns weren't that accurate back then."

"We should get some."

"What?"

"Guns."

I ponder what Brody's just said. I don't think he's ever shot one. It's been a long time since I have—not since the Air Force. Even then, I didn't shoot once I became a JAG. Military lawyers aren't trusted with guns. Growing up, I had a .22 single-shot rifle with an octagon barrel. It was a Christmas present from my parents when I was twelve, I think. I completed a hunter's safety course and then roamed the countryside, shooting cans and rabbits. I later had a shotgun and hunting rifle. I share my reminisces with Brody.

"What happened to them?"

"I sold 'em after you were born." I realize I wish I still had the little rifle. "What do you need a gun for?"

"Shootin' cans and rabbits."

"Would you hunt?"

"Hell yeah. I think it'd be fun."

"We'll think about it." I pull into the campground where we intended to stay the night before.

Brody asks, "What we doin'?"

"I'm hungry… we need to eat those hotdogs."

"Hi, Trichinosis."

I chuckle. "You're cooking. Get 'em well done." I drive through the campground and to the secluded spot we'd selected but not stayed the night before. A raincheck of sorts, I justify. Brody prepares and lights the briquettes, and I read aloud while we wait for the coals to be ready.

━━━

The report of the miraculous lone Indian was unnerving. Crazy Horse was near, but his intended actions now that Sitting Bull was dead, I did not know. Sitting Bull's body, which had been mutilated after the shooting, was wrapped in canvas, consigned to a rough-cut pine coffin fashioned by the Agency carpenter, and transported to Fort Yates. As a pagan, Sitting Bull did not qualify for burial in the Catholic cemetery. The next day his remains were buried in a grave excavated by four prisoners located in the northwest corner of the military cemetery. News of his death spread quickly in the press, and the reactions were mixed between, "If the death of Sitting Bull should prevent an Indian war it would have a most happy effect," to more sinister reports that the government and military knew that Sitting Bull, even under arrest, would continue to be a great source of annoyance and his followers would continue to dance and threaten the neighboring white settlers. As such, "there was a complete understanding from the commanding officer and the Indian Police that the slightest attempt to rescue the old medicine man should be a signal to send Sitting Bull to the happy hunting ground." My name, thankfully, did not appear in the papers.

About one hundred of Sitting Bull's warriors remained unaccounted for. General Miles arrived in Rapid City on December 17, 1890, and established his headquarters at the Hotel Harney, from which he would oversee operations. Brooke was ordered to maintain the cordon around the Badlands, and troops from the Sixth and Eight Cavalry were redirected to "head off and capture" Sitting Bull's "fighting men" feared headed to the Badlands to seek refuge in the Stronghold with the remaining loyal Ghost Dancers. Two days later, it was reported that Sitting Bull's warriors had joined the band of Big Foot, a lesser-known Miniconjous Sioux chief, camped about one hundred miles to the South.

General Brooke fueled concern that Sitting Bull's Indians may influence Big Foot's band to seek refuge in the Stronghold. "The Indians in the Badlands now disclaim any intention to fight and are only preparing for defense. If Big Foot gets there, the hostiles' purpose may change." General Brooke's instincts were correct, although he did not know the extent of the danger. It was not Big Foot he should fear. General Miles ordered more cavalry and infantry into the area.

December 21, 1890, started in relieving fashion. First, it was reported that Big Foot had surrendered, and all of Sitting Bull's Indians had at last been captured. More favorable news followed. Sitting Bull gone, freezing temperatures compounded by several days of high-velocity winds had broken the remaining Stronghold Ghost Dancers. They had surrendered and were moving toward Pine Ridge. My worries diminished. Sitting Bull's influence was no more. His warriors were accounted for. The Indians on Pine Ridge and other Agencies remained docile. The Ghost Dancers in the Stronghold had surrendered and were returning to the Agency. I sat with George Sword, still head of the Indian Police at Pine Ridge, and our spirits were high. I let my guard down. Iktomi, the trickster spirit, again took advantage of my complacency. A policeman entered the office to report that a person dressed in a white blanket claiming to be the long-awaited messiah had arrived in Red Cloud's camp. The Police had him in custody. My heart stopped. I felt cursed.

=====

"You're done."

I stop reading and look at Brody, unsure if he's referring to McGillycuddy or the hot dog he's pushing around his tinfoil pan.

"Did you hear that?"

"What?"

"What I read?"

"Na. Sorry. Gettin' these dogs perfect. Grab a bun."

The smell and sizzle make my stomach growl. They are perfect. "Nice job, Bro." He loads the buns—two for me, three for him.

"Want this last one?"

"Maybe later. Wrap it." We sit at the picnic table and devour our food.

Brody wanting something sweet, is pleased to find a quarter-bag of Bridge Mix remaining in the cubby next to my seat. The candy, my personal selection during our road trip, has never been his favorite, but dire times call for drastic measures. He pours a generous handful and gives me the bag. We enjoy our dessert. The entire meal lasts no more than five minutes, but we're satisfied.

I reread the last paragraph from McGillycuddy's journal for Brody's benefit, to which he confirms his previous assessment in condensed version with, "Should've bolted."

I respond. "He may now. Let's walk." We hike to where we sat, talked, and cried the night before. We again see animals grazing in the valley, but this time it's not the tame Bighorn sheep, but five whitetail deer—one buck and four does. They're about a quarter-mile away. We sit watching them quietly. I break the silence with a half-whisper, "All right, hunter, let's see how close you can get for a shot. The wind's blowing toward us; that'll help."

"Bet." Brody looks at the terrain and back at the deer. "Down here." He steps off the trail to our right and sidesteps down the slope creating mini-avalanches of crumbling sedimentary rock and clay soil with each sliding step. I follow in his wake. We reach the bottom of the gully and walk westward at a normal pace. The gully slowly widens into a narrow flat absent of vegetation. Brody stops to assess his next move. There's a left bend ahead. He looks at the steep hillside above and elects to stay on lower ground. We round the bend slowly. Each step exposes a more expansive view of the green grasses shooting from the wider valley floor that holds our pretend quarry. A shadowed sandy hillside striated with horizontal bands of red, tan, and white soil creates the backdrop. The deer are not visible.

Brody slows his pace even more as he works his way to the base of the hillside to our right. I look ahead and see that a thin, steeply walled finger about thirty feet high extends into the valley floor. Brody stops, points through the sedimentary digit and whispers in my ear. "They're there." He turns quietly, and we retreat until he determines we've gone far enough. He starts up the hillside. The climb is difficult, especially difficult to do quietly, as the ground gives way beneath us with each step. About fifty feet up, the hillside steepens drastically into an almost vertical wall. Brody puts one hand on the face and follows its base back toward the valley. He approaches methodically. Each step is taken with more care, so much so that I start to wonder after each whether he will take another. Step. One… Two… Three… Four… Five. Step. Wait. Eventually, we near the top of the eroded finger that intrudes the valley.

Brody releases his hand from the vertical sandstone face that turns sharply to the right. He drops into a crouched position. His steps slow even more, and his crouch evolves into a belly-down slither for the last remaining thirty feet. I follow his lead. We slide and creep to the crest. Brody reaches first, looks intently, and then turns his head to monitor my approach. I reach his position and look down. The buck is at the base of the cliff below us, the does are on the far side of the valley. None are more than fifty yards away. Brody pretends to raise a rifle to his shoulder and then holds his aim at the buck. Mission accomplished.

We watch the deer for about a minute. Brody stands without care for silence, and still holding his imaginary rifle, yells, "BOOM!" It echoes off the surrounding sandstone walls. The deer raise their heads with wide eyes, freeze and bolt. I don't know why I do what I do next, but it feels right. I grab him around the legs and trip him to the ground. I climb on and start to tickle my twenty-year-old man-child.

"That was awesome! You don't think your brain works!" I tickle harder. "Say it. I'm the man." He's still ticklish, and I'm surprised.

"Stop!" He's laughing hard. Too hard. He coughs and gasps. "Stop!!" I don't let up. I dig my fingers in harder. "Say it. I'm the man." I dig in again.

"I'M THE MAN! I'M THE MAN!"

I give one more push into his armpit and under his ribs and then ease the pressure and roll off him. We lay on our backs, laughing and looking at the maroon sky above. Life is strange. One day we weep; the next we roar with laughter. Maybe the Badlands exaggerate the strangeness.

There hasn't been much conversation back to our camp spot, but we're both in good spirits. It's well into the evening when we get back, and not knowing if we can camp near Wounded Knee, I propose staying put. Brody agrees. We sit at the picnic table until the stars appear. My neck aches pointing out satellites that Brody can't see because he refuses to wear contacts or glasses. Another battle that can wait. We settle into our blankets in the back of the SUV. I lay back, hands crossed across my chest, and relax. Brody lies next to me with headphones on. I take a deep breath and look forward to easing into sleep. A noise. There's somebody outside. I sit up. Another sound. I push Brody. He lifts one speaker away from his ear. "What's up."

"Somebody's out there." Brody pulls the hammer from his side. We both lean toward the back window to look in the darkness. We see our intruder. A raccoon stares back with a face like a true bandit. Brody concludes a perfect day with perfect words, "We left that hot dog out. Enjoy it, Buddy."

———

Albert C. Hopkins is a name I will never forget. The forty-year-old, medium-sized, well-dressed, good-looking man from Nashua, Iowa, had asked to council with Red Cloud, claiming he was the messiah and that he had come because the Sioux had confused his message.

Red Cloud simply told him to go home, saying, "You are no son of God." One of the younger warriors suggested that Hopkins be crucified regardless. He was arrested by the Indian Police instead. The man was obviously daft. I feared I had waited too long to make my escape and had Albert Hopkins instead been Crazy Horse, I would have. I again faced the reality of my predicament. Prudence dictated I immediately gather Fanny and go on the lam. I stood alone, leaning against the paddock fence where Fanny and I had once stabled our pet buffalo calves to contemplate my options. A brisk breeze from the north cleared my head and calmed me. It was never in my nature to run and hide and so unfair it would be to ask Fanny to exchange her life of comfort for a life of seclusion in South America. Iktomi be damned. I would not run. I resigned myself to let the chips fall where they may and accept whatever fate awaited.

While I longed to return to Fanny for Christmas, urgent requests for my stay, primarily from Major Guy Henry, whom I had treated for a bullet wound passing through both cheeks at the Rosebud fourteen years before, pressured me to remain at Pine Ridge for the planned celebrations. Major Henry had become one of the premier cavalry leaders in the army despite his blinded left eye. I also wanted to see the return of the Stronghold holdouts, knowing my influences had contributed to their surrender without bloodshed, but for one warrior's left hand.

Not all of the men would be able to enjoy the Christmas Eve festivities, including Major Henry. A wire from the field reported that Big Foot's band had packed up their few belongings and slipped away in the darkness of the previous night. The army believed a white man, a trader, had entered the camp and told Chief Big Foot the army, then camped five miles away, planned to attack and kill them all. The Indians stampeded like rabbits to the South. I had my own hidden suspicions as to the culprit. General Miles was incensed with the failure, and he acted quickly. Troops were ordered to the field from every direction to capture, disarm, and arrest Big Foot's band and the last of Sitting Bull's warriors.

That evening a "saloon" of sorts was erected by combining several tents in a row, in the middle of which was a long table groaning under its substantial spread of delicious foods flanked by bottles and decanters of every caliber and color. The tents were festooned with evergreen garlands. The number of party patrons now decreased twofold; the remainder of the Seventh Cavalry ate and drank to their hearts' content. Christmas gifts were exchanged, and speeches, songs, toasts and laughter consumed the evening. As the night wore on, the mood shifted. More than once, I heard a trooper say, "Remember Custer," or "We will get our revenge." Few had served at the time of the Little Big Horn, but there was no mistaking that the men of the Seventh harbored

288

an old grudge in need of repayment. I walked to my quarters, hearing a makeshift quartet of drunken cavalrymen singing "The Girl I Left Behind Me."

After several days of severe cold and blizzard, so cold it was reported "the tobacco spit froze when it left the mouth," a battalion of the Seventh Cavalry under Major Whitside spotted Big Foot's column two miles east of an imposing pine-forested knoll called Porcupine Butte. From that summit, he wired by heliograph the following message to Brooke at Pine Ridge:

> I have just arrested Big Foot and one hundred and twenty warriors all well-armed and plenty of ammunition in their belts, and about two hundred and fifty women and children, in the party. Entire outfit is now en route to Wounded Knee Post Office, guarded by my battalion. Big Foot is sick and is riding in my ambulance. I have not disarmed the bucks and do not think it prudent to do so until after they reach camp. I respectfully request that the Second Battalion of the Seventh Cavalry be sent to report to me by daylight tomorrow morning, which will enable me to have sufficient force to disarm the Indians without incident.

The afternoon of December 28, 1890, I left Pine Ridge for the Wounded Knee camp riding with Colonel J.W. Forsythe and the remainder of the Seventh Calvary, including the remaining section of two Hotchkiss Mountain Guns.

We turn off the main highway and see a small cemetery on top of a nearby hill. The cemetery appears enclosed by a chain-link fence from which colorful strips of cloth, mostly red, have been tied and that now flutter in the gentle breeze. There is no sign to indicate that we've arrived at the Wounded Knee Memorial. I drive slowly up the steep pot-holed dirt road taking us to the top of the hill. There are no other visitors. I stop in front of the entrance—two white-painted cinderblock columns decorated by a pattern of interspersed red brick. The concrete foundations on which the columns rest have cracked and settled, causing the columns to lean inward toward the other. But for a metal arch connecting them, it appears the columns may topple.

"Bring the journal." We walk through the little cemetery, not knowing what we're looking at, and sit on the steps of an old wooden building. Brody reads.

====

We reached Wounded Knee shortly after eight-thirty o'clock that night, approaching from the rear flank of the existing troops as not to alarm the Indians in the camp below. The troops unsaddled and bivouacked without shelter. Some walked around to keep warm, others huddled around sporadic campfires, and others slept on the ground in buffalo overcoats. What was readily apparent was that whiskey, brought by barrel donated by trader Palle Lansman flowed freely among the officers as they celebrated Big Foot's capture. Colonel Forsythe assumed command and ordered that he would disarm the Indians in the morning. Whitside would then escort the Indians to Gordon, Nebraska, to board a train bound for Omaha. Forsyth would then return to Pine Ridge to help Brooke deal with the Ghost Dancers arriving from the Stronghold.

Shortly after sunrise, at approximately eight o'clock, Forsythe formed a council area and addressed the Indians. The full force of the Seventh Cavalry surrounded. The battery of four Hotchkiss Guns was on the high ground to the north. Dismounted troops secured the council area, and mounted cavalry cordoned off the Indian camp on the east and to the south. I was positioned between the Hotchkiss Gun battery and the council grounds below, standing shoulder to shoulder with a troop of dismounted troopers.

Forsythe opened with a greeting and then informed the Indians that they were prisoners, and as such, they must surrender all their weapons. He explained the Indians would not be harmed, and they would be compensated for the arms taken with rations. As was usually the case, initial efforts to disarm Indians resulted in them turning in all the antiquated pieces they could gather up but keeping or concealing the good ones. That day at Wounded Knee was no different. The warriors, one hundred and twenty in number and wrapped in blankets, simply waited quietly in a circle with heads bowed. When no weapons were forthcoming, Forsythe ordered a tent-by-tent search of the camp. The soldiers found forty-five guns, many damaged or otherwise unserviceable and some dismantled. This "museum of guns" was brought back to the council area. All attention was then focused on the warriors. Forsyth spoke calmly, telling them that each would be personally searched for concealed weapons and ammunition.

Then a sole Indian, hooded, pushed through the circle of warriors stopping between them and the dismounted troops. I knew I had waited *too long. I took a deep breath imagining the thick canvas being placed over my head. I saw stars as the noose tightened. My heart pounded, but the strangling rope prevented any flow of blood to my brain. My knees went weak, anticipating the floor dropping beneath me.*

Lightheaded, I urged myself to think. What an odd time for a "resurrection," I thought, surrounded by cannons, rifles, infantry and cavalry ten times his number. Surely, he could have separated from the band at any time prior to capture. It baffled me. Perhaps it was because Sitting Bull was dead, and the most faithful of the Stronghold dancers had surrendered, rendering the continuance of his plan futile. Perhaps he refused to again leave Black Shawl Woman. Perhaps he was simply tired and ready to give up the fight. It may have been a combination of it all. I could not explain his reasoning, but it was happening before me.

Crazy Horse turned to address the warriors, dropped the hood, and kneeled to the ground to take a handful of earth that he rubbed over his head. He took another handful, stood, and threw his arms skyward, letting the dirt fly into the air, its cloud of dust passing over them all. His arms remained heavenward as if expecting the earth to open up and swallow the troops. He spoke. I could not make out his words, but I knew what was being said. I waited for the Indians' reaction. Big Foot, who had fought with Crazy Horse at the Little Big Horn, had been laid on the ground in the council area. Despite his infirmity, whatever was being said was resonating with him. He lifted a hand and then tried to stand. The warriors started to move excitedly. Again, Crazy Horse threw dirt into the air. A commotion erupted, with many of the warriors dropping their blankets to reveal the Winchesters they had hidden. They raised their weapons over their heads to heaven as if in votive offering, then brought them down to bear on the troops but yards to their front.

A single gunshot pierced the air.

It was then a blur of confusion. But yards separating the two sides, the first volley dropped twenty-five warriors and about the same number of soldiers. After that, it was excited fire. Much of it misdirected. Hand-to-hand combat ensued. Melee warfare. The Hotchkiss Guns joined the action and quickly changed the tenor of the fight. The battery, as a unit, could fire together twenty-plus rounds per minute. They unleashed a barrage of shrieking canisters shredding tipis and extinguishing all life below. Nothing could restrain them. The only tactic was to kill any Indian seen. When all were dead, the bugle sounded to cease fire. Colonel Forsyth looked white. Heaps of humans lay below me.

In the years to follow, I was asked repeatedly who was responsible for the Wounded Knee Battle. My response to the question was always unwaveringly the same, "Whoever fired the first shot." A more elaborate response would have corrected the presumption in the question that it was a battle. It was no battle. It was a massacre that still haunts me.

Crazy Horse was the first to die in the massacre. All I had to say was, "Revenge the Seventh."

When the firing stopped, I went directly to his body, already freezing into an unnaturally grotesque position. The fingers of his left hand, stiff from rigor mortice, gripped the stone behind his ear firmly. But for the prominent scar creating his ever-present grimace, his face was at rest, his eyes peaceful. I waited near the body while a mass grave was dug for the two hundred plus bodies scattered across the plain. When completed, an army clerk recorded a roster of names as each body was dumped therein. I carried and laid Crazy Horse at the edge and then listened to the discussion that ensued between the scouts, soldiers, half-breeds, whites, and Indians as to the identity of the body. Black Fox, Black Coyote, Sits Straight, Good Thunder, Shakes Bird, Hose-Yanka, and Good For Nothing, were all names proffered. A canary then landed on the high point of a wagon's load, the back of a dead squaw.

"This is Yellow Bird," I said as I rolled Crazy Horse's corpse into the pit. The clerk noted the name accordingly.

Crazy Horse never knowingly allowed his photograph to be taken. Unknowingly, he eventually was. Only once.

The Wounded Knee massacre effectively ended the Ghost Dance craze, and with it came to an end the largest military operation in the United States since the Civil War, punctuated by a spectacular parade at Pine Ridge during a snowstorm. With its sleet, ice and snow, the cheerless, frigid atmosphere was the proper setting to bury in oblivion, decay, and death the once powerful, strong, and resolute Sioux race.

———

From the hillside on which we believe McGillycuddy stood, we imagine the horrific scenes of the massacre he described. Brody and I walk back through the small cemetery with a new understanding and melancholy appreciation of the grounds. I stop to read the engraved Indian names on the polished granite monument sitting over the mass grave below. We walk between the worn, modest headstones that surround us, pushing the weeds and sagebrush aside to inspect each name one by one. Neither the monument nor any headstone bears the name of Yellow Bird.

"Let's go home."

———

Dear Trusted Messenger,

Difficult topics of which I now write, this is my fifteenth draft of this final letter. Forthright, thus, I have been in disclosing the deepest of secrets buried within me for so long. I, like all men, have regrets, but given the chance, there are few things I would change. I was young and full of courage. I was a clear thinker. I made decisions quickly, and I was always unswerving in my purpose. Let history judge me accordingly.

It is my hope that my sins, if sins they are so deemed, will remain in this world upon my passing and my soul, then cleansed, will fly over the divide and through the heavens to be with Fanny and my Creator in pure and holy state. One sin I certainly did commit, that of adultery, only once in a moment of weakness. A child was conceived, and when his Sioux mother, from the Swift Bear clan, died when the child was six years old, his grandmother brought him to my office at Pine Ridge. I reluctantly agreed to take him in. Fanny unaware of the child's history, accepted her new helper graciously. She named him Tommy.

Now at the end of my life, one regret I certainly do have. I was never a father to Tommy. I sent him to the Carlisle Indian School in Pennsylvania when he was seven years old. As previously written, Fanny and I visited him once at the school en route to Washington D.C.. Without a given surname, I learned that he had, of his own accord, taken the name McGillycuddy. He wanted to return to Pine Ridge and live with Fanny and me so badly, but I shrugged his requests. At Carlisle, he would stay for another six years. Only in later years did I learn of the atrocities that Tommy and the other Indian children endured there. Exactly when I do not know, but he later took the surname Lee, undoubtedly in homage to our dear friend Jesse M. Lee at Camp Sheridan, whom Tommy knew well as a child. I inquired once later about Tommy to learn he was no longer at the school.

Years after Fanny's death, I went back to Dakota for Julia, who as a child asked Fanny if she thought I would marry her when Fanny died. No more prophetic words from a child have ever been spoken. It was on this visit, my first return in over twenty years, that I would see Tommy for the last time. I learned that after Carlisle, as a young man of thirteen, he wandered the country for several years before ultimately returning to Pine Ridge to marry a Lakota woman. He had a son named George, whom he did not know well. You are of this lineage.

Julia and I returned to San Francisco and married. I hoped she would bear a son with whom I could share my knowledge, experiences, and love of the outdoors, but it was not to be. I was blessed to have a daughter whom I named Valentine. Throughout her sheltered youth, I harbored hopes that my daughter would meet a decent man of means and give me a grandson. Again, it was not to be. She is now forty years old. I love her dearly, but we grew apart over her desire to marry an Italian man. He was straight off the boat when they met at the age of twenty-six. A Catholic. She has told me she will marry him, against my wishes, immediately upon my death.

So, given that Valentine has shunned me and is now beyond her child-bearing years, this is yours. Do with it as you please.

With contrite heart,

V.T. M'Gillycuddy

═══

Brody's leaving. Content to spin for a few months, Ally never let go of her revolving door. Brody called her on our return from McGillycuddy's adventure, and she swung back into the apartment the day after our return. She said goodbye last night. I'm saying it today before he boards a bus to join a two-month band tour through the South and up the East Coast. A roadie, he said. He'll push equipment, set up and tear down the stage, connect cords and hopefully be able to apply some of the audio engineering knowledge he learned in school. This will be a test. I worry, of course, but he's earned my trust, and I'm optimistic about his future. He returns two days before Christmas. I drive past a lot to our right, seeing two busses and several people milling about.

"You missed the turn, Dad."

"I know." I continue up the block and pull to the curb. "Get out so I can say goodbye." I meet him on the sidewalk. I've had plenty of time to devise the perfect pep talk. There have been many mental drafts and many different arrangements of key bullet points. It was eloquent last night in my mind. Now I know it won't be. Useless preparation. No matter what I tell myself, look him in the eyes. I do. I stand in front of him and put my hands on his shoulders. He towers over me. Still black-dyed, no longer sunken-eyed. He's a healthy beast.

"I'm so proud of you. Have fun… be safe… make good decisions."

"I will, Dad."

I pull him in for a hug. "I love you so much, Brody."

"I love you too. Thank you for everything, Dad." He squeezes and I squeeze back. I feel myself regaining composure and start to pull away. He doesn't let go. Ten more seconds.

"I have something for you." I wipe my eyes, and he does the same. I take the little white leather pouch from my pocket and reach inside to remove a white stone.

"Hell, no."

"Bend down." I wrap the sinewed string around his left ear, letting the white stone dangle behind. "You're bullet-proof, Son. Guard this with your life. Go get it."

He wore the stone when I dropped him off. From inside the Kiva I watched him laughing and shaking hands. He turned away from the crowd to look at me with a smile of nervous excitement. I returned his wave, gave a thumbs-up, and pulled away. I couldn't stay to watch him get on the bus.

EPILOGUE

TWO YEARS DIGGING A HOLE. TWO YEARS CLIMBING OUT. The white stone and many prayers protected him, but it was Brody's willpower and determination to succeed that returned a man for Christmas, stronger and healthier than when he left. He found an octagon barrel, single-shot .22 caliber rifle waiting under the little, now strangely decorated, tree that still adorns our living area. He'll never use it to take the life of an animal. I couldn't be prouder of him.

We're feeling the warm fingerholds of topsoil. Brody's head has cleared the surface, and upon it, the sun shines brightly. He's twenty-one, engaged to Ally, working hard and happy. I'm right behind him. I know it won't happen, but should things give way, I'm ready to catch him and willing to take the full impact should we tumble again to the bottom. If it does, we'll start climbing again. I'm no longer tired.

Valentine. Tommy. George. Kenneth. Lance. Five generations of fathers abandoning their sons. I broke the cycle. I'm a fucking dad.

The bulk of my "inheritance," (the white stone and journals) was given to the Oglala Lakota people, of whom Brody and I are now tribal members. We kept the key.

Of final note, it is my hope that I've fulfilled the unwanted duty of "Trusted Messenger" given me by my great-great-great-grandfather, Valentine. If the revelation of his secrets does "cause much consternation and debate between white and red men alike," and my character is called into question as a result, as Valentine predicted, please remember his words, *"If anyone expresses resentment in my actions or inactions to you, assure him that I was sincere in my judgments and that the responsibility rests solely with me and not with you, my Trusted Messenger."*

Dear Reader,

Thank you for reading my book. I hope you enjoyed it. Writing this note, I sit in the same chair, at the same table, as when I started writing the book. For reasons I can't explain, around 3:00 a.m. on Christmas Eve, 2019, in a moment of self-reflection, I wrote the first five pages. As you now know, those pages contain a running list of painful events. I was emotionally drained. Tears welled as I typed, but I also felt an overwhelming sense of comfort. We were safely in an apartment in a new city. The lights of our little Christmas tree were on. Brody slept soundly on the couch.

There was something about putting those initial words to page that encouraged me to keep writing—to write a story that had bubbled in my mind for seventeen years.

Most of what is written about me and Brody—the childhood stories, our conversations, and our experiences, is true. The rest, at least that pertaining to Crazy Horse and Valentine McGillycuddy post September 5, 1877, and leading to the Wounded Knee massacre, is historical fiction.

I now share with you how I concocted the story. Estranged from my father at an early age, it was not until I was thirty-four years old that I learned of my Lakota ties. Like most finding an interest in the "Sioux", I started reading all I could about Crazy Horse. Perhaps I naturally have a conspiratorial mind, but through the course of my readings I uncovered certain facts that made me ask, simply stated, "what if"?

As a military lawyer, the Chief of Military Justice for the largest training command in the Air Force when starting my research, I was acute to identifying inconsistencies in military reports and witness testimony. The stories surrounding the death of Crazy Horse were rife with such. In the aftermath of the killing, accounts from both the soldiers and the Indians ran the gamut from Crazy Horse being stabbed by a guard, to being stabbed by a fellow Indian, to he had fallen on his own knife trying to fight, to he was only "possuming" and playing a trick on the white man, to he had been ill and died of natural causes.

Searching for the truth, a footnote in *The Death of Crazy Horse: A Tragic Episode in Lakota History,* by Richard G. Handoff, page 147, struck me. He writes, "On September 5, 1877, the guard at Camp Robinson was commanded by James Kennington, Officer-of-the-Day. Also reporting to him was Lt. Henry L. Lemley, Officer of the Guard, who, with E Company, Third Cavalry, was to escort Crazy Horse to Fort Laramie for imprisonment out East. It is further known that Kennington had posted two guards outside the guardhouse during the second shift from 1700 to 1900 hours, the time frame during which Crazy Horse was stabbed…The names of the garrison guard were recorded in a Guard Report Book, which report, dated September 5, 1877, was signed by Kennington. The Nebraska State Historical Society owns a Camp Robinson Guard Report Book for the period September 1877 to July 1878; unfortunately, it commences with September 15, ten days after Crazy Horse was killed. I have not actually examined this ledger, but it appears from the photocopies that a number of pages have been removed from the front of the book, most likely the pages which covered the events around September 5th." My antennae were up.

More I found suspect surrounding the death of Crazy Horse. Most accounts I have found report that the family took Crazy Horse's body by travois to the Spotted Tail Agency about forty miles east of Camp Robinson where it, wrapped in a blanket, was laid into a wooden coffin resting on a scaffold three feet off the ground. Photographs corroborating the initial burial site exist, and one is in the book. This I found unusual. The Lakota placed their dead in the treetops or upon scaffolds fifteen feet off the ground. Although Crazy Horse suffered the consequences of suspicion and jealousy from other Lakota leaders after his surrender, he was by all accounts still admired by many of the people, hence the one thousand warriors storming the parade grounds at Camp Robinson when he was brought in under arrest. Upon death, why was the revered traditionalist warrior and leader not laid to rest in the traditional Lakota fashion?

Adding to my suspicions, a journal entry by Lt. Jesse M. Lee on September 13, 1877, revealed that "Crazy Horse's wife died, and her body was placed on the platform beside his body." (Brininstool, E.A. *Crazy Horse: The Invincible Ogalalla Sioux Chief, Gen. Jesse M. Lee's Account of the Killing of Chief Crazy Horse at Fort Robinson, Nebr.,* Los Angeles, Wetzel Publishing Co., 1949, p. 40.) While Black Shawl Woman suffered from tuberculosis, her nearly simultaneous death to her husband seemed too coincidental, especially since she rode approximately thirty-four miles with Crazy Horse to the Spotted Tail village the day before his arrest. Richard G. Hardoff, in a footnote to the *The Susan Bordeaux Bettelyoun Narrative,* found in his compilation of interviews, narratives, and newspaper accounts entitled *The Death of Crazy Horse: A Tragic Episode in Lakota History,* wrote on page 128, "Since the deceased could not have been Black Shawl, I venture to state that it probably was one of the two Brule wives of Worm (Crazy Horse's father) parenthetical added."

Throughout my readings the name of Valentine McGillycuddy continued to reappear; the doctor at Camp Robinson charged with providing medical care to Crazy Horse's people, including Crazy Horse's wife; the white man who undoubtedly had the most access to Crazy Horse ever; and the self-proclaimed "friend of Crazy Horse." Intrigued by this fascinating man who lived a fascinating life, I purchased an original copy of his memoir dictated to his second wife, Julia, entitled *McGillycuddy Agent,* published in 1941. With excited anticipation I opened the brown-cloth cover. A simple dedication read, "To My Daughter Valentine." The preface, written by Julia now follows in its entirety:

As the second wife of Dr. Valentine T. McGillycuddy—whose first wife I asked, before I was old enough to know better, if she thought the Doctor would marry me when she died—I have listened to his stories since my earliest childhood. After our marriage he jestingly parried requests that his reminiscences be taken down by dictograph or in shorthand for publication.

But when I read aloud to him the fictionalized story of his life which I attempted, in disgust he protested that if I wrote of his experiences I must not deviate from the facts; his life was history, he said, and must be exact. He then began relating the story of his life. Daily I intrigued into my husband into a continuance of the story, including his altercations with government officials, with the press, and with men of the frontier, both white and red.

I am deeply indebted to Marie Sandoz and Mrs. Julia Cooley Altrocchi for information and advice; to General Robert E. Wyllie for assistance in obtaining data from the

War Department; and to the Nebraska State Historical Society for data and encouragement in my sincere effort to make this book historically correct.

If anyone living—either some victim of McGillycuddy's maledictions or a descendent of one—feels resentment at the Doctor's estimate of him, he may rest assured that his judgment at least was sincere and that the responsibility rests with him who has gone "over the divide" and not with his biographer.

J.B.McG.

January 10, 1940

I was hooked and I dove into *McGillycuddy Agent* with gusto. It did not disappoint. Incredible story after incredible story abounded.

I next read *Valentine T. McGillycuddy: Army Surgeon, Agent of the Sioux* by Candy Moulton. Candy Moulton is a historian and brilliant writer. In her preface she states,

> With Valentine T. McGillycuddy, I slipped into the research trap myself, feeling that I could not write the book, or at least could not finish it, until I knew every detail, had every scrap of information possible about my subject. Finally, after eleven years of gathering letters, telegrams, notes, articles, documents, and other sources about McGillycuddy, I told myself, "Quit. Just write the book." And so it is done, in this form, though never finished. For as in all stories of complex, interesting subject matter, another piece of the puzzle always exists.

Thank you, Candy. At the time of discovering McGillycuddy, I was delighted to find you had uncovered so many pieces of the puzzle.

Candy Moulton exposed me to the reality that Dr. McGillycuddy's memoir, as dictated to his wife, was not always entirely "exact." For example, Valentine McGillycuddy was not at the Battle on the Rosebud. Moulton writes, "McGillycuddy often wrote that he was present during the fight at the Rosebud, but his journal effectively refutes those statements." One such example is found in a letter from McGillycuddy to William Garnett dated March 15, 1926, in which he writes, "I want to ask you some questions about the Custer fight on the Little Big Horn on June 25th 1876, as I was surgeon of the 2d Cavalry with Crook in the Rosebud fight on the 17th of June...We were completely taken by surprise at ten o'clock that morning at the Rosebud, and although we had 1100 men we were very glad to see the Indians pull out after a four hour fight..." (Clark, Robert A. *The Killing of Chief Crazy Horse*, University of Nebraska Press, 1988, pgs. 112-113.)

The journals of John Gregory Bourke, the aide-de-camp to General Crook for fourteen years, confirmed that McGillycuddy was absent from the battle on June 17, 1876. Bourke listed by name the four doctors immediately attending to the wounded on the battlefield. McGillycuddy was not one of those named. (*The Diaries of John Gregory Bourke, Volume 1, November 20, 1872-July 28, 1876, edited and annotated by Charles M. Robinson III, Denton, Texas, University of North Texas Press, 2003, p. 329.*) McGillycuddy was at Fort Fetterman on June 17, 1876, where he did care for the wounded in the aftermath of the Rosebud battle on June 27, 1876. He did not arrive at Crook's camp on Goose Creek until July 13, 1876. (Moulton, pgs. 78-79.)

I revisited my earlier readings regarding Crazy Horse from the time of his surrender to the time of his death with a new focus on McGillycuddy, and with a heightened awareness that all I read from the doctor may not be entirely true.

Later in life, McGillycuddy in correspondence with E.A. Brininstool recounted the events of Crazy Horse's death and reported that "I was standing forty feet from him when one of the guard, a private of the Ninth Infantry, lunged his bayonet into the chief's abdomen, and he fell to the ground." (Brininstool, *Dr. V.T. McGillycuddy's Recollections of the Death of Crazy Horse*, p. 45.)

Interestingly, this was not what McGillycuddy first reported, at least not to the Indians. As Crazy Horse lay dying, McGillycuddy tried in vain to convince Crazy Horse's father and Touches the Clouds that the stabbing was caused by a knife, showing them the diameter of both the knife and a bayonet upon penetration into a piece of paper. (Hardoff, *New York Sun, September 14, 1877: The Death of Crazy Horse*, p. 242.)

While McGillycuddy's dissemination of false information was understandable under the circumstances, it further piqued my interest, because it provided valuable insight into the man's character of which I had now come to form a solid opinion. Valentine McGillycuddy, like most, would embellish the truth, if not flat out lie, if it served his self-interest or he believed the ends justified.

Feeling I had exhausted much of what had been written about Crazy Horse and the events surrounding his death, I focused my attention to learning more about the Ghost Dance and the events leading to the Wounded Knee massacre, of which I then had but a vague understanding. I learned that thirteen years after pronouncing Crazy Horse dead, and now a man of means and high society in Rapid City, the Governor of South Dakota appointed McGillycuddy a commander in the National Guard charged to investigate the messianic Ghost Dance religion that had spread through many of the Western tribes with an estimated 50,000 and 100,000 Indians participating.

McGillycuddy's task was to determine the threat of this new religion to the ranchers and settlers in the region. According to McGillycuddy, he reunited with his old nemesis, Chief Red Cloud, who told what he knew of the Ghost Dance as follows: "There came to my people a few sleeps ago, a young Indian from the North; his name is Porcupine. He told us this story. 'I was commanded in a dream to go a great many days' journey to the west where I should come to the great fresh water (Walker's Lake, Nevada). I went as I was told, and in the lodge of Wavoka, the Paiute dreamer, I met a tall white man with golden hair and whiskers and blue eyes. He was a well-spoken man. He spoke to me these words: 'Porcupine, I am the Messiah...I lived among those people more than thirty winters and tried to pull them on the right road, but they would not listen. They tortured me and hung me on a great wooden cross. The Great Spirit was sorry for me and took me back to my home. But it was spoken that some day I should come again.... When the spring comes I will go to visit the tribes, but because of the way I was treated when I was here before, I have arranged songs and dances by which, if I am so received, I shall know that I am among friends...so I would ask you to go ahead of me with these signs and dances and tell the tribes that I will visit my friends when the grass is green in the spring.'"

(McGillycuddy, Julia B. *McGillycuddy Agent*, Stanford University Press, 1941, pgs. 260-261.)

Jerome A. Greene, in his book, *American Carnage: Wounded Knee 1890*, references Porcupine's experience as follows: "I had always thought the Great Father (Christ) was a white man, but this man looked like an Indian... He rose and said he was very glad to see his children...'I am going to talk to you after a while about your relatives who are dead and gone.... I will teach you, too, how to dance the dance.'" Porcupine studied the messiah. "I had heard that Christ had been crucified, and I looked to see, and I saw a scar on his wrist and one on his face, and he seemed to be the man." (pg. 67.)

This passage was striking to me for two reasons. First, and not surprisingly, it did not jibe with Porcupine's description of the messiah as recounted by McGillycuddy; that Porcupine met "a tall white man with golden hair and whiskers and blue eyes." Secondly, it referenced a scar on the messiah's face. No photograph of Crazy Horse was ever taken but it has been well-documented that his most defining physical feature was a distinctive scar on the left side of his face running from nostril, through cheek, to the corner of his mouth giving him an ever-present grimacing appearance.

I searched for Porcupine's full report which I found online on a website entitled: *Oral History of the Dakota Tribes 1800s-1945: As Told to Colonel A.B. Welch,* which claims to have a full transcription of "the interesting account of the visit of Porcupine in search of God, during the Ghost Dancing time in November 1889 that was discovered among the papers of Major McLaughlin and given to me by Charles McLaughlin, his only son living.—A.B. Welch, Mandan,

North Dakota, August 18ᵗʰ, 1926." I have no reason to doubt the authenticity of the documents posted.

In 1889, Porcupine reported seeing "the Christ" on three occasions occurring on three consecutive days. On the first appearance, of which Greene wrote, Porcupine stated, "I had always thought the Great Father (Christ) was a white man, but this man looked like an Indian." Interestingly, Porcupine continued to report, and which Greene negated, that, "In the night when I first saw him I thought he was an Indian, but the next day, when I could see him better, he looked different. He was not so dark as an Indian, nor so light as a white man; he had no beard or whiskers…he was a good-looking man…I saw a scar on his wrist and one on his face, and he seemed to be the man." Regarding the third appearance Porcupine wrote, "This is what they have done to me showing me his scars."

A description of Crazy Horse provided by Susan Bordeaux Bettelyoun immediately came to mind. In her book, *With My Own Eyes*, she describes seeing Crazy Horse at Camp Robinson as follows: "He was a very handsome young man of about thirty-six years or so. He was not so dark. He had hazel eyes, nice long light brown hair; his scalp was ornamented with beads and hung clear to his waist; his braids were wrapped in fur." (pg. 108.)

I also found it interesting that Porcupine reported that "The Christ talked to all of us in our respective tongues." This was corroborated by Short Bull, a member of the Lakota delegation who accompanied Porcupine to Nevada, stating that "after a while a white man came and stood in the middle of them, but no one looked steadily at him. He stood with his head bowed and all at once, surprisingly, he made a speech in the Lakota language." (Andersson, Rani-Henrik, *The Lakota Ghost Dance of 1890*, Lincoln: University of Nebraska Press, 2008, p. 35.)

I found myself confused and apparently so were many others at the time. Andersson writes that "Nobody knew the messiah's identity, or even whether he was an Indian or white…The first news that seemed to give some substance to the rumors reached officials in Washington through the War Department during the summer of 1890. (Porcupine's report.) As late as October 1890, contradictory stories regarding the messiah's identity and whereabouts were reported….No real answers were received until the army took up the investigation. This task was given to the Indian scout Arthur I. Chapman. Under orders to find the 'Indian Christ,' he set out in late November 1890, from San Francisco for Nevada, where the messiah was rumored to live…Remarkably, Chapman's interview with Wovoka took place as late as December 1890, when the army had already been sent to the Lakota reservations."

History now accepts that a Paiute Indian in Nevada named Wovoka was the founder of the Ghost Dance religion, largely based on Chapman's interviews, as well as the reporting of James Mooney, the "Indian Man" as he was known within the Bureau of American Ethnology. Michael Hittman, author of *Wovoka and the Ghost Dance*, writes, "Determined to personally interview the 1890 Ghost Dance Prophet himself, James Mooney left the nation's capital for the field once again; this trip beginning in the middle of November 1891…" [Author's Note: This was over two years after Porcupine's and the Lakota delegation's visit to Pyramid Lake.] "In South Dakota, he was deeply affected by the mass grave containing scores of victims of the December 29, 1890, Wounded Knee massacre and the wooden scaffolding constructed at the grave by mourning Lakotas. Mooney wrote: 'The survivors had fenced off the trench and smeared the posts with paint made from the clay of western Nevada given to Sioux delegates by Wovoka. Since Lakotas were either unwilling or unable yet to discuss their recent tragedy— "The dance was our religion, but the government sent soldiers to kill us on account of it. We will not talk any more about it."'

Mooney also could state with certainty that the prophet was full-blooded. "The impression that he is a half-blood may have arisen from that the fact that his father's name was White Man and that he has a white man's name (Jack Wilson)." In other words, the government ethnologist disputed both rumor and sworn testimony of Plains Indian visitors to Nevada that Jack Wilson/Wovoka, the Messiah or Indian Christ, was light or white skinned. Mooney wrote that the Prophet "...spoke only his own Paiute language, with some little knowledge of English, and "is not acquainted with the sign language, which is hardly known west of the mountains." (pgs. 14-16.)

Surprisingly, neither Porcupine nor any other member of the Lakota delegation ever mention the name "Wovoka," much less state that Wovoka was the new Christ or messiah. Porcupine described the messiah as a light skinned Indian with a scar on his face. Viewing the many photographs of Wovoka that exist, he does not in my opinion fit this description. The messiah spoke Lakota. Wovoka spoke only the Paiute language and did not know the Indian sign language. The messiah spoke of the return of the buffalo. The Paiute, known to the visiting tribes as the "fish-eaters" have no history of hunting buffalo.

The conflicting reports of the Ghost Dance Messiah, as reported by Porcupine and the Lakota delegates were largely dismissed or discounted by investigators, and later by historians. Some have suggested that the members of the Lakota delegations consciously fabricated their stories. I refuse to believe this. James Mooney suggested they were perhaps "under some strange psychological influence not yet explained."

Rather than dismiss or discount the stories of Porcupine and Short Bull as mere fabrications, or as the reports of confused men so overwhelmed by new experiences that they could not comprehend what they witnessed, or the result of drug-induced hallucinations, I choose rather to believe their stories and sworn testimony on their face and ask, "what if?" What if Crazy Horse was the man in Nevada they described?

Obviously, for this to happen, Crazy Horse would have had to have survived his wounds suffered at Camp Robinson.

What if Valentine McGillycuddy had indeed befriended Crazy Horse? Believing Crazy Horse was unfairly arrested and destined to a prison in Florida, what if McGillycuddy, a man willing to lie if he believed the ends justified, chose to falsify Crazy Horse's death?

The rest is history, at least as I imagined it.

BIBLIOGRAPHY

In the event you have a desire to delve into the actual history of which I wrote, I now provide a bibliography of the books I relied upon most.

Andersson, Rani-Henrik. *The Lakota Ghost Dance of 1890*, Lincoln, Nebraska, University of Nebraska Press, 2008.

Bettelyoun, Susan Bordeaux and Josephine Waggoner, *With My Own Eyes: A Lakota Woman Tells Her People's History*, Lincoln, Nebraska, University of Nebraska Press, 1998.

Bourke, John Gregory. The Diaries of John Gregory Bourke Volumes One and Two, edited and annotated by Charles M. Robinson III, Denton, Texas, University of North Texas Press, 2005.

Brininstool, E.A. Crazy Horse: *The Invicible Ogalalla* Sioux Chief, Los Angeles, California, Wetzel Publishing, Co., Inc. 1949.

Greene, Jerome A. *American Carnage, Wounded Knee, 1890.* Norman, Oklahoma, University of Oklahoma Press, 2014.

Hardorff, Richard G. *The Death of Crazy Horse: A Tragic Episode in Lakota History*, Lincoln, Nebraska, University of Nebraska Press, 1998.

Hittman, Michael. *Wovoka and the Ghost Dance*, Lincoln, Nebraska, University of Nebraska Press, 1990.

McGillycuddy, Julia B. *McGillycuddy Agent*, Stanford University, California, Stanford University Press, 1941.

Moulton, Candy. *Valentine T. McGillycuddy: Army Surgeon, Agent to the Sioux*, Norman, Oklahoma, University of Oklahoma Press, 2011.

Sandoz, Mari. *Crazy Horse: The Strange Man of the Oglala*, New York, MJF Books, 1942.

The Killing of Chief Crazy Horse: Three Eyewitness Views by the Indian, Chief He Dog, the Indian-white, William Garnett, the White Doctor, Valentine McGillycuddy, edited , with introduction, by Robert A. Clark, Lincoln, Nebraska, University of Nebraska Press, 1976.

Utley, Robert M. *The Lance and The Shield: The Life and Times of Sitting Bull*, New York, Ballantine Books, 1993.

DANIEL D. LEE first learned of his Oglala Lakota ancestry while on active duty in the U.S. Air Force serving as a Judge Advocate General (a military attorney). Intrigued, he did what many do when first learning about the "Sioux." He read about Crazy Horse. The warrior's story fascinated him.

As Chief of Military Justice of the largest training command in the Air Force, Dan was accustomed to reading military reports and noting inconsistent testimony. The reporting of Crazy Horse's death was full of such inconsistencies. This sparked an interest that he would continue to research for the next seventeen years, during which he was introduced to Valentine McGillycuddy, the self-proclaimed "friend of Crazy Horse" and the first Indian Agent at the Pine Ridge Agency in South Dakota. A story, based on historical facts, that had never before been told slowly emerged and about which he was determined to write. *Stoned* is the culmination of his efforts. The author has one son, Brody, the hero of his first novel, an autobiographical work of historical fiction. Both he and Brody are tribal members of the Oglala Lakota Nation.

Made in the USA
Monee, IL
25 September 2021

78230562R20194